A Lust for Window Sills

A Lust for Window Sills

A lover's guide to British buildings
from portcullis to pebble-dash

Harry Mount

Little, Brown

LITTLE, BROWN

First published in Great Britain in 2008 by Little, Brown

Copyright © Harry Mount 2008

The moral right of the author has been asserted.

A CIP catalogue record for this book
is available from the British Library.

Front endpaper: '17 Ripplevale Grove', © Fred Phipps
Back endpaper: 'The New Houses', etching © Virginia Powell

ISBN 978-1-4087-0090-7

Typeset in Palatino by M Rules
Printed and bound in Great Britain by
Clays Ltd, St Ives plc

Papers used by Little, Brown are natural, renewable and recyclable
products made from wood grown in sustainable forests and certified
in accordance with the rules of the Forest Stewardship Council.

Mixed Sources
Product group from well-managed
forests and other controlled sources
www.fsc.org Cert no. SGS-COC-004081
© 1996 Forest Stewardship Council

FSC

Little, Brown
An imprint of
Little, Brown Book Group
100 Victoria Embankment
London EC4Y 0DY

An Hachette Livre UK Company
www.hachettelivre.co.uk

www.littlebrown.co.uk

For Tommy, Archie and Maya

Contents

We much question whether many noted travellers, men who have pitched their tents perhaps under Mount Sinai, are not still ignorant that there are glories in Wiltshire, Dorsetshire and Somersetshire. We beg that they will go and see.

Anthony Trollope, *Barchester Towers*, 1857

Introduction

or How I Fell in Love with Window Sills on the Way to School

A stone's throw from my childhood home in Islington, north London, there's a plain, red-and-brown-brick building called Canonbury Tower. For years I bicycled past the tower on the way to school and didn't take much notice of it.

Then, one summer afternoon in 1986, when I was fourteen, I got a puncture and had to wheel my bike home. Walking past the tower, I noticed the window sills for the first time. Or, more precisely, the lack of them. Instead of there being the usual deep ledge stepped back from the brickwork, the window was flush with the wall and there was barely any ledge at all.

At school the next day, I looked up Canonbury Tower in the library's Pevsner guide to north London: 'Canonbury Tower stands here, a very happy if accidental group . . . The house was occupied from 1570 to 1610 by the wealthy merchant Sir John Spencer, Mayor

The missing window sills that changed my life, Canonbury Tower, north London, mid-sixteenth century.

of London . . . The brick tower is of uncertain date, perhaps mid-C16.'

Rootling through the library, I discovered why these mid-sixteenth-century windows looked like this.

If a window sill is four inches deep or more, like in the Broadwick Street house below, then the house was built after the Great Fire of London – or, more precisely, after 1709, when legislation was passed to make buildings more fireproof.

Earlier windows, like the Canonbury ones, had been flush, or nearly flush, with the brick façade of the house. As a result, flames licking the building only had to brush the wooden frame's outside edge to consume the whole window, be drawn inside the room and set the entire place alight.

Add in jutting Tudor, timber first floors oversailing the street – banned under Jacobean legislation – and pre-1666 London was one endlessly overlapping line of highly flammable dominoes. Torch a

3

Naked in Soho – a 1723 sash, retracted but exposed, Broadwick Street, London W1. Charles Bridgeman (1690–1738), Queen Anne's head gardener, lived here, as the blue Doulton plaque tells you.

Hidden in Islington – fast forward sixty-six years and the first-floor sashes in Highbury Terrace, north London, are retracted and concealed. Hugh Grant snogged Andie MacDowell here at the end of *Four Weddings and a Funeral* (1994).

bakery in Pudding Lane and you torched 13,500 houses, eighty-seven churches, forty-four guildhalls, the Royal Exchange, the Custom House and St Paul's Cathedral. The crypt of St Paul's – stuffed with paper from the local printers – burnt for a week. The City was a moonscape, buried under four feet of hot ash.

Deeper window frames, stepped back from the wall, meant that just the bricks were scorched, and the interiors would survive such a catastrophe.

There was another fire-fighting window sill Act – in 1774. Under this one, the recessed timber sash frames of the windows now had to be hidden behind the bricks, whereas previously they displayed their outside edge. So you end up with the look of the windows in the Highbury Terrace picture.

Suddenly, magically, London was transforming in front of me. The buildings that surrounded me were telling me how the city grew up – like the way you mark the height of your children on the kitchen wall.

Clothes change over the years, as do eating habits, language, even the climate. But old buildings stay the same.

'You walk straight into a Jane Austen novel,' John Betjeman said of Mildenhall church, Wiltshire – early-thirteenth-century outside and 1816 inside. Each building tells us about a life, or a time. Every style of architecture has a purpose. Once you learn about things like window sills and church furnishings, the pleasure in returning to a building from a past age – and being able to date it precisely – is addictive.

Man liking to have a roof over his head, there are buildings everywhere. Even when they're not the main focus, there they are in the background. Just in the last few days reading the papers, I noticed some engaging little details in the background of news photographs.

First was an old Christmas picture of the boys of Winchester Choir School skating in the shadow of the cathedral. Well, they aren't really in the shadow; most cathedral and church activity takes place on the sunny south side of the building. So entrance porches were on that warm, south side – an airlock, where people met before the service. People were buried on the south side first, too. They only filled plots on the north side in the nineteenth century, once the warmer side had filled up.

In the background of this photo, I noticed the simple pointed windows of the south aisle. Early Gothic, I thought, before going to check in the Pevsner guide to Hampshire. Yes, late thirteenth century, I read with a thrilling little bounce of the heart.

Then, in May 2008, I saw a picture of Tony Blair's new £4-million country house: the South Pavilion at Wotton House, Buckinghamshire – Sir John Gielgud's old home. That steeply hipped roof, those dormer windows, white stone quoins on red brick . . . Turn of the eighteenth century Anglo-Dutch classicism?

Bingo! According to the Pevsner for Buckinghamshire, the pavilion was built in 1704 by John Keene, who was also responsible for Wotton House next door.

What a joy it is to make these jumps from looking at a few news photographs. And I get this joy from buildings several times a day; a joy which rarely comes across in the dry way their history is usually taught.

When I was studying at the Courtauld Institute in London a few years ago, a visiting professor from an obscure Argentinian university gave a lecture in the history of dress. He was outraged when a student quoted from Henry James's *Daisy Miller* (1878) to show how Americans dressed for the Grand Tour. 'My lessons are about clothes, not words,' the professor barked.

Words are rather a good way of describing clothes, I thought; and buildings, too. This book is full of buildings loved and hated by novelists. Buildings like Hetton Abbey, the ghastly Victorian monstrosity that lifted Tony Last's heart in Evelyn Waugh's *A Handful of Dust* (1934), rebuilt in 1864 in the Gothic style and now, according to the local guide book, 'devoid of interest'. It is also, incidentally, based on Madresfield Court, Worcestershire – wrongly thought of as the architectural inspiration for Waugh's Brideshead.

Evelyn Waugh's Hetton Abbey – the epitome of Gothic gloom, specially designed for discomfort with its 'central clock tower where quarterly chimes disturb all but the heaviest sleepers'. (From J.M.D. Harvey's frontispiece to *A Handful of Dust* (1934))

Another Courtauld graduate, Brian Sewell of the *Evening Standard*, is more my cup of tea when it comes to art and architecture. He told the Courtauld's alumni magazine in 2008:

If art history were the one compulsory subject, taught properly, then students would become aware of so many other cultural strands. They have to know the literature of the period, the theology, the philosophy, the medicine. There's no point in standing in the great palace at Würzburg looking at Tiepolo unless we also think of the music of the day.

This book is meant to bring in a few of the things that Henry James and Brian Sewell might go for, while you take a meander through the history of British buildings from the Normans up to the Second World War.

It'll be an informative stroll but, I hope, an effortless, anecdote-rich one; maybe, I fondly imagine, like being shown round Edwardian public baths in Harrogate by Alan Bennett. It's a stroll you can take in little bursts, too; this book is a dipper, not a read-straight-througher.

The approach is roughly chronological; that's why I begin with castles and early churches, and then move on to the places people tend to live in – the terraced houses and cottages that were built later on the whole. Sometimes I'll break the chronology and insert a more general section on building materials, windows or the different ways you can lay bricks. At the end, I've put in some walks, a railway journey and a tour of the M4, to give you a few day-tripper's guides to British buildings.

I'll dip into Anglo-Saxon buildings, but will begin properly with the Normans, because pre-Norman buildings are so thin on the ground. I'll touch on post-Second World War buildings, too, but not in great detail. This isn't because of any particular dislike of them. It's just that architects, from around the 1930s onwards, dispensed with those features – Ionic columns, Decorated windows and so on – that had cropped up, disappeared and been revived over the previous five hundred years or so.

As a result, modern buildings are much more likely to be one-offs that don't mesh into the thousand-year timeline of this book. So it's harder to point out general principles and features that help you date them and relate them to ancient predecessors.

You can look at, say, the Houses of Parliament, built in the mid-nineteenth century, and relate its details to fifteenth-century Gothic churches; its shape to Renaissance palaces. Look at Lord Foster's Swiss Re building (2004), aka 'the Gherkin', in the City of London, and you can't relate its shape or its details to anything much except itself.

Post-war buildings apart, after reading this book, you'll be able to date most buildings on the High Street, any church or any National Trust house to within a couple of decades.

You'll end up being able to work out that Blenheim Palace is early-eighteenth-century, and that Buckingham Palace was finished in the early twentieth century.

You'll see why the porch of your town hall has got those peculiarly shaped pillars on either side, and why the windows of your local church were built in the nineteenth century in imitation of six-hundred-year-old windows.

You'll find out about Doric, Ionic, Corinthian and all that. Early English, Decorated and Perpendicular Gothic, too. But I'll hop between grand places, with all these ancient motifs, and those ordinary houses and flats that most of us live in today. As the French painter Camille Pissarro said in 1893, 'Happy are those who see beauty in modest spots where others see nothing. Everything is beautiful, the whole secret lies in knowing how to interpret it.'

Castles, churches and other grand buildings survived longer than small-scale, domestic architecture because of their scale and significance; that doesn't make domestic architecture any the less interesting, beautiful or full of engaging little mysteries.

Mysteries like why terraced houses across Britain had their tallest room on the first floor and a shorter one on the ground floor. And why were their ground floors covered in white plaster that's cut into horizontal grooves? Or why do classical columns bulge out in the middle?

Why did those terraced houses have back gardens that are lower than street level but higher than the floor of the basement? And what did the landscape round your house look like before it was built?

I'll answer that last one now. If you live in a town or city, look along your garden wall and see how big the trees are along that line. They'll usually be the biggest and oldest ones around – they certainly are in my garden in Kentish Town, north London.

Garden walls ran along old field boundaries – the old hedge-line, home to London's most ancient trees, survivors of several centuries of city development. Take an old map and compare it with a modern street map and you'll see how your garden wall is a perfect fit with old field boundaries. While hedges in the country have been cut and laid flat for years, in town they've grown into full-blown trees.

By the end of this book any urban, suburban or rural view – as long as it's got a building in it – will be illuminated by a little knowledge and anecdote.

This, then, is not just a guide to the great buildings of Britain. You'll find more here on terraced houses than on Chatsworth, more on Victorian pubs than on St Paul's Cathedral. Of course, great buildings will crop up a lot – they were often the juiciest commissions, the ones where architects first tried ideas that then trickled down to, say, those terraced houses.

But the aim is not to identify and praise individual buildings; more to celebrate individual features – Venetian windows, fan vaulting, crenellated church towers. Once you spot these things, you can spot them on smart buildings and humbler ones, too.

What I hope to get across is the excitement of buildings; the excitement you get on turning one of those big, heavy, looped metal handles on a medieval church door, hearing the latch lift – yes! it's open – and stepping in, not knowing what beauties, great and small, quirky and mainstream, lie inside.

The accumulation of vastly different styles over many generations is not unique to Britain or to British churches in particular. But I think the artless, mishmash, make-do-and-mend attitude to this accumulation is. From that random, small-scale, on-the-hoof improvisation, mixed with a pleasing decay, comes the magic.

How bewitching to find in the parish church in Henley-on-Thames, Oxfordshire – a mixture of the fourteenth, fifteenth and sixteenth centuries – a new monument: an oar halfway up the nave wall commemorating the gold medals won by Steve Redgrave and Matthew Pinsent at the 2000 Olympics.

How intriguing, too, the great hodge-podge of British building terms and their history. I like, for example, the fact that naves, like the one at Henley, get their name from the Latin *navis*, 'ship', because of the keel shape of church roofs.

It's not just middle-aged, unmarried men with cravats tucked into upturned collars who can enjoy words like 'nave', 'rococo' or 'squinch'; men like the two art critics in the Fry and Laurie sketch 'Dinner with Digby' from the BBC TV series *A Bit of Fry and Laurie* (1990). Hugh Laurie played Jeremy James Duff, a travel writer and journalist, and Stephen Fry was Susan Digby, an aesthete. They are eating dinner in black tie – Susan Digby is a woman in name only – with classical music in the background and Greek busts on plinths on either side of them.

> Susan Digby: 'I was in Venice last year.'
> Jeremy James Duff: 'Ah, the Serenissima . . .'
> SD: 'You know more about Venice than anybody else in the world.'
> JJD: 'The Queen of the Adriatic . . .'
> SD: '. . . is just one of the things you've been called.'

Well, no need to don a cravat or bow tie. There aren't that many different terms for the ways in which the fronts, sides and tops of buildings have been shaped and twisted over the centuries.

Like people who get by in Naples with restaurant Italian stretching to a couple of hundred words, you'll dramatically increase your pleasure in buildings if you know about forty of these terms. A lot more are listed in the Glossary at the back of this book.

For starters, here are six buildings in Manchester. Guess the date of each building and put them in order. Try again at the end of the book – where the answers are – and see how far you've got.

A [   ]

B [   ]

C [   ]

D [   ]

E [   ]

F [   ]

1

The Philip Larkin Guide to Churches

Ah let me enter, once again, the pew
Where the child nodded as the sermon grew;
Scene of soft slumbers!

N.T. Carrington, 'My Native Village', 1830

I know how Carrington felt. When I was a boy I went mad with boredom in church services – carol services, even – and would yell out, 'Oh come let us ignore him, Oh come let us ignore him, Oh come let us ignore him, Chri-ist, I'm bored.' Not any more. And not because I've let the Lord Jesus into my life. But because I've become interested in buildings.

Churches are the best guide to Britain's architecture from the end of the Dark Ages to the Reformation, that is, from AD 1000 to the 1530s. For most of that time the church was more significant than the King and his barons; and church architecture was more significant than secular architecture, royal or noble. Only after the Reformation – with the collapse in church power – was there a boom in secular masterpieces.

Ninety-nine per cent of surviving pre-Reformation buildings are churches, cathedrals or monasteries; 0.9 per cent are castles, and domestic buildings account for the other 0.1 per cent – the cottages we think of as ancient are rarely more than three hundred years old.

You don't have to be religious to enjoy the beauty of these early religious buildings, even if a monk friend once tried to persuade me otherwise.

'Do you go quiet inside churches?' he asked.

'Yes.'

'And do you take your hat off, if you're wearing one?'

'Yes.'

'And do you feel somehow different when you're in there? Different to the feeling you get in a lovely country house, say?'

14 'Yes.'

'Well, then, you're religious.'

I certainly do feel different in a pretty, secular room, but I often felt moved – perhaps in a less reverent, hushed way than in a church – to the same degree, and with the same sort of emotion; like reading a poignant bit in a book or crying during a film.

Sir John Betjeman (1906–84) said that the churches of the architect Sir Ninian Comper (1864–1960) should bring an agnostic like me to my knees – and they often do.

T.S. Eliot said the same of the odd pocket church of Little Gidding, Huntingdonshire, in 1942:

> You are here to kneel
> Where prayer has been valid. And prayer is more
> Than an order of words . . .
> So, while the light fails
> On a winter's afternoon, in a secluded chapel
> History is now and England.

Little Gidding, Huntingdonshire (1714), with its Hawksmooresque perforated pyramid. Gloomy old T.S. Eliot called it a 'dull facade' in the poem.

In 'Church Going' (1954) Philip Larkin put these thoughts together rather better than I can (doesn't that sound like Margaret Thatcher – 'As God once said, and I think rightly . . .'?):

> For, though I've no idea
> What this accoutred frowsty barn is worth,
> It pleases me to stand in silence here;
> A serious house on serious earth it is.

The story behind the building of these serious houses makes standing in them all the more pleasing.

The Graveyard Shift – Outside the Church

Before you step inside the church, have a look at the nearby buildings. You enter most churches through the lych gate, which is usually Victorian, and often a memorial of some sort. It literally means a corpse gate, lych coming from the Old English *lic*, 'body'. The lych gate was where coffins were sheltered before the vicar turned up for the burial service.

Near the lych gate you'll probably find the pub – usually one of the oldest buildings in the village. In the early days there was often a church house by the graveyard entrance, where churchwardens kept church ales. Betjeman again, in 'Churchyards':

> For churchyards then, though hallowed ground
> Were not so grim as now they sound,
> And horns of ale were handed round
> For which churchwardens used to pay
> On each especial vestry day.
> Twas thus the village drunk its beer
> With its relations buried near,

And that is why we often see
Inns where the alehouse used to be.

There will also probably be a fine, chunky, squarish-looking late-Georgian or Victorian parsonage next to the church or at the end of a footpath through the churchyard. Sir Nikolaus Pevsner (1902–83), the architectural historian, said the church and parsonage together 'make a feature in the villagescape to which the Continent has no parallel'.

The parsonage – the collective term for rectories and vicarages – grew out of the English parish system almost a thousand years ago. Each of the ten thousand parishes in the Middle Ages had a resident priest, or rector, and his deputy, a vicar. And each priest needed somewhere to live.

Some of the earliest surviving parsonages date from the twelfth century, but most are Georgian, Victorian or Edwardian. A gradual collapse in church finances over the past century has triggered a collapse in handsome church housing. Eight thousand parsonages were sold by the Church between 1948 and 1994. The trend was described by Evelyn Waugh in *A Call to the Orders* (1938):

> The rectory too large for the restricted progeny of the new incumbent, let, as often as not, to the local adjutant or a business man who keeps horses there for weekend hunting, but still eloquent of the gossip of Jane Austen's heroines and their orotund, prosaic sermons of happier clerics.

Affection for rectories is now so deep that Charles Moore, formerly editor of the *Daily Telegraph*, set up the Rectory Society in 2006 'to help further interest in all former and existing rectories, vicarages, parsonages and other clergy dwellings'.

Current rectory owners include the thriller writer Robert Harris, the Duchess of Devonshire and Jeffrey Archer, who lives in the one celebrated by Rupert Brooke in 'The Old Vicarage, Grantchester' (1912):

> And spectral dance, before the dawn,
> A hundred vicars down the lawn;
> Curates, long dust, will come and go
> On lissom, clerical, printless toe;
> And oft between the boughs is seen
> The sly shade of a rural dean . . .
> Stands the church clock at ten to three?
> And is there honey still for tea?

Among those brought up in rectories are Jane Austen, the Brontë sisters, Lord Tennyson and David Cameron.

The literary strain is strong in these places. John Betjeman and his family lived in a splendid 1749 rectory in Farnborough on the Berkshire Downs. The rectory at Coxwold, North Yorkshire, was home to Laurence Sterne, author of *Tristram Shandy* (1759), from 1760 to 1768. The clergyman and writer Sydney Smith (1771–1845) lived in the rectory at Combe Florey, Somerset, near the old home of Evelyn and Auberon Waugh. The poet George Herbert lived from 1630 to 1633 in Bemerton rectory, near Salisbury, Wiltshire, where he wrote *The Country Parson*, a guide to the rural priest's life that is still popular among the clergy.

Now the writer Vikram Seth lives there. Passing the house one day, he longed to buy it but couldn't afford it.

'Don't worry,' said his agent, 'your next advance will pay for it, I can assure you.'

Seth got the house. He was so moved that he wrote his poem 'Host' (2008) to Herbert – the 'He' of the poem – which is a sort of interior conversation:

18

Bemerton rectory, on the left, renovated by George Herbert in the 1630s. 'Yet my host stands just out of mind and sight, that I may sit and write,' Vikram Seth wrote of Herbert. (Mary Evans Picture Library)

'He'll change my style.'
'Well, but you could do worse
Than rent his rooms of verse.'

Nowadays most vicars live in the New Rectory, a 1960s box of a house another hundred yards from the church. Even that might have been sold to weekenders, and the vicar will be in the New New Rectory yet another hundred yards further away, on the fringes of the village.

As you walk from the rectory – or the New New Rectory – to the church, look round the graveyard.

Gravestones are a relatively recent innovation. Before the fifteenth century, there were barely any in the graveyard. Although the ground was used for burials, the dead weren't memorialised other than in priests' prayers.

19

DATING TIP

Britain has more brass monuments than all other countries put together – we rule the brass-rubbing world. Made from an alloy of copper, zinc, lead and tin, these monuments peaked from the end of the thirteenth century until the end of the fifteenth century.

The earliest memorials – raised to the grand and the armigerous – were inside the church. The first memorable tombs of the twelfth century incorporated carved stone coffin lids into the floor. Say a prayer as you walk over the ones near the altar.

DATING TIP

The first effigy of an earl sculpted in his robes of estate, and not in armour, was the alabaster one of the 5th Earl of Arundel, who died in 1415 and was buried in the Fitzalan Chapel, Arundel, West Sussex.

Philip Larkin, in 'An Arundel Tomb' (1956), wrote about the effigy of this earl's father – the 4th Earl of Arundel, Richard Fitzalan, buried in Chichester Cathedral next to his wife, their hands touchingly joined together. Sculpted in armour, this Lord Arundel died in 1397.

Side by side, their faces blurred,
The earl and countess lie in stone,
Their proper habits vaguely shown
As jointed armour, stiffened pleat,
And that faint hint of the absurd –
The little dogs under their feet.

Turning our eyes towards the church, the most striking feature is the tower. Even the first builders of Christian churches – the Saxons – built towers. They just didn't build that many – tenth-century St Peter,

The only church – apart from Westminster Abbey – that appears in the Bayeux Tapestry is the little Saxon church at Bosham, West Sussex. King Harold owned Bosham Manor. Harold, on the right, visited the church there before setting sail from Bosham for Normandy in 1064.

Barton upon Humber, Humberside, is one of the few Saxon churches with one. It was only after the Normans arrived that substantial towers and churches became the norm.

Anglo-Saxon Cowboy Builders

A look at the rough-and-ready Saxon church of St Laurence in Bradford-on-Avon, Wiltshire, shows quite how unsophisticated the Saxons could be, with its ultra-simple blind arcading and clumsy attempts at quoins – like a child's drawing of a church.

Built between the early eighth and the eleventh centuries, St Laurence looks like it was knocked up by a dodgy builder who skimped on the plastering. Its lack of sophistication captures the darkness of the Dark Ages, once you compare it with, say, the Colosseum in Rome, built more than seven hundred years earlier. And 'dark' is the word – Saxon churches had high, small windows with no glass in them.

21

Still, it's not as if the rest of northern Europe had done much better since the fall of the Roman Empire. The 140-foot-long Saxon church of Brixworth, Northamptonshire, is the biggest seventh-century basilica north of the Alps, even though the Vikings destroyed an aisle in a pillage in 870.

The Saxons usually built in timber – another reason why few buildings survive. Most buildings in Britain until 1500 were built of wood. The Saxons also used cheap materials: in particular, uneven plaster made of lime, straw, sand and hair, coloured pink, white or yellow. You can still see the plaster on East Anglian cottages, where it has been pargeted – scooped and combed into pretty, decorative friezes, raised above or incised into the wall. It also has a ruder meaning – in his play *Epicoene, or The Silent Woman* (1609–10), Ben Jonson talks of a woman 'above fiftie' who still 'pargets'.

East Anglia, Champion Pargeters of the Seventeenth Century

Suffolk and Essex were strong on pargeting in the seventeenth century – look out for pretty interlaced squares and scalloped herringbone fan designs. Because East Anglia was rich in wool profits but short on stone, elaborate plaster designs boomed. When the wool economy collapsed, pargeting survived because there was no money for upgrading.

There are two types of pargeting: a basic scratch pattern where wet plaster is combed into panels; and freehand modelling in low relief.

One of the last surviving pargeters in East Anglia, Anna Kettle, uses lime-putty mortar mixed with white goat hair for tensile strength. 'Cement hasn't got the right body,' says Mrs Kettle. 'You can't model it into curvy, sexy shapes.'

DATING TIP

This sort of plastering went on long after the Normans arrived and it's a pretty good rule of thumb that any church with walls of ashlar – smooth, cut, bare stone – is from the late fourteenth century or after.

Jesus Christ, Architect

Before you step inside the church, look at its shape. The most striking thing is the traditional cross-plan, as in Christ's cross – with the transepts (or cross bits) standing in for his arms, the nave for his torso and legs, and the chancel for his head.

If the chancel is at an angle to the nave, it's a nodding chancel, in honour of the crucified Christ's lolling head. The chancel is the narrower bit of the church at the east end – so that the altar is closer to Jerusalem. The word comes from the Latin *cancellus*, 'lattice' or 'grille', after the railings around the altar.

There are two sorts of cross shapes in church design. The Latin cross is like a crucifix, with a longer arm below the horizontal crosspiece, a shorter one above. In a Greek cross, all four arms are the same length.

This crucifix church shape took a while to develop. Saxon and Norman churches were usually long halls, not unlike the pagan temples of Roman Britain. You can see a similar outline in the third-century Temple of Mithras in Queen Victoria Street in the City of London. Like us, the Roman congregation gathered in the nave, although they sat in aisles on benches running alongside the walls. The curved chancel area in Roman temples was where they burnt pagan sacrifices.

The modifications for Christian churches were dictated by three demands: a hall for the congregation; a smaller, raised area for the priest to go about his rites; and a set of bells, housed in a tower, to summon them. That's why most churches narrow at one end – there's the narrow choir and chancel for the priest, choir and altar, and a nave for the congregation. Being narrow, the choir and chancel were roofed with expensive stone. The broader, longer nave was roofed in wood – cheaper and more adaptable than stone because it can support itself over longer spans.

The roof, untouched by the feet of the congregation or the hands of iconoclasts, often looks almost new, however ancient. 'Cleaned or restored? Someone would know: I don't,' wrote Larkin in 'Church Going'.

Now for the entrance porch, usually on the warm, south side. Until the Reformation, the porch was the barrier between the secular and the holy worlds. Medieval baptisms and funeral services took place there.

Couples got married in the porch, with or without a priest. All they needed was to provide a ring and declare that they were married. As Chaucer said of the Wife of Bath in *The Canterbury Tales*, 'She'd had five husbands, all at the church door.'

Before the Reformation, only aristocrats got married at the altar. An early-Tudor etiquette book declared that an earl's child could be married by the chancel; a knight could be married just 'within the church and chapel door'. Anyone else, like the Wife of Bath, was kept 'without the church door'.

> **DATING TIP**
>
> From the fourteenth century onwards, porches had a room built above them for a village school, a watchman or as a store for parish records. In Essex, Surrey and Sussex, where stone was in short supply, they were keen on wooden porches.

Before you open the church door, look at the door itself, often the oldest thing in the building. You might take a step down to reach the door – a thousand years of dust and earth has settled around it. Because doors were practical and relatively immune to architectural fashion, they survived while everything around them was manically updated.

The door might also be surrounded by the most ancient stonework in a church. Often the only Norman bits that survived were the concentric semicircles of zigzagging stone over the door.

The oldest door in Britain leads off the cloister in Westminster Abbey, by the Chapter House. Dendrochronologists date the door – the only Anglo-Saxon one in the country – to a tree cut down between 1032 and 1064.

Once you're through the door, you're at the western end of the nave with the font ahead of you – the object with which you are admitted into the Church is at the entrance to the church.

DATING TIP

Holy water was considered so holy in the Middle Ages that the font was covered with a lockable lid in order to keep the water pure. In 1220 the Bishop of Durham ordered that all fonts must be sealed. You can still see early fonts punctured with holes that have since been filled with lead. These holes were slots for rings through which an iron rod was threaded and locked.

The font's importance grew from the fourteenth century, when font covers sprouted into teetering Gothic spires, like the twenty-foot-tall one at Ufford, Suffolk. Some could only be raised and lowered with elaborate pulley systems.

25

The Audrey Hepburn Guide to Church Entrances

Next time you watch the beginning of *My Fair Lady* (1964), look at the church portico where Professor Higgins and Colonel Pickering come across Eliza Doolittle after a night at the opera.

The church is St Paul's, Covent Garden, one of the first classical churches in Britain, built by Inigo Jones in 1633. The piazza around the church was London's first classically inspired, formally designed open space. The church was also the first to be built from scratch in London since the Reformation. Almost no churches were built in England for half a century after 1540, and very few between the death of Elizabeth I in 1603 and the Great Fire of London in 1666.

St Paul's, Covent Garden, was built with the plainest order of them all – Tuscan, nicknamed 'Carpenter's Doric' because anyone could knock up a passable imitation for their garden gazebo. The use of this order here was inspired by a discussion Jones had with his patron, the Earl of Bedford, who didn't want to spend much on the church.

'In short,' said Lord Bedford, 'I would have it not much better than a barn.'

'Well then,' said Jones, 'you shall have the handsomest barn in England!'

Rex Harrison agreed that the church was splendid. When Eliza Doolittle called Henry Higgins a 'squashed cabbage leaf', he called her a 'disgrace to the noble architecture of these columns'.

Because the busy Covent Garden market – where Eliza sold violets – was on the east side of the church, Jones wanted the entrance to St Paul's to be on that popular east side; and you can see a pretty, classical doorway in the background when Rex Harrison sings, 'Why can't the English teach their children how to speak?'

It is, though, a blocked, pretty, classical doorway; blocked because traditionalists, particularly the new Archbishop of Canterbury, William Laud, were horrified that an eastern entrance meant an altar in the

Audrey Hepburn, squashed cabbage leaf and the noble Tuscan columns of Inigo Jones's St Paul's, Covent Garden (1633).

west – that is, the wrong, non-Jerusalem end. So the doorway was blocked up and the altar placed at the east end, with the entrance at the traditional western end.

Back to chancels. The chancel, at that eastern end, was where the clergy gathered. In cathedrals it's where monks and canons sat, along the north and south walls.

Often on the north, or left-hand, side of the chancel in churches of the late Middle Ages, you'll see a recess in the wall, elaborately decorated and in the shape of a sarcophagus. This is the Easter Sepulchre, built in imitation of Christ's tomb. After Maundy Thursday Mass, the host or the cross was placed here for Good Friday and the next day.

Look out for three little seats to the right of the chancel – that is, on the south side. These are sedilia, the Latin word for seats, reserved for the priest in the middle, with the deacon on his right and sub-deacon on his left. They were used during the singing of the Kyrie, the Gloria and the Credo. In several English churches, the sedilia varied in height, with the highest for the priest, the lowest for the subdeacon.

27

Next to the sedilia, look for a small stone pouch set into the wall at around hip height. This is the piscina, or washbasin, originally for water used by the priest to clean his hands at Mass.

Psalm 26.6 says, 'I will wash mine hands in innocency: so will I compass thine altar, O Lord.' The words 'I will wash' were, in Latin, '*lavabo*' – another name for the piscina, and, in modern French, for any old sink.

> **DATING TIP**
>
> In 1204 Pope Innocent III ordered that two separate basins must be used for the rituals before and after Communion, so churches of the thirteenth and fourteenth centuries have double piscinas.

In the early days of the church most of the congregation couldn't read English, let alone the Latin that the priest read so fluently, so his obscure intellectual activities were shielded from the masses. He stood with his back to the congregation and they were lucky to glimpse his back.

You'll be hard-pressed to find any church today where the priest turns his back on you. At the Reformation, the altar at the east end was replaced by a table near the congregation. Altars that were later restored to the east end have recently been dispensed with, so that the priest can face the congregation during Communion.

In the old days the congregation were more likely to see a rood screen rather than a priest. A rood is another word for Christ's cross; the rood was placed above the rood screen which separated nave from chancel. These screens got going in earnest in the mid-thirteenth century.

There were some pretty little variations between screens: the ones in East Anglia – which has the densest concentration of medieval churches in Christendom – were smaller and more elegant; those in the West Country bigger but rougher.

Sometimes, above the rood screen, there was a rood loft, where candles might be lit or members of the congregation stood, prayed and sung – a fifteenth- and sixteenth-century choral singing boom led to a rood loft boom. The rood loft looks like a kind of minstrels' gallery and is also known as a pulpitum, a nod to its occasional use as a pulpit.

In 'Church Going', Larkin teased 'the crew that tap and jot and know what rood-lofts were, some ruin-bibber, randy for antique'. A bit harsh, really – it's rather exciting to find a rood loft; Henry VIII got rid of so many of them from the 1530s onwards that they're pretty rare.

A 1547 decree required that all images – and roods in particular – be stripped from churches. Since roods were practically always wooden, and not stone, they were easily ripped out and burnt. Not a single complete pre-sixteenth-century rood group – with the figures of Christ and usually the Virgin Mary and St John – has survived in Britain.

The three were grouped together in contemporary literature, too. They appear in an anonymous late-fourteenth-century poem called 'The Pearl', about a father who dreams of meeting his dead daughter:

> Crystes mersy and Mary and Jon,
> Thise arn the grounde of alle my blisse.

This poet, also thought to have written *Sir Gawain and the Green Knight*, would probably have seen the three of them together in a rood group in his own church.

The reredos or retable – both words derived from Latin and meaning the tablet at the back – was also ripped out at the Reformation. Also known as altarpieces, these were big panels in stone or painted wood, placed on or above the altar.

Dating all these things was complicated by Queen Mary I (1516–58). After the Reformation the Catholic queen reinstated the Catholic Mass, stopped the removal of images and allowed new ones to be installed, like the rood at St Catherine's, Ludham, Norfolk.

The iconoclasts returned under Elizabeth I. Any murals were painted over, remaining crucifixes were removed and Communion was no longer celebrated at the altar but at a table. These reformers did a pretty good job of smashing stained glass, too. Quite often the oldest glass in a church survived only in high windows where the bashers couldn't reach it.

> **DATING TIP**
>
> Under Elizabeth I, roods were often replaced with big cloths embroidered with the royal coat of arms – the monarch had literally replaced Christ. This was later swapped for wooden royal coats of arms set into the chancel arch – a good sign of post-sixteenth-century work.

Statues of saints were torn away; but look out for paintings and carvings of saints on rood screens, fonts, pulpits and choir stalls – the iconoclasts thought them too minor to bother desecrating.

Even before the Reformation, there were secular monuments to the rich and grand, with the first effigies appearing in the thirteenth century. After the Reformation, there was a tide of memorials – they got really megalomaniac from the late sixteenth century onwards.

Add in the next great iconoclasm under Cromwell in the 1640s, when the Puritans destroyed any Popish images. Then throw in the funeral hatchments – those big lozenges with coats of arms, hung on the nave wall after they were carried in front of funeral processions – and you see why European Catholics often think the churches of England are more godless museums than holy shrines.

Anthony Powell on the Perils of Monuments

The memorial service for Anthony Powell (1905–2000), author of the novel cycle *A Dance to the Music of Time,* was held on 4 May 2000 at the Grosvenor Chapel in Mayfair. This pretty little yellow-brick church with a Tuscan porch was built in 1731 for Sir Richard Grosvenor, ancestor of the current Duke of Westminster, who still owns the surrounding Grosvenor Estate.

Hugh Massingberd (1946–2007), the late presiding genius of the architectural history world, gave the address. 'Welcome, my brethren, to the Eisteddfod,' he began, with a nod to Frankie Howerd, who began his shows that way.

Massingberd moved on to Powell's story of a Norfolk parson who arrived early to officiate at a funeral in a church he hadn't been to before. A keen antiquarian, the vicar took down an iron helmet from the tomb of a knight killed at the Battle of Bosworth in 1485. Unable to control his curiosity, he donned the helmet to see how heavy it was, only to find he couldn't take it off.

As the mourners filed into the church behind the coffin, they were, in Powell's words, 'surprised to be received by a cleric wearing a knight's bascinet'. The priest proceeded to carry out the burial service in this kit.

'I wonder what he went for – visor up or down?' Powell asked Massingberd.

On or close to the line between the chancel and the nave, you'll find the lectern. Lecterns were usually designed in an eagle shape, with outstretched wings supporting the book-rest. The eagle was the symbol of St John the Evangelist, whose Gospel was appropriate to the lectern with its opening line, 'In the beginning was the Word and the Word was with God and the Word was God.'

Brass eagle lecterns in England, often on a circular base supported by three lions, date from the late fifteenth and early sixteenth centuries, although there were nineteenth-century imitations.

On that line between chancel and nave, you'll also find the pulpit. Pulpits only got going in late medieval times. Big Jacobean pulpits with testers – flat sounding boards fixed above the priest's head – flourished during the evangelical golden years, 1600–20.

Look out for intriguing details on Gothic pulpits from the late Middle Ages. They're usually decorated with pictures of the four Fathers of the Western Church: St Ambrose, St Augustine, St Jerome and St Gregory.

Look out, too, for stone medieval pulpits in the West Country, and wooden ones in stone-poor East Anglia.

Bigger churches also developed choirs in front of the altar, with ranks of choir stalls ranged on either side. Most of these date from the late fourteenth and fifteenth centuries. Because choir stalls were elaborately worked – often with a pretty poppy-head design – they survived the brutal modern practice of ripping out plainer pews.

With church coffers swelling before the Reformation, churches expanded; they developed that full cross shape, with transepts and a central crossing tower at the point where the nave met the transepts.

Aisles – long, flanking ranges on either side of the nave – were added in the thirteenth and fourteenth centuries. Because the dark, cold, north side of the church was a less popular spot for graves, there was more building space there. The first aisle was built there, and so the older architecture will be on your left when, like newly married couples, you walk down the nave. By the way, any couple walking down the aisle, happy or otherwise, would end up walking into a transept wall. Pedantic couples should walk down naves.

Nave side-walls also developed a triforium, a first-floor gallery supported by pillars and arches on the ground floor. Above the triforium, in grander churches and cathedrals, a second floor, lined with windows, was built – the clerestory, or 'clear story'.

There are two obstacles to the avid church visitor: the locked door and the cross vicar. The first is easier to handle. There's often a notice in that warm, south-facing porch telling you who the keyholder is – usually somebody living in a nearby cottage.

The cross vicar is more of a challenge. I've met lots who think an interest in buildings is an insult to their faith. 'This isn't a museum, you know,' a purple-faced priest in an engaging-looking nineteenth-century church in north London once barked at me.

Country house visits can be just as tricky. Simon Jenkins, author of *England's Thousand Best Houses* (2003), had some trying times. 'I turned up at one lovely Georgian house to be greeted by the owner,' Jenkins told me in his pretty early Victorian villa in Primrose Hill, north London. 'He said I had five minutes to look round his huge house. I could jog if I wanted, he said. And I did.'

Jenkins had asked for permission to look round. The really brave house maniac turns up unannounced. Lady Diana Cooper (1892–1986), wife of Duff, mother of John Julius Norwich and muse to Evelyn Waugh, popularised the art of 'Sweepers' – sweeping up the drive of some unknown house to have a mooch around. Trespass is, after all, only a civil offence.

Lady Diana liked to go inside the house – big houses were still often unlocked to allow servants, house guests and extended family to move freely without a key. If confronted by someone, she would say, 'Oh, don't worry. I'm a friend of Sir Brian Wyldbore-Smith's.'

Not that Sir Brian (1913–2005), who won a DSO in Italy and was a leading Conservative fund-raiser and friend of Margaret Thatcher's, lived there – just that it was a suitably smart, over-the-top name to throw people off their stride.

The problem came when Lady Diana ended up, unwittingly, at Sir Brian's house.

'I do worry. And you're not,' said Sir Brian, slamming the door in her face.

2

Through the Portcullis

Confessions of a Castle Creeper

When I worked with the late Bill Deedes, I asked him how annoyed he was that Alan Clark now lived in Saltwood Castle – the pile Deedes spent his childhood in.

At that time I was a bit of a castle creeper and rather too keen on big houses; a little like the first Marquess of Curzon (1859–1925), Viceroy of India, who was teased at Oxford for that sort of thing in a bit of anonymous doggerel that stuck to him throughout his life.

> My name is George Nathaniel Curzon,
> I am a most superior person.
> My cheeks are pink, my hair is sleek,
> I dine at Blenheim twice a week.

Having been brought up in a castle, Deedes wasn't nearly as impressed by the things as George Nathaniel Curzon and me. 'Oh no, Saltwood was a horrible, damp place,' he said, his ultra-mobile, expressive lips crumpling into a smile, utterly aware of how ungrand he was being. 'God, I love my double glazing and central heating. Delighted that Alan lives in that horrid place!'

Bill would have hated the Norman castle in its original condition even more – there wasn't any glass in the windows, just oak shutters.

Long before, the Romans had used glass and worked out how to remove its natural greenish colour by adding manganese oxide. But still, even by the end of the twelfth century – when Saltwood was built – glass was only rarely fitted in houses or castles. The poor old freezing Normans relied on stone grilles or linen soaked in oil to let in a tiny bit of light and keep out even less cold. Some peeled slices off cattle horns and flattened the shavings into rudimentary window panes.

A Hand-made Glass Menagerie

Glass has changed immensely over the past eight hundred years – from clumsy, hand-made, uneven stuff, blotted with bulging globs and cloudy drops, to mass-manufactured modern material of a uniform thickness and clarity.

There are endless types of glass, but the main ones are:

Broad sheet glass. This was first manufactured in Sussex in 1226 – handmade by blowing molten glass into a stretched balloon, which was then decapitated at both ends. The remaining glass cylinder was cut and flattened. This process left the glass so uneven that it was cut into small diamonds held together by strips of lead – as in leaded windows.

This glass often had so much lead in it that it rather defeated the purpose, as Charles Cotton revealed in describing the early Elizabethan windows at Chatsworth, in 'The Wonders of the Peake' (1681):

> The glaziers' work before substantial was,
> I must confess, thrice as much lead as glass,
> Which in the sun's meridian cast a light
> As it had been within an hour of night.

Broad sheet died out in the late sixteenth century, to be replaced by other sorts of hand-blown glass, like cylinder glass.

Cylinder glass. A glass cylinder was cut lengthways and unrolled to form a clumsy flat plate of glass. This glass all but disappeared in competition with more expensive, but higher quality, crown glass.

Crown glass. This got going in Britain in the late seventeenth century. Blown into hollow globes, it was then flattened into a disc. Uneven glass – thicker in the middle of the disc – it was cut up and put in window frames, usually with the thicker end down.

▶

These thickened edges at the bottom of the pane fed the myth that glass goes on flowing after it has been set in a frame. Not true – you sometimes get a glazier who has put the thick end at the top. It stays thick, and at the top.

Plate glass. This French invention, first manufactured in Britain in St Helen's, Lancashire, in 1773, was far superior to what went before. Yes, it was thick, but that meant imperfections could be polished and ground away without much danger of cracking.

Sheet glass. Developed in 1838 this glass, being thinner and cheaper, usurped plate glass.

Machine-manufactured glass. This arrived in the twentieth century with the move away from hand-blown glass. It includes float glass (developed by Pilkington's in 1957), machine-drawn cylinder sheet, single and twin ground polished plate, rolled plate and flat drawn sheet glass. This is all crisp, even, clear stuff.

Diamond-paned, leaded casement windows! The location manager certainly knows his Tudor, Natalie. *The Other Boleyn Girl* (2008), starring Natalie Portman and Scarlet Johansson, filmed at Charfield Manor, near Bath. (BBC Films/Focus Features/Kobal Collection/Alex Bailey)

As so often, behind the self-mockery, Deedes was right. Castles were really uncomfortable places and it's only because the inhabited ones have been refitted that we think otherwise.

How the four knights must have shivered at Saltwood on 28 December 1170 before they set off to kill Thomas à Becket at Canterbury the next day; Ranulf de Broc, a baron loyal to Henry II, then owned the castle. When they weren't shivering, they were coughing. The fire the knights huddled round had no chimney to draw its smoke; it escaped through the roof and the windows, blackening the walls with soot.

As so often, behind the self-mockery, Deedes was right. Castles were really uncomfortable places and it's only because the inhabited ones have been refitted that we think otherwise.

So, by the early twentieth century, Lord Emsworth's Blandings Castle had become awfully luxurious – 'one of Shropshire's stateliest homes', as P.G. Wodehouse put it. And so is the place it was based on. Recent Wodehouse scholarship has confirmed that Blandings was inspired by Sudeley Castle, Gloucestershire, while the model for its grounds was Weston Park, Shropshire.

Sudeley Castle, the home of socialite Henry Dent-Brocklehurst and his art-dealer sister Molly, is now beautifully well appointed. It was certainly in fit enough condition to provide a weekend hideaway billet for Liz Hurley after Hugh Grant was caught with the Los Angeles prostitute Divine Brown in 1995.

But Sudeley wasn't always so comfortable. When Ralph Boteler, Lord Sudeley, built the place in 1442, it was the simplest and least celebrity-friendly of castles – no more than a pair of courtyards: one for servants, one for Botelers.

To begin with, castles were brutally simple buildings. The first castles, built by the Normans in wood and then in stone, were basic military forts – 'castle' comes from the Latin *castellum*, 'little camp'. They were defensive outposts – and jumping-off points for occasional rampaging of the environs. The further north you went, the more important defensive towers were; in the Scottish borders, Cumbria and Northumberland, castles were built on the southern banks of rivers as an extra layer of defence against the Scots. Manor houses and country houses in the Welsh Marches and the Scottish borders retained a military air long after English houses shed their armour.

Looks were not a priority of castles, however lovely they might now appear. Arrow slits, crenellations, portcullises and machicolations had an austere beauty, but it was an accidental one.

Even staircases were designed with defence in mind. A castle's staircases rise in a clockwise direction as you climb them. Its defenders could then swipe down and across with their right hand – their sword hand – as they came down the stairs. Attackers climbing the stairs couldn't swing a sword with their right hand because the central post of the staircase got in the way.

The widespread use of gunpowder made castles obsolete in the late fifteenth century. And, once castles were no longer militarily useful, they were no longer built. From then on they were only erected as toy fortresses – like the mock castles built as patriotic gestures during the Napoleonic Wars of the early nineteenth century.

Medieval double glazing. Carew Castle, Pembrokeshire, built in 1100, was given these mullioned, transomed windows in the late sixteenth century.

The Biggest Windows in Wales

In genuine castles, those glassless windows were kept to a minimum, and not for reasons of insulation – most of a castle was necessarily all wall, to keep the baddies out.

A rare exception to the 'big castles, little windows' rule was Carew Castle, Pembrokeshire. When Carew was built in 1100, its windows were tiny, slim defensive jobs. It was only when Sir John Perrott, supposedly Henry VIII's illegitimate son, came along in 1558 that they grew into the mullioned, transomed leviathans they are today.

Sir John got tremendously excited at a promised visit from his Queen; and so he installed those whacking great window frames, made out of expensive Bath stone in contrast with the walls of local silvery Carboniferous limestone.

Sir John waited and waited but the Queen never came. Moreover she later turned nasty, imprisoning him in the Tower of London for treason. He died there in 1592, bankrupt, his only legacy to have been the first man in the county to install the medieval equivalent of double glazing.

Castles began as motte-and-baileys – a curtain wall (a plain, enclosing roofless wall), and sometimes a moat, surrounding an open court, or bailey, with a mound, or motte, in the middle. Bill Deedes used to mow, roll and mark his own cricket square on the lawn of the inner bailey at Saltwood. The only brother to three sisters who did not appreciate the game, he had no one to play with.

A castle's principal defensive building was the keep – a big round or square, free-standing stone tower, the last redoubt in a crisis and the place where the chief nobleman and his retinue lived. William the Conqueror's White Tower in the Tower of London was a classic four-floor keep: his hall and chapel were on the third floor, his bedroom on the fourth. It also contained the first fireplace in Britain, albeit one without a chimney stack.

By the thirteenth century castles acquired a few more home comforts. A hall was built in the walled bailey away from the keep, and a gatehouse added to the entrance.

In the fourteenth century a second bailey was erected and the gate-house built up. The decreasing military threat meant that castles were fitted out more for style than defence. Tower ceilings were vaulted; suites of rooms mushroomed in the inner and outer wards.

The castle ground plans varied. Harlech Castle (1290), Gwynedd, belongs to a group of thirteenth-century symmetrical castles, its pattern of concentric circles borrowed from French and Italian castles of the late twelfth and thirteenth centuries.

At the same time a series of English castles were built on a more irregular plan. At Stokesay Castle (1291), Shropshire, the walls weave a wavy route, squeezing together two of the crucial elements of the castle – the tower and hall. Like a lot of buildings of the period, Stokesay was more fortified manor house than castle. Fortification was a serious matter; crenellation required a licence from the monarch.

The late thirteenth century – when Stokesay went up – was springtime for the romantic castle, even if they were still built with a military role in mind.

'Here was the Middle Age, from the pages of Tennyson, or Scott, at its most elegant: all sordid and painful elements subtly removed,' wrote Anthony Powell in *A Buyer's Market* (1952) of the fictitious Stourwater Castle, based on Hever Castle (1270), Kent. The fantasy look of the restored medieval Stourwater lends it the feel of a film set:

> 'Look, the castle,' said Isobel, 'Nobody warned me it was made of cardboard.'
>
> Cardboard was certainly the material of which walls and keep seemed to be built, as we rounded the final sweep of the drive, standing with absurd unreality against a background of oaks, tortured by their antiquity into elephantine and grotesque shapes.

3

Norman Wisdom

William the Conqueror and the
Round Arch

Grey towers of Durham
Yet well I love thy mixed and massive piles
Half church of God, half castle 'gainst the Scot.
Sir Walter Scott, 'Harold the Dauntless', 1817

I don't quite agree with Sir Walter. As far as Norman cathedrals go, Durham, begun in 1093, was distinctly avant-garde, and certainly light-years ahead of the Norman castles that preceded it.

Still, you can see his point. In its broad outline, Norman Durham Cathedral was not unlike Bill Deedes's Saltwood Castle and other Norman fortresses – a huge square block of masonry built on a scale never seen before in Britain.

The Normans carved mammoth chunks out of the skyline of our cities with their churches, castles and, particularly, their cathedrals. There had been glimpses of these chunky mammoths before the Normans arrived in 1066. Edward the Confessor introduced elements of the style at Westminster Abbey in 1050–65. But it was William the Conqueror who herded the mammoths across Britain: in the 1070s, the

44

Sir Walter Scott's mixed and massive piles – Durham Cathedral (1093).

cathedrals of Canterbury, Winchester, Lincoln, Rochester and Old Sarum. After he died in 1087, Gloucester, Chester, Chichester and Old St Paul's followed.

Another word for the Norman architecture of these cathedrals is 'Romanesque'. The Romanesque style, which flourished under Charlemagne on the Continent two centuries before the Battle of Hastings, was inspired by early Christian basilicas.

Like the Romans, the Normans never cottoned on to the pointed arch, which can carry more weight than round arches. The spiky, lissom buildings of the later Gothic age depended on the pointed arch, the flying buttress and ribbed vaulting to stay up – all of which didn't appear together until the twelfth century.

The most crucial thing to remember about Norman buildings, then, is that they depended on the round arch. Wherever you see great big semicircles of stone, the chances are you're looking at Norman work.

Norman buttresses were weak things, too, so the columns had to be great big, chunky things to bear the weight of the walls and roof. On top of all this, the chunky columns were badly designed. Full of rubble, they weren't as strong as columns made of sturdy cut stone all the way through; so, to be at all robust, they had to be even thicker.

West Country Normans plumped for particularly obese columns with unusually small arches on top; the Peterborough Normans liked rather taller columns.

This fat look was exaggerated by the capitals, or tops, of the columns. Handsome as they are, they look a little primitive and undersized; like trifling little scallops round fat necks; especially when you compare them with the delicate Doric, Ionic, Corinthian and Composite capitals of the classical world.

4

Britain Gets the Point

Twelfth-Century Goths

One may look upon Shakespeare's works as upon an ancient majestic piece of Gothic architecture, compared with a neat modern building; the latter is more elegant and more glaring, but the former is more strong and more solemn.

Alexander Pope, 1725

To compare Shakespeare to Gothic buildings was right. Britain is really a Gothic country. Gothic architecture was only given the name Gothic once classical came along as an alternative in the seventeenth century. Before that, it went without saying. All notable architecture was inevitably Gothic – British architecture *was* Gothic architecture.

In fact, before the Renaissance, northern European architecture as a whole was really Gothic architecture, as the travel writer Philip Glazebrook (1937–2007) said on his deathbed. As he lay dying he asked a friend of mine whether she had been on holiday lately; he so longed to go abroad.

'I've just been to Milan, actually.'

'Aah, I love Milan. I always like travelling up from the south and seeing that great Gothic cathedral and thinking . . . at last, northern Europe!'

The Italians below Milan didn't go in for Gothic much. There is only one Gothic church in Rome – Santa Maria Sopra Minerva, built in 1370. With its ogee arches, its blue and gold-vaulted roof and its pointed, traceried windows, it looks distinctly odd in the middle of classical Rome. That classical dominance down there isn't surprising, really. Italians had so many original classical buildings to copy, unlike us, with our limited collection of antique ruins.

Classical buildings also suited the warm south. Pergolas and chains of columns were custom-made for life al fresco, with open porticoes and walkways shaded from the sun, sheltered from the rain and allowing the free passage of air. The Parthenon was beautifully suited to harsh Athenian sunlight.

Gothic buildings, by contrast, have cold, dark, northern connotations – Hetton Abbey, Evelyn Waugh's Gothic monstrosity in *A Handful of Dust* (1934) has fires lit, whatever the season, to stave off

> the cavernous chill of the more remote corridors where, economising in coke, [Tony] had had the pipes shut off . . . The ecclesiastical gloom of the great hall [was] half-lit by day through lancet windows of armorial stained glass, at night by a vast gasolier of brass and wrought iron, wired now and fitted with 20 electric bulbs.

The mercury was low, too, in the literature that coincided with the nineteenth-century Gothic Revival. When we think of Dickens, we think of snow-frosted Gothic buildings, not sunburnt classical ones. And so did Dickens. Here he is, in *Bleak House* (1853), on a freezing Gothic morning, talking about Lincoln's Inn Hall, a surviving Gothic building of 1489, where the Court of Chancery was held:

> Michaelmas Term lately over, and the Lord Chancellor sitting in Lincoln's Inn Hall.
> Never can there come fog too thick, never can there come mud and mire too deep, to assort with the groping and floundering condition which this High Court of Chancery, most pestilent of hoary sinners, holds this day in the sight of heaven and earth . . .
> Well may the court be dim, with wasting candles here and there; well may the fog hang heavy in it, as if it would never get out; well may the stained-glass windows lose their colour and admit no light of day into the place.'

The miserable connotations of Gothic had been around for a while. Byron said that Lord Elgin was a worse vandal than Alaric, the Goth who sacked Rome in AD 410, and so the most barbaric of thugs. It's funny how barbarian (from the Greek *barbaros*, 'foreign') and vandal

49

(the name of a Gothic tribe that invaded Western Europe in the fourth century AD) were both terms that were originally used to describe foreigners that later became insults. Throughout most of the Georgian period, from around 1700 to around 1830, when classicism ruled, Gothic remained a term of disapproval.

Much later, this dark, gloomy aspect of Goths lent its name to the teenage trolls who stalk British provincial town centres with crimped black hair and white face paint, listening to the Cure. Alaric and his Visigoths from Bulgaria rarely spent their evenings like this – the connotations of the word 'Goth' have changed quite a bit in the last sixteen hundred years.

The Dickensian association between bad weather and a Gothic mood continues today. After the London premiere of that most Gothic of films, *Sweeney Todd: The Demon Barber of Fleet Street*, the rain came down in buckets. The *Daily Telegraph* of 11 January 2008 reported, 'The downpour added to the Gothic atmosphere created in Leicester Square. The square was decked out with Gothic-style lampposts for the occasion.'

Those spiky, black lampposts evoked the gloomy, dark side of all things Gothic. They also got the essential point of Gothic architecture – its pointiness.

Why Did Arches and Windows Get Pointed?

The pointed arch probably grew out of the need to support stone roofs. Some wooden roofs, like Peterborough Cathedral's – the biggest in Europe, built in the early thirteenth century – have survived; but others were forever going up in flames. So it was safer to have stone roofs; but heavier, too, and pointed arches carried that much more weight.

There are plenty more romantic explanations for the birth of the pointed arch. Some say that masons wanted their naves to imitate trees on either side of a forest path, meeting at a leafy, rustling point in the middle. Or that they accidentally created the style when two Norman barrel vaults met at right angles to form pointed cross-arches.

Others think the pointed arch was imported from the Holy Land. The El-Aksa mosque and the Dome of the Rock in Jerusalem had pointed arches as early as the seventh century. Some fantasists connected the pointed arch to the inverted keel of Noah's Ark.

You can see how ferocious – and mad – the battle between classicists and Goths became. Goths claimed it was incredibly expensive to put up all those pediments and porticoes. Classicists said that Gothic windows let in less light than plain rectangles; even that all the fiddly detail in Gothic windows was terrible for collecting dirt.

Whatever your taste – classical or Gothic – it's around 1130 that English architects first worked out this absolutely crucial point: the more pointed an arch was, and the more weight it carried, the taller your building could be.

The principle applies to eggs. Try pressing the two long sides of an egg with your fingers and it'll smash easily; press at the two ends and it's practically impossible to break it. The points can take much more pressure.

You could also make pointed arches as pointed or tall as you want, whereas Norman builders were restricted by the width between two pillars as to the height of the round arch raised above them.

The French built the first pointed arches in the eleventh century at Nevers and Clermont-Ferrand. We didn't catch up until 1128, when Durham Cathedral had the first British pointed arches installed in its nave.

Europe's first fully Gothic church – with a full Gothic set of pointed arches, rib vaults and flying buttresses – was St Denis in Paris, built in 1140.

DATING TIP

Later Romanesque work, after around 1130, was notable for flourishing sculptural work, particularly zigzags – or chevrons – round doorways and capitals. These were particularly profuse in the Lady Chapel at Durham Cathedral, built in 1170–5.

Points on Pointed Architecture

Gothic architecture was once called 'pointed architecture' and divided up into three different periods: Early, Middle and Late Pointed.

Alternative terms – still used today – were invented by Thomas Rickman (1776–1841), a Gothic-obsessed Quaker grocer. In *An Attempt to Discriminate the Styles of English Architecture* (1817), he split medieval architecture into four periods:

Norman – eleventh and twelfth centuries
Early English – late twelfth century until the mid-thirteenth century
Decorated – 1290–1340
Perpendicular – 1340–1530

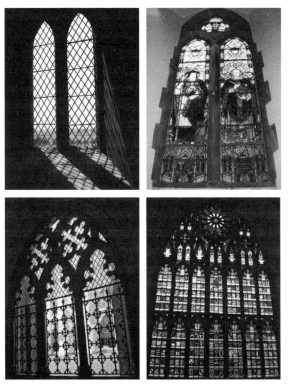

Life cycle of the Gothic window: top left, plain lancets in thirteenth-century St Twynnells, Pembrokeshire; top right, more complicated Early English plate tracery and trefoil, in thirteenth-century St Mary's, Pembroke; bottom left, twirly whirly 1330s Decorated, the cloisters, Westminster Abbey; bottom right, wider, taller, straighter Perpendicular, Lincoln's Inn Chapel, London (1623).

You could also throw in Transitional – for the short transition between Norman and Early English. And Geometrical, too, for the moment between Early English and Decorated. But enough for the time being to know Early English, Decorated and Perpendicular. Then you've already taken in pretty much the first half of British architectural history over the last thousand years; and quite a lot of the second half as well, given that the Victorians started copying Gothic styles all over again in the nineteenth century.

As a rough rule of thumb, Early English windows are plain, narrow and, for the first time, pointed; Decorated ones taller, pointed, wider and tremendously twirly-whirly; Perpendicular enormously tall, wide and pointed, but with a stronger vertical, straight axis than those complicated Decorated windows.

In taking in the development of Gothic architecture, you'll also take in a lot of history, too. It's no coincidence, for example, that the first Gothic cathedrals were as French as William the Conqueror's native Normandy.

Westminster Abbey's Essex Garçon – the French and the Early English

It's helpful that the first stage of English Gothic architecture was called Early English. But, just to make things difficult, Early English was French in inspiration. The style lasted from about 1130 to 1250, through the reigns of Henry I, Stephen, Henry II, Richard I, John and Henry III – a time when England and its architecture had close connections with France.

At Westminster Abbey, much rebuilt under Henry III from 1245, there was a real Frenchness to the Gothicism. The delicate Gallic style even had its own alluring French name – Rayonnant. Among the French touches were the chevet – literally meaning 'head', this was a chancel surrounded by an ambulatory or walkway, with mini-chapels leading off it.

Think tall, thin and elegant Parisian ladies, and you'll get a feel for Westminster Abbey. It had a taller nave than any previous cathedral in England, with shafts extending uninterrupted from ceiling to floor. The walls were exceptionally thin, with no passage to bulk out the clerestory – that upper floor full of windows – as was standard practice before.

The windows were a selection of French greatest hits: a rose window borrowed from Notre Dame's north transept, triangular windows from the Sainte-Chapelle. The tracery – the intersecting masonry ribs that form the window shapes – came from Reims.

For all the French influence, though, there were native unFrench touches to the place and it's still not clear whether Henry de Reynes, the master mason at Westminster, came not from Reims, but from Reynes, Essex.

Early English Dating Tips

As well as the arches, doorways grew pointed, too. So, crucially, did windows – unlike the round-headed windows of Norman days.

The first thin, pointed Early English windows were called lancets, as in the thin, pointed surgical instrument. Lancets were lined up in pairs and triplets – with two shorter ones often flanking a tall one, like in that earlier picture of Bemerton Church, opposite Vikram Seth's rectory. In time, these groups of lancets were topped with an arched hood, or hood mould – a thin, projecting horizontal stone line to stop rain leaking into the church.

In later churches lancets grew closer until they merged into a single window with several panes – or lights. Masons took to piercing a hole in the stone between the hood and the lancets, like in the window of St Mary's, Pembroke (pictured). This hole was then carved into three- or four-lobed shapes – trefoils and quatrefoils. 'Foil' comes from the Latin *folium*, 'leaf'. These first elaborate window shapes – called plate tracery – emerged in around 1200.

Everything grew thinner, taller and lighter in the Early English period, and that included columns. Now made of cut stone, with none of that weak, clumsy rubble inside them, they were stronger and slimmer, grouped in tightly packed quivers. The shafts around these columns stood free, attached to the columns by distinctive rings.

Where the Normans used axes for carving, Early English work was done with a chisel and in much higher relief. Carved leaves that had stuck closely to the capitals in Norman churches now sprouted free of them – so-called 'stiff leaf' carving. And the deep-cut mouldings of the arches were so deep that you could stick your hand right into them.

Other Early English giveaways were the façades of cathedrals – known as poor man's Bibles because they were jam-packed with rows of niches holding statues of saints and holy figures. These cathedrals were colourful places, with pieces of leaded glass in dark red, brownish pink, blue and olive, divided by heavy black, lead outlines. The walls were covered with red and black paint – all gone now, leaving behind our monochrome cathedrals.

St Anne Brookfield, Highgate, north London – John Betjeman's childhood church, where he was baptised – was built in a Victorian imitation of the Early English style.

> Soft the light suburban evening caught our ashlar-speckled
>   spire,
> 1860 Early English, as the mighty elms retire
> Either side of Brookfield Mansions, flashing fine French
>   window fire.

In the poem, 'Parliament Hill Fields' (1940), Betjeman was slightly out in giving it a date of 1860: St Anne's was built in 1853.

In the thirteenth century, another magical device to support all this heavy stone emerged – the flying buttress. With its help, walls grew miraculously tall and thin. The sideways pressure of the cathedral walls

The ashlar-speckled tower of John Betjeman's childhood – St Anne Brookfield, Highgate, London (1853).

was carried outwards, then downwards, by these delicate buttresses that curved like a spider's legs away from the body of the church.

Builders take Monastic Orders in the Twelfth and Thirteenth Centuries

Just before the Reformation of the 1530s, the fortunes held by the monasteries were immense, with as much as a third of England's wealth in their hands. Fountains Abbey alone owned twenty thousand sheep and more than a million acres.

Monasteries had thrived in England and Wales throughout the twelfth and thirteenth centuries. Cistercian abbeys – like Rievaulx and Fountains (both 1132), Yorkshire, and Tintern (1131), Monmouthshire – are particularly stirring today, even after their severe bashing during the Reformation. The Cistercians were largely responsible for spreading the Gothic style through Wales.

56

These epic building projects combined deep pockets with a puritanical approach to decoration.

One of the rules of the Cistercians – originally from Cîteaux, near Dijon, and called the White Monks for their pale woollen habits – was that ornament was forbidden; no stained glass, no crosses, no sculpture, no painting. The poor Cistercian mason was allowed to score a little moulding along the line of his arches but nothing more.

If ever beauty through form was achieved, it was by the Cistercians. The allure of their abbeys depended on those soaring, pointed ribs holding together ultra-delicate skeletons. And those spare, ruined bones were made that much more stark once Henry VIII got hold of them.

We're lucky to have even the bones. Of the 650 monasteries Henry VIII took over in the 1530s, a third have gone completely, a third are in ruins and another third became churches – like Bath's – or cathedrals, like St Albans, Hertfordshire.

Westminster Abbey only escaped the wrecking ball because of its unique royal status. The place for the burial and coronation of monarchs, it always had a governmental role: the Chapel of the Pyx was the King's Treasury; William Langland called the Chapter House the 'parliament-house' in the fourteenth-century poem *Piers Plowman*.

The dissolvers of the monasteries were a mercenary bunch and the only really valuable, reusable stones were square blocks. Round blocks could be recycled for millstones. But arches, pinnacles and capitals, all precise one-offs, couldn't be reused, thank God, so they were left where they lay, alone in the valleys and dales of England and Wales.

5

The First Snobs

To the Manor House Drawn in the
Thirteenth Century

Drawing room or lounge? Couch or sofa? Where do these wicked questions come from? The answer lies in the thirteenth-century fortified manor house.

In the early middle ages the grandest noble in the land dined with his servants in the main hall of the house. Then, slowly, slowly, the grandees withdrew from the hall. Eventually they ended up eating and sleeping apart from their servants, except for the moments when they were waited on.

After the Danish king Hrothgar's victory in the eighth-century Anglo-Saxon epic *Beowulf*, the first thing he did was 'build himself a hall, a large and noble feasting hall, whose splendours men would rave about. The hall towered high, lofty and broad-gabled'. It is in a big communal hall like this that the Venerable Bede (AD 673–735), in Book II of his *Ecclesiastical History*, set his analogy for the shortness of human life:

> The life of men on earth, in comparison with that time which to us is uncertain, is as if when on a winter's night you sit feasting with your ealdormen – and a simple sparrow should fly into the hall, and, coming in at one door, instantly fly out through another. In that time in which it is indoors, it is indeed not touched by the fury of the winter; but yet, this smallest space of calmness being passed almost in a flash, from winter going into winter again, it is lost to our eyes.

Even in the early days of Hrothgar and Bede, the noble host slept apart from his minions. In *Beowulf* the separation took place after a heavy evening's wassailing: 'When evening came, the king departed to his private bower to his couch, and the others cleared away the benches, and covered the floor with beds and bolsters.' (This ritual of building a bed from scratch on the ground is the origin of 'making your bed'.)

By the time of the romance *Sir Gawain and the Green Knight*, in 1400, guests were withdrawing from the hall to sleep, too. Before he has his revenge match with the Green Knight, Sir Gawain has a night of feasting, and then:

> Gawan gef hym god day, de godmon hym lachchez,
> Ledes hym to his awen chambre, de chymne bysyde.
> [Gawain said good night; his kind host took hold of him, and
>   led him to his own chamber beside the chimney.]

Noble and servant still dined together in the hall, though. In the thirteenth century, Grosseteste, the Bishop of Lincoln, recommended that eating outside the hall should be banned.

At the actual supper table, though, the separation between noble and servant was extreme. Nobles may have stayed in the same room as their servants, but they dined on a literally higher level. The lord and his party ate on a raised dais at one end of the hall, while everyone else sat on a lower level on benches at right angles to this high table. The lord's followers sat on one side of these tables on either side of the room, with their backs to the wall, facing a fire in the middle of the room. The smoke drifted out through the louvred ceiling – that is, a wooden turret open at the sides. The timbers, dating from AD 890, in Britain's oldest inhabited timber-framed house – Fyfield Hall, Ongar, Essex, on sale for £1.85 million in June 2008 – are still blackened with smoke from the open fire dug into the mud floor.

High table is still reserved for benchers – leading barristers – in the halls of the legal Inns of Court; and it's still where the dons eat at Oxford and Cambridge.

At the turn of the fifteenth century, big windows – the first bay windows, in fact – were built at this dais end of the hall to reflect the grandness of the people who ate there.

In *Sir Gawain and the Green Knight*, King Arthur, Queen Guinevere and the king's nephews, Gawain and Agravian, all ate at Camelot's high table:

Dise were dist on de des and derwordly serued,
And sipen mony siker segge at de sidbordez.
[They dined on the dais and ate daintily,
And many fine knights were below at the side tables.]

This is where 'below the salt' comes from. Salt was expensive in these northern climes, where there were no salt beds of evaporated sea water. So the salt was kept on the high table on the raised dais, and the poor, saltless people sat at the lower tables. 'His fashion is not to take knowledge of him that is beneath him in clothes. He never drinks below the salt,' wrote Ben Jonson in *Cynthia's Revels* (1599).

The separation between high and low table extended to language, too. Norman noblemen used the French name for food at high table – *boeuf* (beef), *mouton* (mutton) and *porc* (pork). The poor bloody peasants stuck to Anglo-Saxon to describe the animals they looked after to provide all this meat – cow, sheep and pig.

As they got richer, the boeuf-munchers developed more and more rooms to separate themselves further from the cow-eaters. Around the thirteenth century a parlour – a place to talk in, from the French *parler* – emerged on the ground floor. This was a room to withdraw to from the hall – thus withdrawing room, thus drawing room. Talking rooms, by the way, continued into the twentieth century, when the Americans invented 'the conversation pit' – a socialising well sunk in the middle of the sitting room.

This vexed question of drawing rooms – or withdrawing rooms – and, later, lounges, has been getting up people's noses for nearly 650 years now. 'The hall has come to a pretty pass when the lord and lady avoid it at mealtimes, dining every day in a private parlour to get away from the poor,' records Langland in *Piers Plowman*.

The withdrawing process accelerated through the fifteenth century, as castles changed from defensive garrisons to splendid houses. The nobles' need for privacy and comfort led to the high table being moved to a separate room: the light, airy solar, or great chamber, on the first floor at the dais end of the hall.

It wasn't just writers who took against the withdrawal. In 1526, King Henry VIII complained, 'Sundrie noblemen and gentlemen and others doe muche delighte and use to dyne in corners and secret places, not repayring to the kinges chamber or hall.'

As the great chamber expanded, so the service quarters in manor houses built up. At one end of the hall were the kitchens, separated from the hall by a screen and the screens passage behind it.

In the fourteenth century a buttery – not for butter, but for beer, from the Anglo-Latin *butta*, 'cask' or 'bottle' – was added between the hall and the kitchens, with a guest room above it. Alongside the buttery there was a pantry – from 'paneterie', Old French for bread room. Above the screen went the crucial accessory for a satisfactory night's wassailing – the minstrels' gallery.

While these extra rooms were tacked on to grand manor houses, lower down the social scale the hall remained the heart of the house.

The classic yeoman's house of the late fifteenth century was based around a hall with a parlour at one end. This more modest hall combined a kitchen, sitting room and dining room – a model you can still see in farmhouses across Britain, albeit much modernised as the farmhouse kitchen.

The ancient farmhouse was the basic model for Heathcliff's home, built around 1500, in *Wuthering Heights* (1847) by Emily Brontë. It's rather different from 10 Downing Street.

One step brought us into the family sitting-room, without any introductory lobby or passage: they call it here 'the house' pre-eminently. It includes kitchen and parlour, generally; but I believe at Wuthering Heights the kitchen is forced to retreat altogether into another quarter.

The war between 'drawing room' and 'lounge' kicked off relatively recently. The first mention of 'lounge' as a noun – as opposed to the verb, from the Old French *lungis*, 'a lout' – was in 1881. But it wasn't used widely until the twentieth century. *The Daily Mail Book of Bungalows* (1922) still referred to the word as part of a hyphenated term: 'lounge-hall' or 'dining-lounge'. Over the next thirty years it acquired its evil class connotations, as illustrated by Betjeman's 'A Few Late Chrysanthemums' (1954):

> It's ever so close in the lounge, dear
> But the vestibule's comfy for tea.

By the time of the BBC TV series *To the Manor Born* (1979–81 and a regrettable 2007 Christmas Special), snobbery reached its peak in the form of Penelope Keith's Audrey fforbes-Hamilton. The architectural division of class was now absolute.

Cricket House in Cricket St Thomas, Somerset, was the model for the manor house in the fictional village of Grantleigh in the series. At the time of filming it belonged to the father-in-law of Peter Spence, the programme's creator and writer.

64

She'd call it a drawing room – Penelope Keith and Cricket House, Somerset, Audrey fforbes-Hamilton's old home, built by Sir John Soane in 1804. (BBC)

Sir John Soane and the Red Phone Box

The architect of Cricket House was also responsible for that British icon, the red telephone box, or the K6 as it's officially called. It was designed by Sir Giles Gilbert Scott (1880–1960), the architect of Liverpool's Anglican Cathedral (1910–48) and Bankside Power Station (1947), now Tate Modern. But Scott proudly admitted that he borrowed the phone box's starfish-shaped roof – or cross-vaulted ceiling – from Sir John Soane (1753–1837).

Soane dreamt it up in 1792 for the breakfast room of his house in Lincoln's Inn Fields, London, now the Sir John Soane's Museum. Soane said of this room – its ceiling dotted with a series of little mirrors and a magician's box of fanciful effects – that he had evoked the 'poetry of architecture'. The starfish ceiling cropped up again in his tomb in Old St Pancras Churchyard, which he built in 1816 for his wife.

Scott designed the K6 in 1935 after doing the groundwork in the K2 of 1926. Since 1920 there had been five models of phone box – K1 to K5 – but it's the K6 we all recognise.

Made of eighteen sections, joined by two hundred screws, sixty thousand K6s were produced until 1967 in one of three Scottish locations – Kirkintilloch, Glasgow or Falkirk. On each box there's a maker's plate which tells you where it was built. K7 (from 1959) and K8 (from 1968) were not popular – the K8, with its big windows, was particularly prey to vandalism. After the K8, British Telecom moved on to the ugly aluminium KX100 and KX100 Plus.

There are now 62,000 pay phones in Britain; 13,000 of them are red boxes.

The tomb of Sir John Soane and his wife at Old St Pancras Church, London (1816); Sir Giles Gilbert Scott's K6, Whitehall (1935).

Although it has fourteenth-century origins, Cricket House is essentially an early-nineteenth-century house built by Sir John Soane. It illustrates what great social changes had taken place since Sir Gawain dined with King Arthur's Court – and King Arthur's servants – in the big old hall at Camelot. The hall has mutated into the dining room and drawing room. The servants have been cleared from what was once the grandest room in the house – the hall – and installed in low-ceilinged quarters in the basement or the attic.

The hall had been the focus of the house since the Anglo-Saxons – the Latin *focus* means 'fireplace' – and it was where the main fire in the house used to be. Now it was fast becoming the place where you hang your coat before making for the kitchen. Do you ever sit in your hall, let alone sleep or eat in it, like King Arthur with his servants at Camelot?

Audrey fforbes-Hamilton's hall was still enormous but she wouldn't have eaten there in a million years, and certainly not with her old butler, Brabinger, however far below the salt he sat. Things were a little more cramped when she moved into the Old Lodge after Peter Bowles's Richard DeVere took over the manor house. But she still didn't eat with Brabinger.

6

Byron's Mouldering Abbey

Merrie England Gets Decorated

Newstead! What saddening change of scene is thine!
Thy yawning arch betokens slow decay;
The last and youngest of a noble line,
Now holds thy mouldering turrets in his sway.

George Gordon Byron, 'Elegy on Newstead Abbey', 1807

Byron's years at his ruined family pile – Newstead Abbey, near Mansfield, Nottinghamshire – were not happy. He had grown up nearby in a little Georgian house, waiting for his inheritance. But once he got Newstead he never had enough money to keep the place going and eventually flogged it to an old friend when he was twenty-eight.

Since Henry VIII granted the priory to Sir John Byron for £810 during the dissolution of the monasteries, it had passed down to the poet, the 6th and last Lord Byron, 'the wreck of the line'. When he inherited in 1798, aged ten, the oaks along the drive had been chopped down to pay the grocer; hay bales were stacked high in the hall; the

Byron's yawning arch at Newstead Abbey (late thirteenth century), Nottinghamshire. (Getty Images)

corridors were given over to cattle. Byron was forced to let Newstead out and live in the lodge during holidays from Harrow.

Occasionally Byron went shooting on the estate with his tenant, Lord Grey de Ruthyn. When the peer took to molesting Byron, the poet fled Newstead, returning a few years later to live in the prior's chamber above the cloister. One of the few improvements he made was a classical monument to his dog Boatswain, buried by the high altar of the old church in 1808.

Byron did have some golden hours there with friends from Trinity College, Cambridge. In the summer of 1809 they dressed up as the 'merry monks' of Newstead and drank until three in the morning from a monk's skull; dug up in the abbey's gardens, the skull had been made into a goblet set in a silver base. When they weren't drinking they played badminton or teased Byron's pet wolf and bear.

These irreverent games cropped up in *Childe Harold's Pilgrimage* (1818), where Newstead – 'Monastic dome! Condemned to uses vile!' – was the model for the abbey inherited by the poem's hero.

For all Byron's troubles with the place, Newstead is a good spot to study Decorated architecture. It was begun in the late twelfth century as a priory for Augustinian canons; its thirteenth-century front has some fine Decorated work.

Byron's 'yawning arch' survives, as do the blind arches on either side. Those cinquefoil and sexfoil windows were characteristic of the time. Look how those mullions curve away from the vertical at the top – classic Decorated.

Decorated England was Merrie England, the England of the three King Edwards, among them the flamboyantly gay Edward II, with his close pal Piers Gaveston.

It was a relatively peaceful time when people let their hair – and their drawbridges – down. The wool economy was booming, the barons were rich and the buildings got flasher. And the most obviously flash feature of the Decorated style was the growth and greater sophistication of those windows, like at Newstead. Where those Early English lancets were separated by strips of masonry, Decorated windows were brought together in one big glass frame, narrowing at the top in a network of intertwining tracery.

Tracery began to get more elegant like this in around 1250, with mullions bent like tree branches into so-called bar tracery. From around 1300 you get intersecting tracery, a mesh of slim ribs forming jagged clover shapes and ogees; and then the utterly enchanting reticulated tracery – a net of ogees – took off from the early fourteenth century.

Ogees were a real giveaway to the Decorated style. An ogee is a double curve and an ogee arch a pair of double curves, concave then convex, meeting to form the top of a doorway or arch.

The adjective for ogee-shaped things is 'ogive'. The two words are pronounced 'oh gee' and 'oh jive' – appropriate shouts of joy for such lovely things.

The other giveaway to the Decorated style was, as the name implies, a proliferation of decoration, in the form of thick encrustations of pinnacles, crockets and ballflowers. Pinnacles are small, ornamental turrets, usually ending in a pyramid or a cone. The crockets nestling on those pinnacles are little hooks, often in the shape of buds or curled leaves. And ballflower is exactly what it sounds like: stone balls wrapped in three-petalled flowers.

Decorated columns, too, continued their upward, crash-dieting climb. Those shafts that stood proud of Early English pillars were now absorbed into a clustered sheaf of tall, thin beanpoles. At the top of these columns, ribs sprouted out across the ceiling like palm trees.

Because Britain was not well endowed with stone quarries, a lot of Decorated work was carved in timber in the thirteenth and fourteenth centuries, often by joiners who'd done plenty of ship-building.

To see the Decorated style at its height, head for Ely Cathedral

DATING TIP

The first ogee in England appeared on the Eleanor Crosses built by Edward I in 1291–4 along the funeral route of his wife, Queen Eleanor, from Lincolnshire to Westminster Abbey. The most famous one is Charing Cross, although today's cross, by the railway station, is an 1863 replica, designed by E.M. Barry, the son of Sir Charles Barry who helped to build Parliament. The original Charing Cross was south of Nelson's Column where the statue of King Charles I now stands. A plaque nearby says that distances from London on British road signs are still measured from here.

In 1290 King Edward was in Scotland, waiting for Queen Eleanor. On the way she caught a fever and died soon after at a manor house near Lincoln. The Queen's body was taken from Lincoln to Westminster Abbey for a state funeral. The grief-stricken king ordered that a memorial cross be installed at each of the twelve stopping points of the funeral procession along its 172-mile route.

The twelve sites were: Lincoln, Grantham, Stamford, Geddington, Hardingstone, Stony Stratford, Woburn, Dunstable, St Albans, Waltham, Cheapside and Charing Cross. Only three original crosses remain: at Geddington, Hardingstone and Waltham. The last of these was the first historic building in Britain to be given official protection. In 1721 the Reverend William Stukeley, a Lincolnshire vicar and the first secretary of the Society of Antiquaries, paid four shillings for a set of wooden bollards to protect the cross from traffic.

(1335–53), Cambridgeshire. The 1342 octagon beneath the crossing tower was a confidence trick – wood imitating stone, sculpted into ornate bosses, tracery and vaults.

Ely's Lady Chapel of 1349 showed how English masons could do stone, too, when they had the material. Reversing the pattern of the octagon, stone was treated like wood, rippling and curving in the slimmest, most liquid lines. A star-shaped vault covered one of the most ornate rooms in Britain. Imagine what it looked like when it was painted in its original lurid colours, before the Puritans had their way with all that stained glass.

The tracery was ornate but delicate, allowing plenty of light in to flood the crockets, pinnacles, gables and arcade of ogees which lined the walls – a parsley bed of sculpture, one critic called it. You can also see a heart-stopping set of nodding ogees – ogee arches that swell forwards as well as sideways.

Henry VIII, sheltered by nodding ogees – King's College, Cambridge.

7

Myrna Loy's
Favourite Style

Perpendicular Gothic

In 1934, when John Betjeman was the *Evening Standard*'s film critic, he found himself short of things to say in an interview with Myrna Loy, star of *The Thin Man*.

'Would you mind if I said you liked English Perpendicular?'

'It's fine by me, honey,' she cooed.

You can't blame Myrna Loy, a Montana girl, for not knowing much about Perpendicular, a form of Gothic architecture that's rare everywhere except Britain. Some say it's the only true British Gothic style.

With walls made almost entirely of window, Perpendicular lantern churches would have been eye-scorching cauldrons in a Spanish summer. In the soft light and temperate summers of Britain, they were ideal. Our weather produced the only exclusively British architecture. And Perpendicular spires gave exclamation points to a skyline obscured by all-consuming, damp greyness.

See a Perpendicular Gothic church against the horizon and look how much light passes through it, and in what varied shapes; not just through those big windows, but through the light, airy, crocketed and perforated spires.

> DATING TIP
>
> Perpendicular was the longest period of Gothic architecture, stretching from 1340 to 1530 – the earliest surviving Perpendicular work is in the choir of Gloucester Cathedral.

Perpendicular windows were made up of panel tracery – the accumulation of straight-sided panels with mullions soaring straight to the top of the window. One of the original meanings of the word 'perpendicular' was 'nearly vertical' or 'very steep'. These panels often had cusped heads – that is, with sharp points, from the Latin *cuspis*, 'point'.

Perpendicular windows in the Chapel Royal (1530s), built by Henry VIII, St James's Palace, London. If you'd looked through these windows on 10 February 1840 you'd have seen Prince Albert marrying Queen Victoria. This is also the church where George V was married and where the Duchess of Cornwall's granddaughter, Lola Parker Bowles, was christened in June 2008.

The overall effect was of immense height and straightness – long shafts of glass heading north, with none of that Decorated diversion into twirly-whirly ornament.

Vaulting Ambitions

> With what rich precision the stonework soars and springs
> To fountain out a spreading vault – a shower that never falls.
>
> *John Betjeman, 'Sunday Morning, King's Cambridge'*

75

Treasure Vaults – King's College Chapel, Cambridge (1515).

No chunk of a British building has been more praised than the Perpendicular fan vaults of the chapel of King's College, Cambridge – commissioned by Henry VI in the late fifteenth century but not finished until 1515, after his death.

Wordsworth wrote about how ruinously expensive they were when he visited Cambridge in 1820 to see his brother, then Master of Trinity College. His sonnet 'Within King's College Chapel, Cambridge' praised Henry VI – 'the royal saint' in the poem – for spending so much on such a splendid building:

Tax not the royal saint with vain expense
. . . high Heaven rejects the lore
Of nicely-calculated less or more:
So deemed the man who fashioned for the sense
These lofty pillars, spread that branching roof
Self-poised, and scooped into ten thousand cells
Where light and shade repose, where music dwells
Lingering – and wandering on as loth to die.

George Santayana (1863–1952), the Spanish-American philosopher, spent a year at the college in 1897. The question was not whether the fan vaults were worth it, but whether the dons were. 'The birds are not worthy of the cage,' he wrote.

These inspirational fan vaults – the biggest in the world – are great sprays of stone ribs streaming out of the edges of the ceiling, curving and criss-crossing in a kaleidoscopic frenzy. They marked the high-water point for vaults – the name for those pretty threads of masonry holding up the ceiling of the nave and aisles of a church.

Other sorts of vaults, with their slim stone spines, help to support the weight of the ceiling – the pressure of one stone on another holds the vault together. But fan vaults – stone convex cones covered with heavy webs of decorative masonry – actually add to the weight. King's College's vaults had to be supported by huge external buttresses. These buttresses also allowed the glittering walls of stained glass to be uninterrupted by heavy piers.

Vaults are vital dating tips, too. First remember: the more complicated the vault, the later it is. The latest – and most ornate – Gothic vaults were those fan vaults, built in the Perpendicular period, from 1340 to 1530. The earlier types of vaults are listed in the Glossary.

8

From Hovel to Bolthole

A Brief History of Cottaging from the
Fourteenth Century Onwards

The transformation of the cottage – from downtrodden peasant's ultra-basic crash pad to hedge-fund manager's downtime battery-recharger – took a long time.

It was only in the late fourteenth century that Rural Man upshifted from a wattle-and-daub, one-room shanty roofed with straw or reed to the sort of permanent structure that has survived into modern times.

These new cottages usually had two rooms: a hall with the hearth, and the chamber or bower – that is, the bedroom. In the north and west of the country, the earliest cottages were cruck-framed, that is, built round an A-frame provided by a curving tree split in half. The two halves, or crucks (like crutch, both meaning 'fork-shaped'), rested against each other. To get that all-important bend in the timber, builders cut down trees that grew horizontally out of a river bank before sprouting upwards.

You can still spot crucks in ancient cottages, both on the outside and inside. The smallest cottages had two pairs of crucks, a pair at either end. Bigger cottages repeated these pairs every sixteen feet or so – this sixteen-foot span, called a bay, was the average stable size for a pair of oxen. Cattle sheds and stables were attached to cottages – in Wales, you can still sometimes see the medieval colour scheme in the old longhouses: a red house connected to a white byre.

Gaps between crucks were filled with wattle and daub. Wattle is a net of hazel wands woven with reeds and branches, then matted – or daubed – with a mixture of horsehair, clay and dung.

Once those crucks were painted black, and the wattle and daub white, you ended up with the familiar black and white – or magpie – look. That look is better known in later box-framed houses, squarer than the A-shaped, cruck-framed jobs.

In the late seventeenth century, if those wattle and daub panels rotted, they were replaced by brick nogging – lines of bricks, set at decorative angles.

Before 1450, great big triangular spaces between the crucks – sometimes divided into large rectangles – were common. After 1450, the frames were divided into smaller and more decorative squares and rectangles; the more timber you used, the richer you were.

What Mock Tudor was Mocking

> Imitation, if extensive enough, really does debauch one's taste for the genuine. It is almost impossible now to take any real delight in Elizabethan half-timber – logical and honourable as it is – because we are so sickened with the miles of shoddy imitation with which we are surrounded.
>
> *Evelyn Waugh,* A Call to the Orders, *1938*

The former Deputy Prime Minister, John Prescott, got a real kicking when his expenses were published in May 2008. Not only had he spent £6707 of taxpayers' money on home improvements. The killer detail was the style of that home. Prescott spent the money on – shock, horror – mock-Tudor panels.

Snobbery about mock Tudor has been intense for seventy years, ever since the architectural and comic strip cartoonist Osbert Lancaster (1908–86) first attacked it.

Stockbroker's Tudor, as drawn by Osbert Lancaster, *Pillar to Post* (1938).

People love mock-Georgian terraces and Gothic Revival houses. But mock Tudor gets it in the neck. The style can actually look very nice; it just has to be done well. Liberty's flagship shop off Regent Street, London, built in 1923, gets the traditional Tudor profusion of gables and repeated panels just right. The materials are right, too: the shop was built from nice old wooden bits of eighteenth-century men-of-war – the *Impregnable* and the *Hindustan* – and put together in the original way with mortises and pegs. The whole thing was built around a seasoned oak cage, with proper leaded windows and handmade roofing tiles. It looks lovely – a real work of art that even Prescott-haters couldn't take against.

The problem with mock Tudor comes when it's not Tudor enough; like Osbert Lancaster's 'Roadhouse Tudor' – semi-detached houses, often strung alongside arterial roads, with a single gable to one side. Or his 'Stockbroker's Tudor' – mock-Tudor executive homes, standing in their own grounds, with gables sprinkled about at will. Still, Stockbroker's Tudor was tremendously popular, however much it was mocked in 1930s satires like the *Song of the Sussex House-Agent*:

> Four postes round my bed,
> Oake beams overhead,
> Olde rugs on ye floor,
> No stockbroker could ask for more.

Most mock Tudor is a thin attempt at the real thing, using only the odd panel and half-timbered gable to achieve its flimsy effects. Real Tudor houses – the sort you find in rows in ancient towns like Chester and Shrewsbury – were a more regimented accumulation of units: block after block, panel after panel, gable after gable, jettied window after jettied window.

As for their layout, the ground-floor hall of the average Tudor town-house remained the most important room, as it was in early medieval houses. The bedroom was on the first floor. Bay windows projected more and got wider the higher you went.

Most genuine Tudor houses in London were destroyed in the Great Fire. Even before that, in 1605, James I banned new timber house fronts, but only in London. James I said of London that he had found the 'City and suburbs of stickes and left them of Bricke'; one down from Emperor Augustus, who boasted that he found Rome brick and left it marble.

Regardless of the Fire, the Tudor house lasted longer in the provinces because of cultural drag. In 1664, when the classical terraced house was born in London, you could still find Tudor houses going up in Bristol.

Real Tudor gables, like the mock ones, could just be plain triangles. They could also be rather more elaborate, looping things, with scrolled volutes (twirled endings) at either end, topped off with a shell pattern. Pretty as these gables were, they weren't merely decorative. Gables raised above the roof stopped the wind getting under and lifting up the thatching or the tiles.

One casualty of the 1667 Act for Rebuilding the City of London after the Great Fire were these pretty gables. Although they were not actually disallowed by the Act, the rules on the height of ceilings made the gable's soaring roof impractical. They soon went out of fashion.

By the seventeenth century, the rich graduated to brick and stone, leaving old-fashioned, Tudor, black-and-white framing techniques to humbler homes. Lots of frames were later concealed behind plaster, weatherboarding or tiles.

Still, the rich were unlikely, in the seventeenth century, to gravitate to a cottage. The cult of the well-appointed, upmarket cottage – built for beauty, not pragmatism – only got going in the late eighteenth century.

At the same time, the great bulk of cottages – for the rural poor – also improved. It had become increasingly unacceptable for them to be housed in hovels. In *Hints to Gentlemen of Landed Property* (1775),

Emu's Tudor Perch

In the late 1980s, the comedian Rod Hull, best known for his TV double act with his feathered partner Emu, bought Restoration House in Rochester, Kent. For £387,000 he got one of the finest Elizabethan townhouses in Britain. He had also sown the seeds of his death.

The house was in such a terrible state that Hull went bankrupt trying to restore it. His wife left him and he was reduced to living in a shepherd's cottage in East Sussex. It was from the roof of this cottage that he fell to his death in March 1999, aged sixty-three. He had clambered on to the roof to adjust the TV aerial to get a sharper picture of Inter Milan versus Manchester United in the Quarter Final, Second Leg, of the UEFA Champions League.

You can see why Hull went for Restoration House. It appears to have been built in two phases – in the sixteenth century and the mid-seventeenth century. As a result it's a charming mix of Dutch gables and classical pilasters – columns that are flattened in low profile against a wall. Much harder to fall off a roof fringed with gables, too.

Restoration House also captivated Dickens, who lived nearby and used it as the model for Miss Havisham's house in *Great Expectations* (1861): 'Of old brick, and dismal . . . The cold wind seemed to blow colder there, than outside the gate.' He called it Satis House after another house in Rochester. Queen Elizabeth I stayed there; when asked whether she'd been comfortable, she said, 'Satis', the Latin word for 'enough'.

The young hero of *Great Expectations*, Pip, asked Miss Havisham's adopted daughter, Estella, about the house's history:

'Is Manor House the name of this house, miss?'

'One of its names, boy.'

'It has more than one, then, miss?'

'One more. Its other name was Satis; which is Greek, or Latin, or Hebrew, or all three – or all one to me – for enough.'

'Enough House,' said I; 'that's a curious name, miss.'

'Yes,' she replied; 'but it meant more than it said. It meant, when it was given, that whoever had this house, could want nothing else. They must have been easily satisfied in those days, I should think.'

Nathaniel Kent hinted that it was a little absurd for landlords to provide elaborate stables and kennels while skimping on cottages.

Not long after, in 1781, John Wood, the man who dreamt up Bath's Royal Crescent, wrote another book devoted to the cottage, aimed at the grander end of the market.

Sir John Soane and John Nash also designed pretty little cottages; Nash was keen on the cottage orné, literally 'adorned cottage'. These were big houses disguised as thatched cottages, with bargeboards (ornamental boards running along the edge of the gable) – pet peasant housing for the chic client. Nash introduced the cottage orné in the dairy of Blaise Castle, Avon, in 1802. Nearby, at Blaise Hamlet, he built nine cottages in an artfully picturesque range around a green.

By the time the Duke and Duchess of Kent took their baby – later Queen Victoria – on holiday to Woolbrook Cottage in Sidmouth, Devon, in the early 1820s, the cottage fashion had taken off. The arch, dingly-dell school of weekend-cottage architecture had arrived.

Modern cottage owners will be reassured to know that the great arbiter of elegant life, Jane Austen, lived in one. They'll be less pleased to find that she thought living in a cottage was a little downmarket.

In real life, Jane Austen was perfectly comfortable at Chawton Cottage, an eighteenth-century red-brick house on her brother's estate in Chawton, Hampshire, where she moved with her sister and mother in 1809, after her father's death. But, despite the name, Chawton Cottage was in fact a big, handsome, five-bay house, which Austen lavishly praised to her brother, Captain Francis Austen:

> Our Chawton Home, how much we find
> Already in it to our mind:
> And now convinced, that when complete
> It will have all other houses beat
> That either have been made or mended,
> With rooms concise or rooms distended.

85

'Twas like taking bread to the top of the world' – classic sixteenth-century cottages, Gold Hill, Shaftesbury, Dorset, also known as Hovis Hill since the 1973 TV advert. (www.advertisingarchives.co.uk)

In Austen's novels, though, cottage life wasn't quite as accepted as it is now among the well-to-do. It is a big comedown for the Dashwood girls in *Sense and Sensibility* (1811) when they're forced by their brother out of smart Norland Park and into a cottage: 'Barton Cottage, though small, was comfortable and compact; but as a cottage it was defective, for the building was regular, the roof was tiled, the window-shutters were not painted green, nor were the walls covered with honeysuckles.'

The lack of dingly-dell motifs didn't bother the Dashwoods much. What did bother Mrs Dashwood was the cottage's size and lack of a suitable drawing room:

A narrow passage led directly through the house into the garden behind. On each side of the entrance was a sitting room about 16 feet square; and beyond them were the offices and the stairs. Four bedrooms and two garrets formed the rest of the house . . .

These parlours are both too small for such parties of our friends as I hope to see often collected here; and I have some thoughts of throwing the passage into one of them, with perhaps a part of the other, and so leave the remainder of that other for an entrance; this, with a new drawing-room which may be easily added, and a bed-chamber and garret above, will make it a very snug little cottage.

That passage through the middle of the house was a familiar feature in older cottages. Most cottage owners have since taken Mrs Dashwood's advice and filled it in to make more space.

Jane Austen didn't say how much rent Mrs Dashwood paid, but it was probably less than £1300 a week. That's how much you'll pay in high season for the cottage used in BBC TV's 2008 version of *Sense and Sensibility*. Blackpool Mill, on the north Devon coast, is owned by Sir Hugh and Lady Stucley, of nearby Hartland Abbey. The fifteenth-century, four-bedroom cottage was given dormer windows, fake shutters and an extra chimney to play the nineteenth-century cottage in the TV series.

9

A Very Big House in the Country

The Birth of the Country House in the Sixteenth Century

If anyone spots
The Queen of Scots
In a hand-embroidered shroud,
We're proud
Of the Stately Homes of England.
Noël Coward, 'The Stately Homes of England', 1938

Noël Coward's knowledge of architectural history was – like his pronunciation, timing and courtliness – impeccable. The life of Mary Queen of Scots (1542–87) coincided with, or just predated, the construction of the first great generation of English country houses – Burghley, Longleat, Hardwick and Hatfield among them. There had of course been fine palaces and manor houses before, but nothing to match this tide of masterpieces in such a concentrated period.

These so-called 'prodigy houses' were erected to impress Queen Elizabeth I, who built no palaces herself but relied on courtiers to have her to stay during the summer when she left London.

With defensive castles no longer needed, Tudor fortunes were spent on comfort and beauty rather than arrow slits. Some defensive features remained – towers and battlements in particular – but these were increasingly for show.

These new palaces had suites of state apartments, long galleries for indoor walks and formal gardens with terraces, fountains and yew walks.

While castles turned into pretty pleasure houses, so their old military characteristics were borrowed for decorative features. Oxford and Cambridge colleges developed crenellated walls; Perpendicular churches grew mock battlements on top of their towers and along their parapet walls; elaborate tomb canopies sprouted crenellations.

Desire for beauty instead of defence also led to a change in the use of towers. In the twelfth and thirteenth centuries, the most important tower, the keep, was in the middle of the castle and was made of stone – the ideal place for brave last stands. Through the fifteenth century, towers were increasingly made of flimsy brick – fashionable, and easier to build with and cheaper than stone. Caister Castle (1446), Norfolk, was the first castle with a brick tower, built by Sir John Fastolf, as in Shakespeare's Falstaff.

Towers were now decorative things, displayed at the most prominent point of a building – its entrance. Brick gatehouse towers became a classic Tudor device. Look out for corner turrets on gatehouses, with wide central arches for horses and carriages, and narrow side arches for pedestrians. Those turrets were mostly octagonal – the concept was expanded for Tudor palaces, where the builders erected huge octagonal towers on either end of the façade, with the gatehouse in the middle.

The boom in turrets, alongside pepperpot domes on top of pinnacles, combined with a spreading vogue for gables. These busy Tudor skylines were made even busier by corkscrew-shaped chimneys. Under Elizabeth I those Tudor corkscrew columns untwisted into rectangular classical columns grouped in twos and threes.

Burghley House (1577), Lincolnshire, had the bristliest skyline in the country: chimneys disguised as classical columns jostled with pepperpot towers and stone pyramids.

An Elizabethan and Jacobean agricultural boom led to a chimney explosion – Hampton Court alone has 571 chimneys. In his *Description of England*, published in the year (1577) that Burghley sprouted its chimneys, William Harrison noticed them not just on palaces, but all over the humble houses of Radwinter, Essex. A generation before, you'd be lucky to get three chimneys in a village full of cottages. By 1577 there was a 'multitude of chimneys lately erected'.

The agricultural boom affected other household comforts, too. In

DATING TIP

In the seventeenth century, a new fashion emerged for building chimney shafts at an angle to their base. You can see this at Rudyard Kipling's 1634 house, Bateman's, in Burwash, East Sussex. Its six chimneys are all at an angle.

Chimney pots first became popular under George III in the late eighteenth century. Not everyone liked them. In the nineteenth century, Tennyson asked, in 'The "How" and the "Why"' (1830):

Why the church is with a steeple built;
And the house with a chimney pot?

The Victorians didn't share his attitude; chimney pots spread across Britain throughout the century.

the 1570s the British started throwing out those so-last-year logs they used for pillows, and replaced them with bolsters.

Humbler houses were fitted with upmarket materials like oak panelling and plaster-of-Paris ceilings. Façades were also covered in plaster, for decorative reasons – like that East Anglian pargeting mentioned earlier – and for fireproofing.

Chimneys spread with the growing taste for coal – a new fuel after centuries of wood fires. And, where smoke previously seeped out through the roof or in a basic flue through an outside wall, fireplaces could now be installed on inner walls – a great breakthrough.

DATING TIP

Chimneys were increasingly made of brick or stone – again nice and fireproof. As a result, houses built on the cusp of the 1570s chimney boom were a fetching mix of timber fronts and brick chimney stacks.

Letting fireplaces into the wall meant you could roof over the hall at first-floor level and stick a great chamber above it, with its own fireplace. This rang the death-knell for the hall as a place for grandees – there was now an equally big room directly above it, and plenty of other warm rooms to gather in, like the long gallery, an Elizabethan favourite. By 1600, nobles withdrew from the hall completely, leaving it a mere vestibule and a place for the servants.

Now that nobles entertained in these new great chambers, upper floors became altogether smarter.

The breakthrough came at Hardwick Hall (1597), Derbyshire, built by Bess of Hardwick, the Countess of Shrewsbury (1527–1608). Bess, the second most powerful woman in the kingdom after Elizabeth I, put all the finest rooms – the best bedroom, the great chamber and the long gallery – on the second floor, to take advantage of that new fashionable thing: a room with a view. The pattern of building bedrooms upstairs was copied lower down the social order, too. In the 1620s rural cottages were gentrified, with the hall roofed in at first-floor level and a bedroom inserted into the new space.

With smarter rooms moving up from the ground floor, the staircases to reach them were kitted out more smartly, too, with richly carved newels and balusters.

These new great chambers on the first floor led off the grandest bedroom, which usually had the best bed. Beds were so crucial to status that even the second-best bed – like the one Shakespeare left to his wife in his will in 1616 – was valuable.

They were enormous things; the idea of the twin bed was anathema to the Elizabethans, only arriving on the scene in the late eighteenth century. The Great Bed of Ware, built in 1590, for Ware Park, Hertfordshire – and now in the V&A – can sleep fifteen people – if you can find a duvet that's ten feet by eleven feet. In Shakespeare's *Twelfth Night* (1601), Sir Toby Belch says, 'As many lies as will lie in thy sheet of paper, although the sheet were big enough for the bed of Ware in England, set 'em down.'

The same bed appeared in Jonson's *Epicoene*:

Sir John Daw: Why, we have been . . .
Sir Amorous La-Foole: . . . in the great bed at Ware together in our time.

The Elizabethans filled every square inch with ornament. Tudor linen-fold panelling – wood carved to imitate folded cloth, with nice, plain bottom edges, to make it easy to dust – gave way to carved, chiselled and patterned woodwork. Windows filled up with luridly coloured coats of arms. Plaster ceilings with elaborate geometrical patterns took off. Structural advances meant that hammerbeam roofs with heavy pendants were no longer needed. Still the Elizabethans stuck with them because they liked the look of those pendants dripping with plaster, like the fan-vault ceiling in the Henry VII Chapel at Westminster Abbey – built, as stipulated in Henry's will, so that ten thousand masses could be said for his soul.

These plaster stalactites were matched with plaster panelling in the Elizabethan and Jacobean periods. All this lavish decor on the walls was anchored in place by black and white marble chessboard floors. You had to be in a robust, sober frame of mind to take in the onslaught of strapwork, lozenges and early attempts at classical pillars, pilasters and friezes. Strapwork – a series of interwoven straps of elaborate join-ery – originated in Antwerp in the late sixteenth century.

Henry VIII, Father of British Classicism

As all these gatehouses, chimneys and pinnacles sprang up outside royal palaces, something unprecedented was going on inside them; something that echoed through British architecture for ever – the arrival of classicism.

When Henry VIII got in the sculptor Pietro Torrigiano (1472–1522) to design his father's classical, realistic and sophisticated tomb in Westminster

Abbey in 1512, it was a crucial moment. The new Renaissance influence heralded the end of Anglo-French architecture.

Torrigiano – who in his childhood broke Michelangelo's nose in a row over the frescoes they were copying in Santa Maria del Carmine,

95

What a difference a reign makes: Henry VII's birthplace, Pembroke Castle (1204), and his tomb in the Henry VII Chapel, Westminster Abbey (1512). (Corbis)

Florence – brought the Renaissance to Britain, several hundred years after it developed in Italy. Our first distinguished classical architect, Inigo Jones, was born in 1573, nearly two centuries after the first great Italian Renaissance architect, Filippo Brunelleschi, the man who built Florence's Duomo.

One reason for the delay was the Channel. But a greater barrier to classical architecture than a twenty-one-mile-wide stretch of water was the Reformation: Henry VIII's religious revolution and Elizabeth I's isolationism meant that not a single Italian architect was invited to Britain in the sixteenth century. There were, though, plenty of Italian craftsmen who made the journey.

And it's no mystery that Italians should have been called in; English craftsmen just weren't capable of that sort of work. A series of his compatriots, all much in demand, followed in Torrigiano's wake. Antonio Toro became court painter and, in 1535, a group of Italians designed the screen and stalls at King's College, Cambridge.

To get a picture of how much art and architecture changed in the fifteenth and sixteenth centuries, look at medieval Pembroke Castle – where Henry VII was born in 1457 – and then at his Renaissance effigy of half a century later.

The End of Britishness – We Go Symmetrical

The gardening writer Vita Sackville-West (1892–1962) said that the Renaissance wasn't really an English style, that it was far too Continental, and that the only true English buildings grew organically from purely English influences – like her childhood home, Knole, or the home of her adulthood, Sissinghurst, both in Kent.

She had a point. Because we weren't used to classicism, our first attempts in the late sixteenth century were pretty ham-fisted. The columns were fat and stumpy, with lashings of Elizabethan strapwork sprayed all over them.

Still, in the late sixteenth century, Renaissance symmetry gradually emerged in the new palaces. Longleat, Wiltshire, begun in 1554, was symmetrical to north and south and to east and west. Each façade was also itself symmetrical.

Hardwick Hall was the first house to take the symmetry inside, and the first to have a 'cross-hall' – laid right across the middle of the house along the building's central axis, with visitors entering through the middle of the façade, straight into the hall. The hall there also did without the traditional screens passage and the dais where nobles used to dine at high table. The fireplace – previously in the middle of one long side of the hall – was now moved to the far end.

Both Longleat and Hardwick, as well as Wollaton Hall, Nottinghamshire, and Burghley, were designed by the chief architect of the age, Robert Smythson (1535–1614). This mason turned surveyor was the first man to have 'architect' written on his tomb. His gravestone at Wollaton church reads: 'Architecter and Surveyor unto the most worthy house of Wollaton with divers others of great account.'

Until then there had been no real concept of an architect. There were masons, joiners and patrons who paid for buildings. But there was no notion of Westminster Abbey or Canterbury Cathedral having a single architect who signed the plans. The profession – or trade, as it was to begin with, given the lowly position of early architects – only got going in the sixteenth century. And even at this date architects were not recognised as significant figures. The word 'architecture' doesn't appear in Shakespeare.

DATING TIP

Look out for bay windows on late Elizabethan and Jacobean houses. These big, rectangular, jutting chunks of glazed masonry provided lots of movement on Longleat's façade. With these vast ranges of windows, they were called lantern houses. 'Hardwick Hall, more glass than wall,' as one wag put it.

H blocks and E types

Look out for E- and H-plans on classic Elizabethan houses. Big as these palaces were, they were in fact a cut-down version of the courtyard manor house that came before. Those manor houses were ranged around a whole square courtyard; the new E- and H-plan houses took up only three sides of the square.

The E-plan was popular from 1590 to 1620; E had the added bonus of being the first letter of Queen Elizabeth's name. This plan had wings coming forward on either side, with a central porch forming the E's middle horizontal stroke. The hall ran along the vertical stroke of the E. The top and bottom horizontal strokes – truncations of the old courtyard – contained living rooms and the kitchens.

Sometimes, as at Hatfield (1611), Hertfordshire, the middle stroke of the E was nothing more than a porch, parallel to those great thrusting wings on either side.

DATING TIP

The first H-plan came in Armada year, 1588, at Wimbledon House. It lasted through the 1580s and 1590s and became the standard plan of the Jacobean period in the 1600s – examples included Montacute House, Somerset, and Charlton House, Greenwich.

Hall, entrance porch and principal staircases were placed on the horizontal line of the H, other rooms on the two vertical lines. Ogee-capped turrets on the corners of the roof were favourite motifs. The Jacobeans went in for cupolas and Dutch gables, too.

10

Material Considerations

What Are All These Places Made Of?

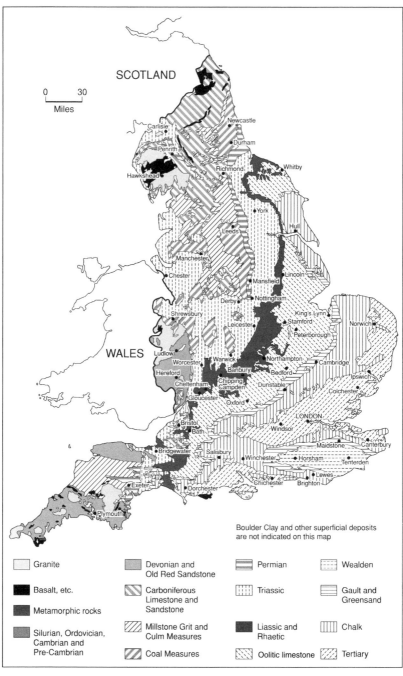

Granite	Devonian and Old Red Sandstone	Permian	Wealden
Basalt, etc.	Carboniferous Limestone and Sandstone	Triassic	Gault and Greensand
Metamorphic rocks	Millstone Grit and Culm Measures	Liassic and Rhaetic	Chalk
Silurian, Ordovician, Cambrian and Pre-Cambrian	Coal Measures	Oolitic limestone	Tertiary

What lies beneath – the stones of England.

Until you reach the modern age – of lugging granite kitchen surfaces from Aberdeen to Notting Hill, and oak floors from Shropshire to Islington – houses were built from the stuff in the ground beneath them. Only with the eighteenth- and nineteenth-century boom in canals and railways did it become cheap enough to, say, roof London houses with Welsh slate.

Look at the geological map of Britain, and you're also looking at what the houses on the different geological strips were made out of. So, you'll find stone cottages along that broad sash of oolitic limestone running diagonally across England's torso from Yorkshire through Nottinghamshire, Leicestershire, Oxfordshire, Wiltshire and Gloucestershire down to Somerset and Dorset. If you want to see a variety of stones, it's best to take a journey heading north-west to south-east, rather than following the line of the torso.

Britain's best stone churches also lie along this stone belt. Stone spires are particularly frequent there – the word 'steeplechase' came from the spires of Northamptonshire, Rutland and Leicestershire, where races from steeple to steeple were popular. In places where there was no local stone – only flint and timber – church towers kept their short wooden Norman spires. Where there was access to both timber and stone, they often combined the two, with a stone tower and a wooden bell-turret – the more flexible timber kept the bell from shaking the stone of the tower to pieces.

T.S. Eliot was so taken with the Ham Hill limestone of the church at East Coker, Somerset, that his ashes were buried in the churchyard in 1965. His ancestors had left the village for Boston, Massachusetts, in 1660. In 'East Coker' (1940) he wrote:

> In a warm haze the sultry light
> Is absorbed, not refracted, by grey stone.

Ham Hill is actually a fine, golden-brown, coarse-grained, shelly, Lower Jurassic limestone, quarried near Montacute, Somerset, since the Romans. Still, poetic licence and all that.

Real pros can tell the difference between those stones; not just from the colour, but from the microscopic whirls and whorls you can see close up, like stone fingerprints. The committed aesthete is never without a magnifying glass on his travels, to take in the little dints and curls of a nice oolitic limestone; and even little fragments of seashell. Oolitic (literally, in Greek, *egg stone,* from its shape under the microscope) limestone is a sedimentary calcium carbonate stone, part-formed from the shells of sea creatures.

A real pro can spot the difference between the Carboniferous sandstone used to build Glasgow until 1890, when the local quarries ran out of the stuff; and the Triassic sandstone – a pink colour, from sand grains covered in red iron oxide – imported afterwards from Dumfries and Ayrshire. The Stone of Scone, or Stone of Destiny, once under the Coronation Chair at Westminster Abbey and now in the crown room in Edinburgh Castle, is a lump of Perthshire sandstone.

The colour of those stones bleeds into the earth, too. So the Devonian Old Red Sandstone under Herefordshire is reflected in red soil, red churches and red houses. The use of local stone in local landscape produces a natural harmony, and the opposite is true – thus the oddness of Kinloch Castle (1897), on the island of Rum in the Hebrides. Its incongruous orangey-brown sandstone was carried miles over the sea from Annan, Dumfriesshire.

Stones vary enormously in strength. In the seventeenth and eighteenth centuries, Oxford builders used Headington freestone from the city's eastern fringes. Easily worked, it was also coarse and porous – that's why millions of pounds have been spent in the past half-century refacing the blackened, pitted university buildings. When Nathaniel Hawthorne, the American novelist, visited Oxford in 1856, he said, 'If you strike one of the old walls with a stick, a portion of it comes powdering down.'

Medieval Birmingham was built of another workable but flimsy stone – the local sandstone. You can still see it in the fifteenth-century tower of Aston church and the medieval tower of St Martin in the Bull Ring. The city's sandy soil was, by contrast, excellent for brick-making, so Birmingham turned to brick in the sixteenth century.

> **DATING TIP**
>
> Over several million years, layers of stone, sand, clay, and earth have been laid down, one on top of another. The closer you get to the surface, the more recently the stuff was laid down.
>
> This calculation becomes a little trickier if the layers of stone are tilted at an angle to the earth. So there's a long, multi-decker sandwich of stones – Great Oolite and Forest Marble among them – that tilts downwards towards London from the north-west. This means that the stone near the surface in London is younger than, say, the stone near the surface in the Midlands.

The Hard Man of Scottish Geology

Aberdeen is Britain's most exotic stone city. It's almost entirely built of the immensely hard local stone, granite; a stone so rich in radium that an Aberdeen Geiger counter never rests.

The city's granite comes in all sorts of colours, too. On Aberdeen's beach, in fifteen minutes on a wet day in 1952, John Betjeman found fifteen types of granite – grey, silver, pink, red, crimson, white, green purple, pink-red among them. 'Where the waves had washed the pebbles so that they were still wet, they glowed with an intenser colour just as the city of Aberdeen glows a deeper, richer silver after rain.'

Where stone was thin on the ground, or under it, houses used other materials. Oak, medieval Britain's most common tree, grows best on clay, so houses built of brick and timber are common in clay districts. 103

There are often precise regional differences in materials. In north Powys there's plenty of stone, but it splits easily, so everything except churches and castles was built of local oak. When that began to run out in about 1700, brick took over.

Brick, flint and plaster houses run along the chalk strips of England – east Dorset, Hampshire, Salisbury Plain, Wiltshire, Kent, the Berkshire Downs, the North and South Downs, the Chiltern Hills, Suffolk, Norfolk and east Yorkshire.

Timber-framed and weatherboarded houses cropped up across timber-rich Kent, Sussex and Surrey from the sixteenth century onwards. Weatherboarding – overlapping horizontal boards – worked beautifully for throwing rain away from the walls.

You'll find timber-and-stone cottages where the stone uplands meet the wooded plain in Gloucestershire. Cottages with drystone walls – plastered or whitewashed, with thatched roofs or stone slates – suited the bleak uplands and moorlands of Dartmoor, North Wales and the Scottish Highlands. Stones on those cottages were rough and ready; unlike the smooth, expensively cut stone of the big house.

At the humbler end of the market, pretty much any building material would do. In Norfolk, Suffolk and Cambridgeshire, they were keen on clay lumps pressed into moulds. In Devon, Dorset, Somerset and Wiltshire, they went for cob (called wichert in Buckinghamshire), a mixture of straw, mud and small stones. Cob was popular from the sixteenth century and was not replaced by brick until the nineteenth century.

Cob was put down in layers on a stone foundation over several months, with each layer trodden down and left to dry. The result was unusually strong except at the corners, which were rounded to prevent the cracking that came with square edges. Window- and door-frames were built into the wall as the layers piled up. A thatched roof was then jammed on top. Look out for the steep pitch of a thatched roof, designed to throw off the rain; slate roofs do the job with a shallower pitch.

The most popular and beautiful thatching material was long-stemmed wheat straw, currently in short supply because it doesn't yield as much wheat as short-stemmed wheat. Long straw is gradually giving way to less alluring water reed – 'Euro-style thatch', as it is damned by the Thatching Information Service of Levens Green, Hertfordshire. Water reed does, though, last sixty years compared with wheat straw's twenty.

Water reed used to be banned by English Heritage on any of its thirty thousand listed thatched buildings, except in East Anglia, where the stuff is grown. They relaxed the ban only after a disastrous harvest of long-stemmed wheat straw in 2008, when thatching straw zoomed from £600 to £1500 a tonne.

Thatching style varied according to location, as it still does in the sixty thousand thatched buildings that survive in Britain. In Cornwall and the Isle of Man they like domes of thatch tied down with straw ropes and held in place by slate pegs or weighed down with rocks. In Norfolk the water reed is laid in fetching patterns, with hazel used to ornament the ridge, verge and eaves.

Roofs varied according to location. Dutch gables and pantiled roofs went down well on East Anglian cottages – far from the slate mines of Wales and close to the Low Countries.

It wasn't just stone and brick that were scooped from the ground. Iron for the railings round St Paul's Cathedral came from the iron-ore soil under the forest of the Weald. It was forged at a foundry in Lamberhurst, Kent.

Stucco – Britain gets Plastered

While stucco, or fine plaster, comes in many different forms, all stuccos are combinations of an aggregate, a binder and water. The aggregate is the base reinforcement material – sand, gravel or crushed stone.

Traditional stucco was made from sand, lime and water; now it's usually made from Portland cement, sand and water. Applied in three coats (the scratch coat, brown coat and finish coat), it goes on wet and is shaped with wooden moulds over brickwork or timber lathes.

Usually stucco was painted beige or grey to imitate stone. Inigo Jones was keen on the stuff, combining it with Portland stone at the Queen's Chapel by St James's Palace and the Queen's House at Greenwich.

Stucco became less popular through the seventeenth century. Christopher Wren preferred brick and stone and the early Palladians were devoted to stone. But stucco took off again in the late eighteenth century. Robert Adam went crazy for it at Kenwood House (1767), Hampstead. One day in 1778 his family company covered some houses in Bloomsbury Square with stucco. The architect of these houses, John Nash, liked it so much that he eventually became London's stucco king; most strikingly in his terraces that snake down the eastern and western edges of Regent's Park. A special clause was inserted in the leases of these terraces that the lessees covenanted to renew the stucco every 4 August. Nash's predilection for stucco was lampooned in the *Quarterly Review* of June 1826:

> Augustus at Rome was for building renowned,
> For of marble he left what of brick he had found;
> But is not our Nash, too, a very great master?
> He finds us all brick and he leaves us all plaster.

On sunny Tuesday and Thursday afternoons in my childhood, the glare off the creamy-white stucco burnt into my barely formed retinas half a mile away on the school cricket pitch in the middle of the park. If I'd known it at the time, I'd have pointed out to my fellow fielders that Nash was partial to Parker's Stucco, made by a certain James Parker from clay on the Isle of Sheppey, Essex.

Other popular varieties of render – which is what stucco really is – were Lord Stanhope's Composition and Hamlin's Mastic. Nash used both.

Coade Stone, the most famous material of the time, was an artificial stone concocted by Mrs Eleanor Coade on the site of the Festival Hall in London between 1769 and 1833. Durable Coade Stone lasted a lot longer than lots of real stones. Apart from having a matte tone, it isn't easy to spot because it varies in colour, from light grey through light yellow to beige. The fireproof stone became particularly popular after the Building Act of 1774, which drastically reduced the amount of wood in the decoration of façades.

Eleanor Coade took her recipe for the stone to the grave, but it has recently been rediscovered by Stephen Pettifer, a Wiltshire sculptor. Rootling through the order books of the south Devon quarry where she got her materials, he worked out the exact proportion of clay she used. He deduced that the stone was made of 10 per cent grog (crushed ceramic pitchers), 5–10 per cent crushed flint, 5–10 per cent fine quartz (to reduce shrinkage), 10 per cent crushed soda lime glass and 60–70 per cent Ball clay from Devon and Dorset.

Mr Pettifer is now using Coade Stone for the statue of a huge Triton, a sea god, for Lord Rothermere, owner of the *Daily Mail*, at his house in Ferne Park, Dorset.

Coade Stone remained fashionable until the 1830s, when it was replaced by another artificial stone, Portland Cement. By then it had been used by a Debrettsful of grand clients, and it can still be found on places as varied as St Paul's Cathedral, Nelson's Memorial at Burnham, Norfolk, and Captain Bligh's tomb in the graveyard of St Mary's, Lambeth. The shop front of Twining's, the tea company, opposite the Royal Courts of Justice in the Strand, was recently cleaned to reveal immaculate Coade Stone beneath a century of soot.

Our Favourite Building Material

Even brick has its charm, and thank God for that – in a country like Britain, rich in brick earth and in many areas poor in stone. More British houses today are made of brick than any other material.

There's a real pleasure in noticing the different ways of laying bricks – or bonding as it's called. Bricks are laid lengthwise ('stretchers') or sideways ('headers'). A single layer of bricks is called a course.

There are all sorts of complicated bonding patterns, with alluring names like Rat-trap Bond and Flemish Garden Wall Bond. But let's stick to the two most common: English bond and Flemish bond. The first alternated header courses with stretcher courses, while the second alternated headers with stretchers in a single course.

> DATING TIP
>
> English bond dominated until the 1630s, when Flemish bond took over. Flemish bond prevailed until the early nineteenth century, when the Gothic Revivalists returned to the national style. Nowadays bricklayers vary between the two – the modern Englishman uses Flemish bond, and, I daresay, the modern Fleming uses English.

Bond, Flemish Bond – Heffer's Bookshop, Cambridge. English bond on an oriel window, Gonville and Caius College, Cambridge. There's some good English bond in the picture of Canonbury Tower at the beginning of this book.

DATING TIP

Bricks were first used by the Romans but the practice died out when they left in the early fifth century AD. When William the Conqueror came to build Colchester Castle, he had to use old Roman bricks – the Normans just didn't make them. Domestic brick-making wasn't revived in earnest for a thousand years after the Romans; in the fourteenth century the use of brick in northern France and the Low Countries became fashionable here. Later on, the Tudors loved the stuff, particularly in the south-east, so handy for the early brick importers of Holland. It wasn't until the fifteenth century that the word 'brick' was used regularly – the first mention of the word is by Flemings at work on Stonor Park, Oxfordshire, in 1416. Until then a brick had been called a 'waltyle', wall-tile. The Tudors were keen on diapering – diamond and zigzag patterns of red and black bricks. They made black bricks by over-burning grey ones.

DATING TIP

In 1625 Charles I decreed that the standard brick must be nine inches by 4⅜ inches by 2¼ inches.

There were no set dimensions for earlier Tudor bricks. They were priced by the thousand, though, so manufacturers made them as small as possible. The bigger and the more even the brick, and the thinner the joints, the later the building. Inigo Jones was the first to use rubbed or gauged bricks. These red and soft-orange bricks were sanded down to make fine, ultra-thin joints.

Modern bricks follow the British Standard of 215 millimetres by 102.5 millimetres by 65 millimetres – a bit fat, I think.

Under the Tudors, bricks spread from their East Anglian heartland throughout the country. Bricks were imported from the Lowlands as ballast in ships returning from delivering wool to the Continent. Belgian and Dutch brickmakers even set up shop in East Anglia. Tudor bricks were often laid vertically or in a herringbone pattern; in these formations they couldn't support anything very much and were really there for show.

By the seventeenth century, architects got more daring with brick colours. A mixture of red brick with white cornices and quoins, hipped roofs, dormer windows and cupolas was a Dutch idea, imported by the British architect Hugh May in the 1660s. Wren was keen on the look, combining bright-red brick of an even hue to contrast with his favourite gleaming white Portland stone. Nicholas Hawksmoor and Sir John Vanbrugh liked white Portland stone with brown and red bricks, as at their 1704 orangery at Kensington Palace.

Colours varied according to the clay the bricks were made of. Red brick goes red because the iron in the clay oxidises during firing. In industrial Lancashire, shale – rock formed from clay or mud – produced screaming red bricks called Accrington bloods. In the Chilterns, the clay, rich in lime, with no iron, produces lovely silver-grey bricks. There's a cottage in Cuxham near Watlington, Oxfordshire, with red, iron-rich bricks on the sides and grey, limey ones on the front.

Grey, red and purple bricks were popular from the late seventeenth century until around 1730, when they were replaced by pinkish-grey and brown-and-grey ones. In around 1800, grey gave way to yellow marl brick. This brick, used for the terrace-building boom, became known as London marl or London stock brick. The chalk in the soft Kent clay used for these bricks turns a yellowish-brown when it is fired.

As Osama bin Laden says, London is a yellow city. When my cousin, Fred, painted a picture of my parents' early-Victorian house in Ripplevale Grove, Islington in the 1970s, the bright yellow he chose for the façade was accurate (see the front endpaper). Note also the Flemish bond of the brickwork.

Looking at that brick now, there are dozens of colours. There are shades of brown, red, off-blacks and greys, and the off-white of the mortar between the bricks. Endless yellows, too: bright splashes of recent gougings into the middle of the brick; the muted yellow of bricks sheltered from a century and a half of smog, soot and weathering; a shade of black on those bricks that got a full blast of smog and soot – now something of a prized antique since the Clean Air Act of 1956. Soot was once everywhere: when St Paul's Cathedral was cleaned for the first time forty years ago, seven million gallons of water was used to remove an inch-thick layer of soot from the west front.

By the 1850s and 1860s the mechanisation of brick manufacture led to a collapse in independent brick-makers and a smaller variety of colours. The standard bright-red brick had arrived. It has never settled happily into the landscape. In one of his rare jokes, Pevsner called Ludlow's Victorian market hall – built of machine-made, eye-blisteringly red bricks – 'Ludlow's bad luck'.

11

Inigo Jones the Doric, Jones the Ionic and Jones the Corinthian

DICC. Forgive the vulgarity, but no single word tells you so much about buildings – not just in Britain, but throughout the world. If you remember one thing from this book, remember DICC, and a walk along every single high street in Europe – or any part of the world influenced by Europe – will change for ever.

Doric, Ionic, Corinthian and Composite are the four orders of classical architecture, referring to the style of columns used in buildings. (A fifth order, Tuscan, was a much later invention, recorded for the first time by Palladio and Serlio in the sixteenth century.) DICC also gives the orders' chronological sequence. Progressing from short, fat, stumpy, plain Doric columns in the seventh century BC, the orders grew taller and slimmer, with more complicated capitals, first under the Greeks, then under the Romans.

Doric, Ionic and Corinthian were all Greek inventions; Composite was Roman. The idea of this chronological sequence became embedded in the Renaissance mind – a reverent view of antiquity meant classical ideas were enshrined in stone.

Whenever there was more than one floor to a classical building, the hierarchy of the orders was strictly observed: strong, chunky Doric did

The five orders of architecture from Vignola's *Regole delle Cinque Ordini d'architettura* (1562).

all the supporting on the ground floor, then thinner, less robust, more elegant Ionic on the first floor, and so on. You didn't have to have all the orders on one building, and you didn't have to start with Doric at the bottom; but, where you had more than one, they had to follow the hierarchy.

If the hierarchy of the orders was broken, it was broken for a very definite reason. At Culzean Castle (1792), Ayrshire, Robert Adam put Corinthian columns below Ionic ones in the oval staircase hall, because more people used the lower, Corinthian floor – the private quarters of the Earl of Cassillis were on the upper, Ionic floor – and so they got a chance to admire the more elaborate order.

> ### Entasis
>
> Look closely and you'll see that all classical columns bulge outwards in the middle. This is called entasis. The ancient Greeks worked out that the human eye tends to squeeze the middle bit inwards when it looks at a pair of straight lines. To compensate for this optical illusion, they added the bulge.

Because the origins of the orders were lost in the mists of time, fantasists came up with mythical stories to explain their derivation. Sir William Chambers (1723–96), the neo-classical architect who built Somerset House in the Strand, thought the orders came from tree trunks used for prehistoric shelters – an idea that originated with the French Jesuit priest and architectural theorist Abbé Laugier (1713–69). The tree's proportions were reflected in the stone pillars; the capitals were versions of the branches and leaves growing out of the top of the trunks; the panels in the friezes on top of the pillars reflected where the stumps of the trees, laid flat on the roof, protruded.

There are four basic sections to all classical columns. First, there's the simplest bit of the column – the shaft or the trunk. Then, on top of the column, there's the capital – the bit that sprouts out to the sides. Doric capitals are simple, Ionic ones more complicated; and so the complicating process goes on through the orders. Beneath the column there's the base on a plinth; above the column, the layers of stone that the column carries – the entablature. This entablature comprises three sections. Moving upwards, they are the architrave, frieze and cornice. Looking at the Vignola picture of the orders, the architrave is the rectangular block immediately above the capital. The frieze is the squarish block above that. And finally, on top, comes the jutting wafer of the cornice.

Doric Columns

Everything about the Doric column is nice and plain, which makes them the easiest to recognise. Greek Doric columns, first erected in the seventh century BC, often have no base (although Roman Doric ones, a later variation, do.)

116

Simple, male genius – Auberon Waugh (1939–2001) and Roman Doric column, by Nicholas Garland.

The only real decoration is the fluting – vertical grooves – that often runs down the shaft. This can be pretty deep. When Sir John Soane was on holiday in Agrigento, Sicily – in the Valley of the Temples – he dozed in the giant groove of a Doric column lying on its side.

Doric capitals are simple and undecorated.

Those thick, chunky Doric columns were supposed to mirror thick, chunky Greek men. The order's proportions were said by Vitruvius, the first architectural historian, to come from the ratio of the length of a man's foot to his height.

Ionic Columns

First used in the sixth century BC, Ionic columns were the feminine order: elegant, slim, with those little volutes or twirls at the top suggesting a pretty young girl's curls.

T.S. Eliot, in *The Waste Land* (1922), fell for the Ionic columns in Wren's church of St Magnus Martyr, by the Thames in the City of London:

> The walls of Magnus Martyr hold
> Inexplicable splendour of Ionian white and gold.

Corinthian Columns

The Corinthian column, first erected in 400 BC, was the last order invented by the Greeks. Corinthian capitals are ornate things, sprouting bunches of acanthus leaves topped with little volutes.

Composite Columns

The Composite column was a mixture of the Ionic and Corinthian orders, first used on the Arch of Titus in the Roman forum in AD 82.

It's the biggest show-off of the orders, with the upper part of their capitals growing big, twirly Ionic volutes, while all that Corinthian acanthus pours out below. Composite is also the transvestite's order, with those little girls' curls attached to an unusually tall body.

Tuscan Columns

This is ultra-simple, like a Doric column with a base and no fluting. The column in the Little, Brown symbol on the spine of this book's dustjacket and on the title page is Tuscan.

The Orders of the British Empire

British architects took more than 550 years after the Normans arrived – and 1200 years after the Romans left – before they got classical architecture right. To get it right, after such a long gap, took an unusual talent – that of Inigo Jones (1573–1652). Jones was a human watershed: until his arrival on the scene in 1610, British columns were fat and squashy, unGrecian, unRoman and wrong, their entablatures flimsy; after 1610, columns were slim, Italian, antique and correct, with their entablatures in even proportion.

Inigo Jones was an Englishman, born in Smithfield, London, where his Welsh Catholic father was a cloth-maker. Crucially, he studied Italian buildings in the flesh, or in the stone, during two grand tours with the Earls of Rutland and Arundel in 1608–11 and 1613–14. When he returned to Britain he created his own Little Italy – St Paul's in Covent Garden, the Banqueting House in Whitehall, the Queen's House, Greenwich and the Queen's Chapel by St James's Palace. These buildings were straight out of Italy, the first correctly classical buildings in Britain since the Romans.

How revolutionary they must have looked – almost impossible to appreciate today, when classicism has been the default style in

European architecture for four hundred years, with occasional Gothic Revivals intervening.

Jones was the first British architect to closely study the great Roman and Italian architectural writers Marcus Vitruvius Pollio (c.75 BC – c.15 BC), Leon Battista Alberti (1404–72) and Sebastiano Serlio (1475–1554). But the most influential of his models was Andrea Palladio (1508–80), whose *I Quattro Libri dell'Architettura*, scrawled with Jones's tiny notes in fading brown ink, survives in Worcester College, Oxford. Palladio's five hundredth birthday is to be celebrated imminently with a big show at the Royal Academy.

There had already been successful stabs at classical buildings. And several books on classical architecture had appeared; engravings of the orders were first published in England in 1565. But nobody had got close to Jones's levels of understanding of the classical rules. He was responsible for a tremendous series of firsts. The first British architect to get classical details absolutely right; among the first to use a Venetian window; the first to build long, trailing concave wings leading to the front door of the country house, with pavilions at either end. He dreamt these up at Stoke Bruerne, Northamptonshire, in 1635.

You'll see these concave wings curling away in British buildings throughout the seventeenth and eighteenth centuries – notably at Castle Howard, Blenheim Palace and Hopetoun House in Scotland.

Inigo Jones imported classicism into Britain and customised it. This thoroughly Jonesian classicism was later exported across the world. Those sweeping wings can also be seen at George Washington's Mount Vernon (1735) in Virginia.

12

1666 and All That

Professor Dr Sir Christopher Wren
Arrives

Henry, a culture-hating friend of mine, hates those brown signs that you see on motorways, directing you to country houses.

While he was at Edinburgh University, he used to drive up and down from London with his flatmate, an avid castle creeper. The flatmate was so obsessed with taking detours to this or that house that Henry used to time his motorway driving so that he was always overtaking a lorry whenever they passed a brown sign.

'I'm sure this is the turn-off for Chatsworth,' the friend would say.

'Nooope,' Henry would reply, gently accelerating past the Eddie Stobart lorry in the slow lane. 'There'd have been a brown sign, wouldn't there?'

Despite hating country houses, Henry knew rather a lot about them.

'I hate Sir Roger Pratt,' he once said, out of the blue, as we were driving along the fast lane of the M4 in Wiltshire, overtaking a Scania lorry concealing the sign to Bowood House.

'Oh really. Why?'

'He's the one whose houses inspired the brown sign, isn't he?'

He was quite right – the classic country house depicted on those signs is pure Roger Pratt (1620–84). Pratt came on the scene after the Restoration in 1660, just before Wren. Like Wren, he carved out a uniquely British form of classicism. You should remember two things about Pratt: the double pile and the E-type.

A Short History of the Corridor

'Double pile' described houses that were two rooms deep in a single rectangular block, as opposed to old-fashioned plans that were one-room deep, snaking round a courtyard. The scheme was popularised by Sir Roger Pratt at Coleshill, Oxfordshire, built in 1662 and burnt down in 1952.

The plan had a central corridor running along the long axis of the house, with a symmetrical set of rooms on either side of it. This corridor divided the house into the classic double pile.

At Castle Howard, Sir John Vanbrugh placed the corridor along the northern façade – a thermal buffer for the house's coldest side. Like most houses, Castle Howard had its entrance front on this cold, north side, and the more regularly used rooms were on the warm, south side. Drawing rooms went on being built on the south front of houses into the modern age.

Corridors weren't new, really. As Vanbrugh said to the Duchess of Marlborough, his tricky boss at Blenheim Palace, in 1716, 'The corridore, Madame, is foreign, and signifies in plain English no more than a passage.'

Still, using prominent corridors to give dramatic long views – as opposed to their being hidden but necessary circulation routes – was new. Showy corridors were added to Longleat in 1805 and Wilton in 1811 – long after the main houses were built.

The corridor's popularity in Britain contrasted with the Continental habit of running rooms *enfilade*, or in a row (from the French *fil*, 'thread'), so that each room was also a passage. Where Continental rooms had communicating doors between rooms, British rooms – particularly in the nineteenth century – led off the corridor.

'The English room is a sort of cage,' Hermann Muthesius (1861–1927), cultural attaché to the German embassy in London and author of *The English House* (1904), wrote admiringly, 'in which the inmate is entirely cut off from the next room . . . [This comes from] one of their most conspicuous needs, their desire for privacy, for seclusion.' He was so impressed by our jigsaw of rooms around a central core, each with as few doors as possible, each with a fireplace, that he successfully imported *das Englische Haus* into the fashionable suburbs of Berlin at the turn of the twentieth century.

As a result of this harmonious pattern, the British, Muthesius noted approvingly, had no word for *Schwellenangst*, or 'threshold anxiety', a phobia of moving from one room to the next. In fact, the British had no real thresholds at all – floorboards ran straight through from room to room. The only side-effect of these free-flowing plans was the draught that came through the gap under the door.

As for Pratt's E-type, it looked like a classical version of the Tudor E-plan. A side wing projected either side of a central entrance section – usually of three bays with a pediment on top.

Pratt learnt his classical proportions abroad. The Grand Tour got going in the late seventeenth century, and it was now unremarkable for architects and gentlemen – and gentlemen architects like Pratt – to hoover up the Continent's art and architecture. He spent six years in Italy, Holland, France and Flanders, and knew his classicism inside out.

The classicism was very much more inside than out, in fact, on his buildings.

The ultimate Pratt country house look – Belton House, Lincolnshire (1685).
(Alamy Images)

Sir Roger used orders sparingly on his exteriors. The proportions were dictated by an imaginary order that was then left out: the cornice of this imaginary order was at the same level as the roofline; the upper line of the basement was where the bases of the imaginary columns would have been. His first go at this type was Clarendon House in Piccadilly in 1664 (demolished twenty years later). William Winde is thought to be the architect of a close imitation at Belton House, Lincolnshire.

The Pratt look – a central pediment flanked by projecting wings – is *the* classic country-house shape, loved by caricaturists, cartoonists and the designer of that brown sign.

Wrenaissance Man

Never a cleverer dipped his pen/Than clever Sir Christopher, Christopher Wren.

In the year of his death the ninety-year-old Sir Christopher Wren (1632–1723) visited St Paul's Cathedral. The building had been finished in 1708 – the first cathedral to be completed within an architect's lifetime since the Hagia Sophia church in Istanbul, built in 532–7 for the Emperor Justinian. Other cathedrals could take centuries to build – Belfast Cathedral, begun in 1899, only got its spire in 2007; Westminster Cathedral, begun in 1895, is still unfinished.

Wren enjoyed revisiting St Paul's; even at the age of seventy-four he had been hauled up to the roof in a basket by a rope attached to a hook under the dome. Now, turning the corner of Cheapside, he saw his masterpiece looming above the City and burst into tears. A new balustrade had been built along the parapet.

The balustrade was useless. It performed no protective role – no one ever walked up there. It was too far away from the ground to be aesthetically worthwhile. And Wren had never included it in his original design.

'Ladies like nothing so well as an edging,' he moaned.

Still, he couldn't stay away from his mutilated masterpiece. On a later visit he caught a chill and died. It was his son, also Christopher, who composed the epitaph for his tomb in the crypt of St Paul's: '*Lector, si monumentum requiris, circumspice*' ('Reader, if you seek a monument, look around').

I heard the story about the balustrade from a Wren-obsessive who is a counter-tenor and loves singing in Wren churches, particularly the chapel of Emmanuel College, Cambridge (1673). The acoustics work beautifully, he says.

It's hard enough to build a beautiful building; much more difficult to build one that fits its purpose. But then Wren is such a part of Britain's furniture – and built and inspired so much of that furniture – that it's easy to forget quite how much he did.

Born to an eminent priest who later became the Dean of Windsor, Sir Christopher Wren the architect was also Dr Christopher Wren the scientist, a founder member of the Royal Society, the Savilian Professor at Astronomy and a Fellow of All Souls, Oxford. No surprise, then, that he knew how to build churches – fifty-three of them in the City of London alone, in addition to St Paul's Cathedral – for acoustics.

At St Paul's, Wren used all his engineering know-how to maximise beauty while concealing the practical workings that supported the whole thing. So the familiar outer dome was just a timber frame to provide the famous outline. The heavy stone spire on top was supported by a hidden brick cone that can't be seen from the outside because of the timber frame. Nor from the inside, in fact, as the cone was hidden by an elaborately painted inner dome.

At the top of each of the three domes, Wren pierced a hole to allow a lazy laser beam of sunlight to move gently around the cathedral. The weight of these three great shells was then borne by flying buttresses. These are impossible to see, hidden by fake outer walls that do nothing to support the cathedral.

The Finest View in Europe – Gothic Meets Classical

One brunchtime in early June 1993, I was sitting in the Queen's Lane Coffee House in Oxford's High Street, one of the earliest coffee houses in Britain, founded in 1654, shortly after the taste for coffee caught on.

Halfway through my Full English Breakfast, I was joined by a thin, old man in a long, green, creased mac, who had an air of decayed gentility.

'Do you mind if I join you?' he said, pointing the palm of his right hand at my table.

'Not at all.'

'Actually, I'm terribly sorry, but do you mind if I take your seat?'

'Erm, oh no.'

'I know it sounds odd. But the thing is, I come here once a year, just to have a look at the view from this café. And your seat's got the best view.'

Simon had been at Queen's College – the classical building in the foreground of the view below – half a century before. He had not

'Restored Norman and revived Gothic . . . travesties of Venice and Athens' – Oxford as described by Evelyn Waugh in *Brideshead Revisited*.

prospered since. A career as a failed lawyer was followed by spells teaching English as a foreign language in London and Bristol.

He hadn't particularly enjoyed Oxford, but he had liked his breakfasts in the coffee house. To begin with, he didn't steal people's seats to get his fix. But in recent years he had become obsessed with the view, convinced he'd struck upon accidental perfection.

'Look how it curves away from you, but never curving at the same angle. Isn't a curve so much lovelier than a straight line? Of course, the buildings gradually get smaller the further they get away from you, but then you get sudden highs – like a graphic equaliser. And look at the change in style, constantly flipping,' Simon said, emphasising the dates like a primary-school teacher. 'Classical Queen's, 1711, Decorated St Mary's with all that ballflower, 1325, Dean Aldrich's classical spire of All Saints, 1708.'

I later discovered that the early-nineteenth-century architect John Nash had also been inspired by the view when he designed Regent's Park in London: 'Individuality and variety of design . . . may produce the same effect to the eye as the High Street of Oxford so generally admired.'

It's now unremarkable to mix Gothic and classical styles. David and Victoria Beckham do it – Beckingham Palace in Sawbridgeworth, Hertfordshire, is classical while the faux-ruined chapel in the garden, covered in briar roses, is Gothic.

But, before Wren came along, it would have been revolutionary for anyone to mix the styles like this. As well as being the first architect to build a college chapel in Oxford or Cambridge that had no Gothic influence – Pembroke College Chapel, Cambridge (1665) – he dipped back into the Gothic world, and even combined the style with classicism.

In his 1682 Tom Tower at Christ Church, Oxford, he took an essentially classical design – a dome surrounded by supplementary mini-domes – and fitted them out with Tudor ogee hats and crocketed Gothic spires.

While Wren was doing all this revolutionary mixing and matching, less daring architects stuck to Gothic.

Surefire Bet Number One

Stroll down to Westminster Abbey, and bet anyone they can't date the towers (pictured) to within twenty years.

Medieval, they're bound to say – thirteenth century, like the inside?

The towers were in fact designed by Nicholas Hawksmoor and finished in 1745, nine years after he died. Although the towers certainly have a Gothic feel – with those nice little ogees near the top – you'll see that those rounded pediments over the clock on the left and the wheel-shaped roundel on the right are distinctly classical.

If you go under Tom Tower and head towards Christ Church hall, above the staircase leading into the hall you'll see a magnificent, but dated, Perpendicular Gothic ceiling. This ceiling, built in 1640 – thirty years after Inigo Jones came on the scene – wouldn't have looked out of place a century earlier.

This Gothic lag continued for a long time – Gothic churches were built well into the seventeenth century. Barns were fitted out with Gothic roofs and buttresses for centuries after that, their builders happy to ignore the classical houses in vogue among the rich and grand.

Gothic or classical? You decide.

Inspiring Spires

> Methinks already, from this chemic flame,
> I see a city of more precious mould:
> Rich as the town which gives the Indies name,
> With silver paved, and all divine with gold.
>
> *John Dryden, 'The New London'*

Dryden wrote these lines several years after the Great Fire in 1666. Most of that more precious mould was provided by Christopher Wren – in St Paul's, of course, but also in his City churches.

Again Wren was happy to use Gothic alongside classical.

Because this was the first big church-building scheme since the Reformation, it was also the first time that proper thought was given to what a Protestant church should look like. Wren was inventive, using all sorts of models – ancient Rome, the seventeenth-century Netherlands, and the Italian Baroque among them. His main concern was that:

> in our reformed religion, it should seem vain to make a parish church larger than that all who are present can both hear and see. The Romanists, indeed, may build larger churches; it is enough if they hear the murmur of the mass, and see the elevation of the host, but ours are to be fitted for auditories.

So Wren's churches – however small the site, however cramped by the pre-Fire streets that he tried in vain to rearrange on neat radial lines – were remarkably airy, with big windows, galleries for overspill crowds, and lots of gleaming gold and white plaster. The altar was often brought forward from the east wall towards the congregation so they could see and hear the action better.

Among the fifty-one churches rebuilt after the fire were several Gothic ones by Wren – notably St Dunstan-in-the-East. Many others show a Gothic influence, particularly in their spires, where he was essentially dressing a medieval form in classical clothes. Spires were a medieval invention of Gothic origin.

On the back cover of this book you'll see Wren's spire at St Bride's, Fleet Street (1703) – the journalists' church, and the inspiration for the wedding cake. W.E. Henley wrote about the church in 'The Song of the Sword' (1892):

> The while the fanciful, formal finicking charm
> Of Bride's, that madrigal of stone,
> Grows flushed and warm
> And beauteous with a beauty not its own.

Wren's spire at St Vedast, Foster Lane, was daringly Baroque. 'Here architecture does what all the best architecture should do,' Betjeman said of this, his favourite spire. 'It moves as you go past it and changes to make another and another and another perfect picture.'

The most familiar spire arrangement today is the one where the spire is slap bang in the middle of the church façade, rising from the top of a great big pediment over a portico.

This was all a huge break with the classical rules. The Romans and the Greeks didn't go in for spires at all – their 'churches' were temples, and temples were really classical boxes that didn't have towers.

The combination of portico and tower was first done at St Martin-in-the-Fields, as in '"You owe me three farthings," say the Bells of St Martin's.' St Martin's, whose perforated spire looms over the northeast corner of Trafalgar Square, was built by James Gibbs (1682–1754) in 1726, and refurbished in 2008 at a cost of £36 million.

If the combination was popular in Britain, it was even more so in America, where it's the most influential building type in the country. Christ Church, Philadelphia, designed by Dr John Kearsley in 1727, was the first American church to copy Gibbs's design. Now you'll see

131

it all over the place, from Maine to Mexico – but particularly in Maine, where St Martin's inspired the classic New England lil' ole white clapboard church, usually right next door to a classical court house and town hall.

British architects were at last comfortable with the classical language of architecture; and confident enough now to break the rules and create their own peculiarly British form of classicism.

Inigo Jones's buildings were certainly British and would look a little odd if they were transplanted straight back to Italy. Even so, they would just about fit, as there were few individual elements that Jones didn't borrow from the Continent, however unique his combination of them was.

What came after Jones – Wren in particular – grew further and further away from Palladio, and became more and more idiosyncratically British.

New England in Old England – St Mary-le-Strand (1717), the Strand, London, by James Gibbs. Somerset House (1780) by William Chambers is on the right.

13

Know Your Mullions

Casement Gives Way to Sash

A mob-capped chambermaid throwing open the casement window of a manor house on a frosty morning . . . The ideal atmospheric scene-setter for the Elizabethan feel of Sunday teatime telly.

Where would BBC period drama directors be without casement windows – those ancient windows that open outwards on hinges? And where would Keats have been without the medieval romance conjured up by casement windows? In 'The Eve of St Agnes' (1820), rose-tinted light falls on the heroine's breast beneath 'a casement high and triple-arched all garlanded with carven imageries'. And the bird's song in 'Ode to a Nightingale' (1819) 'charmed magic casements, opening on the foam of perilous seas in faery lands forlorn'.

Casement windows weren't so good for the poor chambermaid, though. She could only regulate the temperature of her mistress's Elizabethan manor house by opening or closing the casement, and aligning the holes pierced in its handle with a fixed peg on the window frame. It didn't help that, in those glimmering walls of leaded Elizabethan windows, there was often only one light that actually opened.

Casements weren't so good, either, for the classically minded man who liked his windows slim and lissom – unlike the clumsy, thick lines of those mullioned, transomed casements. With sash windows you could support the glass on thin stretches of wood or painted metal. Glazing bars got thinner through the eighteenth century, and by the early nineteenth century they were only half an inch thick.

Casements became even clumsier when the windows were thrown open, out into a third dimension, messing with the flat, symmetrical lines of the neighbouring brickwork.

Enter the sash window. Now you could regulate the temperature inch by inch – literally, by lifting or dropping the sash (the word for each frame of the two-framed window). You could open the window directly to the breeze, whereas the half-open casement acted as a sort of shield to fresh air. The sash window was invaluable to Sir Alexander

C.S. Lewis's view, Magdalen College, Oxford. The clean lines of the sash window in classical New Buildings (1733) overlook the chunky casement windows and crocketed, jagged lines of the Perpendicular cloisters and tower.

Fleming. On 28 September 1928 Fleming left several festering culture dishes out in his lab at St Mary's Hospital, Paddington, only to find a few hours later that some helpful penicillium mould spores had drifted unimpeded through the open window. A casement window would have kept the spores out, prevented the discovery of penicillin and led to the death of millions.

And all this sash-window magic came with little effort. The window cords, usually hidden, are attached to carefully calibrated weights that almost balance the weight of the sash. An opened window stays in place, and only a little pressure is needed to shift it.

135

In Laurence Sterne's novel *The Life and Opinions of Tristram Shandy, Gentleman* (1759), Shandy had an unfortunate accident courtesy of sash weights. His Uncle Toby needed as much metal as possible to build his battle reconstruction tableaux. 'He had taken the two leaden weights from the nursery window: and as the sash pullies, when the lead was gone, were of no kind of use, he had taken them away also, to make a couple of wheels for one of their carriages.' This sash later fell, just as the child Tristram, at his nurse's insistence, was relieving himself out of the window; with disastrous consequences for the House of Shandy.

Typically the first sashes each had nine, twelve or sixteen lights, and only the lower sash moved. By the Regency period the classic sash window was three lights across by two down. So, with a pair of sashes, you got a total of twelve lights – or six over six, as they're called. The Victorians cut the number down to two over two or, in smarter houses, one over one. Removing so many glazing bars made the window weaker. To strengthen it, little protrusions, called horns, were added below the centre bar on either side.

The sash reigned supreme until the late nineteenth century, when the casement made a comeback. The Arts and Crafts movement encouraged a return to the Olde English look.

In the 1981 TV version of Evelyn Waugh's *Brideshead Revisited*, the window that Sebastian Flyte was sick into after an evening with Oxford's Bullingdon Club was a classic sash. It's still there, in the front quad of Hertford College – Waugh's old college, where Anthony Andrews was filmed throwing up. Charles Ryder's Hertford rooms were 'large, with deeply recessed windows and painted, eighteenth-century panelling', with gillyflowers in the window box.

There's a battle over who invented the sash window. The East Anglian architect William Samwell (1628–76) installed an early version at Charles II's Newmarket Palace in around 1671. Some say he was beaten by the architect and scientist Robert Hooke (1635–1703), as in Hooke's Law of Elasticity.

'The wines were too various; it was neither the quality nor the quantity that was at fault. It was the mixture.' Front quad (1895), Hertford College, by Sir Thomas Jackson (1835–1924).

Others claim it was Christopher Wren who dreamt up the window in 1669 for a house in Tring, Hertfordshire. Certainly, by 1685, in Whitehall Palace, 'very strong shasses with their frames and brass pulleys' were being manufactured.

Soon after, there was a mass replacement of casement windows with sashes. So, for example, only one significant thing has changed on the Banqueting House in Whitehall since Inigo Jones built it in 1622: the original mullioned and transomed casement windows were swapped for sash windows in 1713. By 1720 the sash was standard issue across Britain.

14

The *Brideshead Revisited* School of Baroque Architecture

After Anthony Andrews and Jeremy Irons, the third star of the 1981 television adaptation of *Brideshead Revisited* was Castle Howard, the Baroque masterpiece begun in 1700 by John Vanbrugh and Nicholas Hawksmoor.

It's also the only star that reappeared in the 2008 feature-film version. Castle Howard isn't a bad match with Waugh's description of Brideshead – he wrote of a 1670s house, set in open parkland designed in the 1790s, with a central dome plus colonnade and flanking pavilions.

If you look at a timeline of classical architecture in Britain, Castle Howard appeared at the peak – the moment in the early eighteenth century when we cool, unadventurous northerners got closest to the seething, curly-whirly, tempestuous ways of wild southern Europeans.

You can see just a little of the detail of Castle Howard's north front on the cover of the TV tie-in paperback – some of the windows, pilasters, statues, pillars, niches, friezes, putti, garlands, military emblems and rustication that coat the façade.

Ah, rustication – before we continue with Castle Howard, it's worth a closer look.

'Below us, half a mile distant, grey and gold amid a screen of boskage, shone the dome and columns of an old house' – Aloysius, Anthony Andrews, Diana Quick and Jeremy Irons at Castle Howard, North Yorkshire.

Bertie Wooster Gets Rusticated

Rustication was the Italian Renaissance technique of scoring the exterior walls of a building's lower floors with thick horizontal – and sometimes vertical – grooves and roughening the stone. These techniques gave an impression of solidity and simplicity, originally of a rustic kind. Soon, though, rustication lost any rustic element and became a popular way of giving strength and solidity to a ground floor.

Rustication cropped up in P.G. Wodehouse, on a nineteenth-century folly – the Octagon at Aunt Agatha's lair, Woollam Chersey, Hertfordshire. In *Jeeves and the Impending Doom* (1927), Bertie Wooster, trying to rescue the Right Hon A.B. Filmer, who has taken to the roof, was grateful for the rustication of the Octagon, based on a folly at Hunstanton House, Norfolk:

> Whoever built the Octagon might have constructed it especially for this sort of crisis. Its walls had grooves at regular intervals which were just right for the hands and feet, and it wasn't very long before I was parked up on the roof beside the Right Hon, gazing down at one of the largest and shortest-tempered swans I had ever seen.

These grooves were banded rustication – long, horizontal lines running along the wall. Rustication was often more elaborate than this – a criss-cross of vertical and horizontal grooves producing a chequered grid across the ground or lower-ground floor.

Panels formed by rustication could also be glacial (carved into mini-icicle shapes), diamond-faced (mini-pyramids), cyclopean (a rough, rocky surface) or vermiculated. The last, from the Latin *vermis*, 'worm', means a series of pitted ticks and swirls, like the tracks of a worm.

Anyway, back to Castle Howard. Along with all that ornament, there was lots of frantic movement in the façade – a trademark of the Baroque. Doric pilasters jump forwards and backwards, pushing the Ionic columns of the porch forward, bringing their architraves with them.

There are also a lot of planes, or vertical surfaces. There's one in the middle, others on the side, along with the sunken grooves of the rustication. Even the friezes above the pilasters jut beyond the friezes above the window bays.

The roofline, too, bounces all over the place, particularly around that distinctive dome with its tall drum clustered round with all those pilasters. It leaps wildly over statues, trophies and busts, and then negotiates the balustrade along the wings.

Who was responsible for all this frantic Baroque agitation – Vanbrugh and/or Hawksmoor? This is one of the conundrums of British architecture. It's still not clear which of their confections of art and fantasy were collaborations and which solo works.

Sir John Vanbrugh (1664–1726) led an eccentric life before turning to architecture. He worked in India for the East India Company, joined the army, was imprisoned in the Bastille as a spy, wrote a hit play entitled *The Relapse* (1696) and joined the Whiggish Kit-Cat Club. He brought this spark and breezy flair to his buildings – some of his drawings show smoke coming out of the chimneys. In 1706, Jonathan Swift said of his dilettante career, 'Van's genius, without thought or lecture, Is hugely turned to architecture.'

Vanbrugh's brilliant amateurism contrasted with the diffident professionalism of Nicholas Hawksmoor (1661–1736). Born of humble origins in Nottinghamshire, Hawksmoor served a long apprenticeship under Christopher Wren.

Whatever the division of their skills, between them Vanbrugh and Hawksmoor displayed the new fluidity of British building styles. Although ostensibly classical, their buildings often had the outline of medieval castles or Gothic cathedrals.

Look at Vanbrugh's Seaton Delaval (1729), Northumberland, or Grimsthorpe (1722), Lincolnshire, with eyes half closed, and you might be looking at an ancient fortress. Vanbrugh even talked about giving Kimbolton Castle (1707), near Huntingdon, 'the castle air'.

In London, look from a distance at the broach spire of Hawksmoor's

Christ Church, Spitalfields (1729), or his turreted tower at St Anne, Limehouse (1724), and you could be forgiven for thinking you were looking at a medieval parish church. Only when you get up close do you see that the details are all classical – these buildings could only have been built since the arrival of Inigo Jones.

DATING TIP

Broach spires were the most recognisable sort of Decorated Gothic church tower. They were much copied, not just by Hawksmoor, but by lots of nineteenth-century Gothic Revival architects, particularly Pugin.

The classic broach design began with a square tower at the base which then, using pyramids at the corners, sprouted into an octagonal spire on top. Broach spires were often punctuated with lucarnes – little windows cut into the spire with their own little hoods.

The freedom of interpretation of the classical rules shows how far Vanbrugh and Hawksmoor had taken British classicism into the hot, southern-European waters of the Baroque.

We very rarely got the hang of the Baroque. Perhaps because, as Vita Sackville-West said, the Renaissance was essentially unEnglish, the English were a little scared of its wildest incarnation – Baroque. It's no coincidence that the word itself was originally pejorative – the Portuguese word *barroco* means a misshapen pearl.

Evelyn Waugh said of the style, 'It has been related to the holidays – a memory of the happy days in sunglasses, washing away the dust of the Southern roads with heady Southern wines.'

Alexander Pope's jokey reaction to Blenheim – '"Thanks, sir," cried I, "'tis very fine, but where do you sleep or where d'ye dine?"' – hinted how suspicious we were of showing off too much.

Besides, English anti-Catholicism in the seventeenth century didn't encourage a voyage of exploration of these rash, Italianate, Popish church features across the Channel.

The Old Faith in the old style – broach spire and lucarne, in the Catholic church of Our Lady and the English Martyrs, Hills Road, Cambridge (1890), by H.H. Dunn and J.A. Hansom.

Even so, there were touches of the Baroque in Wren's work, particularly on those City church spires and on the curved transept ends of St Paul's.

Some 1684 interiors at Windsor Castle by Hugh May, Antonio Verrio and the great wood carver Grinling Gibbons were also astonishingly Baroque.

Vanbrugh, Hawksmoor, William Talman (1650–1719, the man who built much of Chatsworth) and Thomas Archer (1668–1743) were the only British architects who got really close to injecting some of that Mediterranean heat into the cool, hard rules of classicism. The heart of Archer's Baroque – borrowed from the Roman master Francesco Borromini (1599–1667) – lay in those distinctly unItalian areas Birmingham (in his cathedral of St Philip's) and Deptford (in his St Paul's church).

Auberon Waugh's Aim in Life

Another architect who let his hair down and took up the swirling lines of the Baroque was James Gibbs, the one who came up with the

Midlands Baroque – St Philip's Cathedral (1725), Birmingham, by Thomas Archer. (Alamy Images)

portico-and-tower combination. Hawksmoor and Vanbrugh never made it to Rome, but Gibbs had actually studied there.

He devised the Gibbs surround in 1719. These windows are easily spotted – a series of stones laid along the edge of the window, with gaps between each stone. Easy to construct, they are expensive to replace, as the late Auberon Waugh discovered in his renovation of his house in Combe Florey, Somerset. Evelyn Waugh's last house, Combe Florey was built out of fine, red sandstone in 1665 by Thomas Francis. The house was sold, in July 2008, by Auberon Waugh's widow, Lady Teresa Waugh, for £2.25 million. Included in the price is Evelyn Waugh's sign, engraved in stone, at the entrance, saying, 'No Admittance on Business'.

In his autobiogaphy, *Will This Do?* (1991), Auberon Waugh wrote:

My father described Combe Florey as 'a plain, square house on a hill' in a letter to my mother-in-law in 1961. In fact it is a large, extremely grand and handsome house, not square at all, finished in

145

Evelyn Waugh, perron and Gibbs surrounds, Combe Florey, Somerset (1665).

red sandstone in the 1740s, with an imposing grand portico on an elevated perron [an outside staircase with a platform, from the Old French word for a large stone], the doorway being noted (like the window surrounds) for Gibbs rustications. The only thing which spoiled it were some heavy plate-glass lattice windows put in by the previous owners at the turn of the century . . .

I hope to replace them all with the money from the publisher's advance on delivery of the manuscript of this autobiography . . .

They will be my monument. There they will remain until the house is burned down, or taken over by the local authority as a hostel for unmarried mothers, who will no doubt wish to restore plate glass throughout.

In fact, these features are called Gibbs surrounds, not rustications. And that doorway hasn't got Gibbs surrounds or rustications either. Those columns with square blocks of stone either side of the door are 'banded columns'. I hate to correct Waugh, but pedantry will out.

15

Mr Darcy's Palladian House

or the BBC Location Manager's Guide
to the Eighteenth Century

Earlier this year, at around four o'clock on a surprisingly warm late-April afternoon, I was lying on the lawn of a Scottish country house that must remain nameless.

The original house, for the first Lord Mc****, was late-seventeenth-century Anglo-Dutch classical; it was utterly changed in the early nineteenth century by a follower of Sir John Soane. That is to say, it remained classical, but slimline classical, with ceilings like trampolines bulging upwards, and cornices stripped down to lean threads.

I had just been playing tennis on the potholed asphalt tennis court the colour of pink bubblegum, buried in a dell a few hundred yards from the house, its wire fence concealed by rhododendrons, rampant on all four sides.

A banked lawn led from the terrace outside the library towards a ha-ha – a concealed ditch to keep deer off the lawn – and then down to a dammed stream designed by the third Lord Mc**** to form a lake in the shape of a thistle.

I had got myself an apple-juice spritzer from the drinks cabinet and was lying on the bank, eyes closed, when I heard the soft footfall of someone approaching. I opened my eyes to see Tommy Fitz*****, leading interior designer of the Pimlico–Chelsea borders, heartbeat of the ruching and stippling world.

Tommy had a glass of Chablis in his hand but managed to tumble on to the bank without spilling a drop. Lying beside me, he adopted my pose – right knee raised, left leg flat on the ground, eyes aimed at the sky.

'Marvellous house, isn't it?' he said after a moment's silence.

'Absolutely lovely.'

'Are you interested in architecture?'

'Yes, very. I did a master's in it at the Courtauld Institute, in fact.'

'Oh, really?' Tommy said, raising himself on his left elbow so his face blotted out the sun. It was a good-looking face in its mid-fifties. The face's rounded, doughy babyishness was enhanced by the slight puffiness brought on by his functioning alcoholism, and damaged by the blotchy redness that came with the condition.

'What's your favourite house?'

'Well, there are lots. But I really love higgledy-piggledy houses added to and knocked around a bit for years, like Knole.'

'Oh, I know Knole. Used to stay there in the old days. Haven't been there for years . . . It's got that lovely courtyard with that early Tuscan colonnade, hasn't it? Goes a bit like this . . .'

Tommy started to sketch out the long, low gallery at Knole. Along the bony ridge of my calf. Holding the Chablis in his left hand, he marked out an accurate line of the entablature of the colonnade – he was right; it is Tuscan – with the stiff index finger of his right hand, moving north from the top edge of my rumpled tennis sock.

What a relief when he ran out of Tuscan pillars as he reached my knee – the outside edge of the final pillar in the colonnade coincided with the concave curve of the top of my kneecap.

'Erm, that's right. Built by the first Earl of Dorset. 1605-ish, I think.'

'Yes, and it has that wonderful drive, doesn't it? Now I remember. Starts on the outskirts of Sevenoaks, then dips down over that little hillock . . .' His index finger hopped down the slope of my kneecap, still heading north. 'And then it winds . . . up the hill!' he said, with a girlish whinny of delight.

His finger slowed now and slackened a bit as it described a bending course along the upper slope of my thigh.

'And then it takes that marvellous right-hand swooping turn down through the woods.'

Tommy's finger had now come up against the shiny, black, nylon edge of my old football shorts, cut short as was the fashion in the middle nineties, when I played for my college.

'Then you come to that most magnificent view of the house.'

The finger dropped down the slope of my inside leg and began to burrow under the tight nylon.

'Yup. Vita was always in tears by the time she got to the turn . . . Oh, isn't that the gong for lunch?' I said, my voice straining only a little as I leapt to my feet and drained my spritzer.

Thank God I hadn't picked a mammoth Palladian house like Wentworth Woodhouse, near Rotherham, South Yorkshire, whose 606-foot-long façade is the longest in Europe. Built in 1733 by Henry Flitcroft, Wentworth Woodhouse has a room for each day of the year. If Tommy had sketched out its façade, starting at the bottom end of my calf, he would have reached the area I didn't want him to reach, long before he got halfway across the house's rolling front.

Wentworth Woodhouse's façade darts in and out, up and down for all those hundreds of feet. How nimble and strong Tommy's fingers would have to have been to cover all that stonework.

One useful way, then, to work out whether something is Palladian or not is to trace its façade along the upper reaches of your thigh. Does it stretch from top edge of rumpled sock to the fringe of your tight nylon shorts? And does its skyline jump up and down, and its façade move in and out, with the love of playful movement that was close to Palladian hearts?

Another way is to think, might Mr Darcy have lived there?

Directors of TV period drama always give nice helpful dating tips – they like to film in houses built at the same time as the action takes place, as if no houses on earth had been built before the era they are filming.

So, if they're doing a 1930s Agatha Christie, Hercule Poirot gathers the murder suspects in the 1930s drawing room of a big Art Deco house in Berkshire. And when Stephen Fry and Hugh Laurie played Jeeves tending to Bertie Wooster's hangover in his London flat in the thirties, Bertie's flat was played by the Senate House in London – the Art Deco headquarters of London University, built by Charles Holden in 1937. London's first skyscraper, the Senate House housed the Ministry of Information during the War and inspired the Ministry of Truth in George Orwell's *1984* (1949):

Bertie Wooster's pied-à-terre –
Charles Holden's Senate House
(1937). A thousand rocket
bombs would not batter it
down, said George Orwell.

It was an enormous pyramidal structure of glittering white concrete,
soaring up, terrace after terrace, three hundred metres into the air.
From where Winston stood it was just possible to read, picked out
on its white face in elegant lettering, the three slogans of the Party:
WAR IS PEACE
FREEDOM IS SLAVERY
IGNORANCE IS STRENGTH.

When those period-drama directors want emanations of grandness,
though, they go Palladian, irrespective of period. Location managers
went Palladian for Stephen Fry's house in *Peter's Friends* (1992), set in the
early 1990s, or *Gosford Park* (2001), set in the 1930s, or, most recently, for
the Dashwoods' house in *Sense and Sensibility* (2008), set in 1811.

In fact, all three films used the same house – Wrotham Park,
Hertfordshire. Designed by Isaac Ware in 1754, the house is still owned
by the Byngs, descendants of Admiral John Byng, who built it. His   151

Hollywood's favourite country house – Wrotham Park (1754), Hertfordshire. (Alamy Images)

father was Admiral Sir George Byng, executed in 1757 for failing to save Minorca from the French – the execution that provoked Voltaire to say, 'In this country it pays well, from time to time, to kill an admiral *pour encourager les autres.*'

Ware had a direct link to one of the fathers of English Palladianism, Lord Burlington. It was Burlington who discovered the young Isaac Ware as a chimneysweep's boy cheerfully sketching Inigo Jones's Banqueting House in chalk on the pavement.

Wrotham Park is the most filmed country house in history. It hosted Colin Firth's modern Mr Darcy in *Bridget Jones's Diary* (2001); Lady Chatterley, twice, in *Lady Chatterley's Lover* (1981, 1993); and King Ralph in the eponymous film of 1991, where it stood in for Buckingham Palace.

So, when film producers do something set in the eighteenth or early nineteenth century – when the Palladians were actually building Palladian houses – they are even more likely to go Palladian; particularly when it comes to Jane Austen.

In *Pride and Prejudice* (1994), Colin Firth's Darcy's Pemberley was played by Lyme Park, Disley, Cheshire, a great big Palladian house built by the Venetian architect Giacomo Leoni in the 1720s. Leoni was so devoted to Palladio that he translated his *I Quattro Libri dell'Architettura* into English.

BBC location scouts have got plenty of Palladian houses to choose from. When Palladianism went into overdrive in the 1720s, it was boom time for Whigs after George I's accession to the throne. With the economy in rude health, they had the money to get a country house boom going, too.

Palladian houses, for all their Italian origins, became quintessential British palaces. Evelyn Waugh wrote:

> Dominating and completing the landscape, the great palaces of the Whig oligarchs, with their lakes and bridges and grand avenues, orangeries and follies, their immense façades and towering porticoes, their colonnades and pavilions and terraces; those most commodious of all palaces, planned to provide a sequestered family life; concealing beyond the saloons and galleries and state apartments an intimate system of little breakfast rooms and sun-lit studies; very homely palaces, even now when the cold light of electricity has cast its chill over rooms once warmed by a Christmas-tree blaze of tapers.
>
> A Call to the Orders, *1938*

Dating a Palladian house is tricky, particularly since there was a time-lag in the spread of the style, with the provinces catching on to innovations a decade after the cities. Enough to point out some general giveaways to a Palladian house of 1720–1800. They were based on Palladio's works, of course, and Inigo Jones's, but not slavishly so. Repeated motifs included rusticated ground floors, central pedimented porticoes, wings on either side ending in pavilions, and Venetian windows on the first floor. Wrotham Park has all these features.

Another Palladian invention was to make the staircase a main feature of the house. Until then, staircases, however grand, were kept in separate staircase halls. Lord Burlington (1694–1753) and William Kent (1685–1748) were the first to do this, at Holkham Hall, Norfolk, where a sweeping staircase dominates the hall. Holkham was also the first house with a gallery dedicated to antique sculptures displayed in Roman niches, built in 1753.

The alternative was an outer staircase leading straight up to the *piano nobile* – Italian for the grand floor, meaning the first floor – meaning there was no need for a big inner staircase.

Grand staircases were all the rage until the arrival of the hydraulic lift, introduced by Elisha Otis in a New York hotel in 1859. Otis (1811–61), whose lifts are still found worldwide, invented the safety device that stopped lifts from plummeting to the ground if the hoisting cable snapped.

Within decades, London hotels were cutting back on grand staircases, limiting them to a single sweeping flight between ground floor and first floor, like the one at the Savoy in the Strand, built in 1889.

The American influence on hotels also led to an explosion in bathrooms. The Victoria Hotel, built in 1887 in nearby Northumberland Avenue, had four bathrooms for five hundred guests; two years later, again at the Savoy, Richard D'Oyly Carte installed seventy bathrooms. 'Are you catering for amphibian guests?' Collins B. Young, the Savoy's architect, asked him.

Back to the Palladians. The champion of the movement was a Scottish architect, Colen Campbell (1676–1729). As well as designing houses such as Houghton Hall (1722), Norfolk, and Mereworth (1723), Kent, he wrote the first great handbook to British country houses, *Vitruvius Britannicus*, published in three volumes between 1715 and 1725. In these books Campbell provided a solid archetype for the quintessentially British country house – even though most of the features were Italian, ancient and modern – that echoes all the way down to BBC location managers three centuries later.

Campbell also featured his own buildings prominently in the books, implying he was the modern counterpart of Marcus Vitruvius Pollio (80–15 BC), usually known as Vitruvius, the Roman author of *De Architectura*, the seminal book on classical architecture.

The Perception of Doors – The Seventeenth Century to the 1930s

The grandeur and size of 10 Downing Street's rooms are quite a shock when you walk through the humble front door of the most famous terraced house in the country.

I have walked through that door three times. Each time I was struck by the big inside behind the humble outside – like strolling into a Palladian Tardis.

Number Ten's front dates from 1775 when the original 1683 house was refaced by Kenton Couse. The most famous front door in the world, with its fanlight and wrought-iron overthrow, was part of the

Palladian Tardis – six-panel door, author and six-over-six sash window, June 1983. Note the Flemish bond, too.

same job. It is a classic six-panel door: two shorter panels at the top, four longer ones below. By the mid-eighteenth century the six-panel door was standard, as were its proportions – six foot by three, big enough to accommodate the tallest, fattest Georgian.

The history of doors followed a meandering route from the late seventeenth century to the nineteenth century.

Early doors, as Ron Atkinson might say, were ornate. Look at this one, overleaf, designed for the barristers of 5 King's Bench Walk, Inner Temple, by Christopher Wren in 1676 – an early example of a doorway with columns. With those gauged brick columns and capitals carved out of stone, it's a remarkably grand entrance.

Those Corinthian pillars are practically free-standing. With that grand, later ironwork lamp holder above, it's a mini-temple front – the sort of thing Renaissance architects in Italy did.

Wren and the early door-makers were free and ornate in their doorcases – the rectangular frames around a door. Cornices, soffits and scrolls sprouted all around these early doors.

To begin with, all this was done in fine English oak. As terrace construction boomed in the mid-eighteenth century, this gave way to cheaper Scandinavian soft woods like pine and fir, both also known as deal. More vulnerable to the English weather than oak, which hardened with weathering, this cheap foreign wood was painted in thick layers of white lead paint.

In the late seventeenth century, two-panel doors became popular. The tall top panel and small bottom one reflected the proportions of seventeenth-century rooms; their walls were divided by the low dado rail that ran around the room roughly three foot from the floor. The original point of the dado was to stop chairs scuffing the wall.

Big enough to accommodate barrister plus suitcase full of briefs – a Wren door (1676), 5 King's Bench Walk, Inner Temple, London. Clive Anderson is a door tenant at number six.

During the early eighteenth century, eight- and ten-panel doors were common. By the time the door of 10 Downing Street was refurbished in the late eighteenth century, six-panel doors reigned supreme. They lasted into the Regency period, when reeded doorcase surrounds and bull's eyes in the corners of the doorcase were popular.

During the early Victorian terrace boom, the four-panel door took over – like in my childhood home, pictured in the front endpaper. The Edwardians liked a single panel on the top third of the door and a series of slim, vertical panels below.

The world of doors loosened up in the 1930s. Doors with horizontal panels took off; as did doors filled with glass etched in opaque, reeded, sunray and sash-window patterns. The doorway in Tunbridge Wells on the back of this book is a good example.

You know you've arrived in the twentieth century when the fanlight opens at the same time as the door because they're attached to each other.

Behind that front door, 10 Downing Street is a grand mansion – two 1683 houses knocked into one in 1735 for the first Prime Minister, Sir Robert Walpole, by the Palladian architect William Kent. Kent also worked on Houghton Hall, Walpole's Palladian home in Norfolk.

Among the architects who have since spruced up Downing Street's interior are Sir John Soane and Quinlan Terry, who in 1989 ultra-Palladianised the place for Mrs Thatcher.

That was the look I saw when I returned to 10 Downing Street as a leader writer for the *Daily Telegraph* in 2004. As I sat listening to Tony Blair defend his plans to remove grammar schools from Ulster, I noticed a little Terry joke in the frieze over the new doorway in the Terracotta Room on the first floor – a little plaster model of a thatcher, thatching away with characteristic industry and determination.

I paused to look again at the famous façade before I headed back to my office. The genius of the place is that the outside gives a democratic impression of ordinariness – what other leader's official house is a

English Shyness and the Way Doors Open

In the early summer of 2001 I made the mistake of wearing black tie to a dinner in a fetching Gothic Revival mansion on the edge of the Grünewald – the Green Wood – in the upmarket Berlin suburb of Charlottenburg-Wilmersdorf.

As I opened the double doors to the drawing room, I saw my friends – Berlin journalists, mostly – in fetchingly faded red jeans, open-necked blue shirts and crumpled linen jackets.

Even though I'd only opened the doors an inch or so, it was too late. They'd spotted me.

'Oh Harry, you've made an effort!' said Peter Kamm, a political writer on *Der Spiegel*.

It wouldn't have happened in Britain.

In *The English House* (1904), Hermann Muthesius noticed an odd thing about British doors. Where Continental doors open in pairs into the middle of the wall, the shy English put their single doors to one side of the room. The Englishman 'insists on having as few openings in his wall as possible'.

What's more, he hung them so that the door hid the newcomer as he entered the room. This gave the shy Englishman a chance to slip into the room relatively unnoticed. And anyone already there had a few moments to prepare themselves for the new arrival – impossible to do if every new guest marched through open double doors placed in the middle of the wall. So, if a new guest wants to hide a bow tie on ginger-ly entering a Continental drawing room, he doesn't stand a chance.

terraced house and not even number one in the street? Number one was demolished when the Treasury was built in the early nineteenth century. Most of the rest of the street fell to Sir George Gilbert Scott's Foreign Office in 1862.

Downing Street was certainly at the grand end of the terraced house market, I thought, as I headed off on my bicycle towards Canary Wharf; but its charm comes from its ordinariness, from the features shared with every other terraced house in the country.

16

On the Georgian Terraces, 1700–1830

The Most Popular Building in Britain

Know a little about the terraced house and you know something about most of the buildings put up in Britain between 1700 and 1830 – the boom years of the Georgian terraced house. Given that most Victorian terraces after 1830 also copied the look, the terraced house accounts for more buildings than any other style in Britain.

First of all, why were they called terraced houses? Well, before you could build a row of houses, you scraped away the earth until you got a literal 'terrace' – a level, secure surface to place your foundations on. Some early-eighteenth-century terraced houses, then, weren't literally terraces in this sense of the word – they were built in pairs or on single sites on an undulating ground level.

Digging the foundations to an even depth also explains why terraced houses have back gardens that are lower than street level but higher than the floor of the basement. The spoil from digging out the house's foundations was used to build up the road in front.

So, imagine you're digging the foundations of your eighteenth-century house. If you dig down four feet and use the spoil to build up the road, you end up with an eight-foot drop from road surface to basement floor in the front; and a four-foot drop from garden level to basement floor – and sometimes more, after several hundred years' worth of compost has been emptied on to your lawn.

That explains the mini ha-ha between your rear basement window and the garden behind, and the one between your front basement window and the street in front.

Your garden, then, is on the ancient ground level of your neighbourhood. That explains the little trot downhill you make when you walk off the main road down into a mews or side street – those mewses and side streets weren't built up with the spoil from the terrace excavations.

The gardens of terraced houses were unusually big in comparison to the house footprint. When developers marked out a building plot, they divided the street into narrow, long strips – usually around twelve feet wide – moving at a right angle back from the road. These narrow strips went on until they hit another terrace coming in the opposite direction.

So an aerial view shows houses cramped together with all that space behind – thus the popularity of 'back additions', or extensions, stretching further and further into the garden. These were built on an ad hoc basis and were often a bit chaotic, unlike the even, symmetrical façades on the street side. Terraced houses also grew loft extensions, making for an uneven skyline. Some ground floors even sprouted shop fronts over the front garden, with the old front room becoming the shop's back parlour. The only way terraced houses couldn't expand was sideways.

The new terraces were remarkably adaptable in scale and cost for all classes. Here, unlike on the Continent, palaces weren't feasible for anyone except the really grand, who occupied ducal homes like Spencer House and Devonshire House. British developers liked erecting as many buildings as quickly as possible – and one-off palaces weren't as remunerative as miles and miles of terraces.

Britain's land-owning structure, in which large areas of cities were owned by individuals, also meant that organised building of long strings of terraces was possible. On the Continent, fragmented land ownership prevented such ambitious projects. The smart rich in Paris, for example, lived in free-standing *hôtels*, or private houses, with a high wall and courtyard separating them from the street. Meanwhile the British rich lived cheek by jowl in the terraces of Mayfair.

So we must yield to Italy and France at the grand end of the market, in urban palaces and individual mansions. But when it came to pretty, flexible housing that slots easily into any town, for any resident, terraced houses were a triumph of domestic architecture that could be stretched to almost any length. Silkstone Row, Lower Altofts, Yorkshire, demolished in the 1970s, was over eight hundred feet long.

For all their adaptability, it is extraordinary that terraced houses exist nowhere else in the world except where the British exported them; particularly since the quintessentially British terrace owes its origins to European palaces. All terraced houses trace their roots back to the Palladian *palazzi* of Italy and, further back, to ancient Roman palaces. The word 'palace' comes from Palatium, the Latin name for the Palatine Hill, where Emperor Augustus built his splendid palace.

The terraced house is born: Palladio's alternative plans for Palazzo Porto (1570), Vicenza, and Lindsey House (1640), London. (Alamy Images)

Look at the similarity between the right-hand half of Palladio's plan for Palazzo Porto, Vicenza, and the earliest surviving pair of terraced houses in Britain – Lindsey House, Lincoln's Inn Fields, London, built in 1640. The terraced house began life in 1637, when William Newton, a rich Bedfordshire property developer, built a row of fourteen houses in Great Queen Street, Covent Garden. This no longer survives, so the earliest standing example is Lindsey House.

The pattern for the grand British terraced house had been set. A rusticated ground floor – or lower ground floor in some terraces – supported a grand, first floor (or *piano nobile* with pillars or pilasters adorning it. Above there was a low attic.

Simpler terraced houses had no rustication but a nod to the distinction was made by covering the ground floor in white plaster and leaving the upper floors in exposed brick.

Like the Italian *piano nobile*, the first floor of the terraced house had taller windows than the ground floor and those ground floor windows were taller than the attic floor – as at Lindsey House and the Palazzo Porto. The same varying proportions went for the ceilings. The badly lit attic rooms with their low ceilings and small windows were used by servants.

In grander houses a second floor was inserted, with windows shorter than in the *piano nobile* beneath and taller than in the attic above. This basic Georgian terrace shape – rusticated ground or lower-ground floor, tall *piano nobile*, shallower second floor and/or attic – remained remarkably resilient through the whole period 1700 to 1830.

There were, though, intriguing little changes along the way.

With the passing decades of the Georgian age, the pillars framing the main door moved back through the orders, getting less complicated. By around 1720, the Corinthian order gave way to Ionic and Doric doorcases; sixty years later, simple Tuscan or Doric pillars with plain friezes were all the rage.

One feature, the fanlight above the door, went in the opposite direction, getting more complex. In the 1760s Robert Adam took a great liking to the things. He applied all his delicate, lacy touches to the fanlight, now divided up like segments of an ornate orange and rich in Greek honeysuckle motifs. The Adam influence went on into the 1820s with fanlights sprouting into great looping spider's webs of iron.

The plan of the town house was established in those first terraces of the late 1630s. On the ground floor there was a small hall, a parlour and dining room; on the first floor, a big drawing room and principal bedroom; above that, more bedrooms and closets; on the bottom floor came something borrowed from late-sixteenth-century Italy – the basement kitchen.

Jane Austen Downshifts Again – The Drawing Room and the Parlour

Having the most important floor upstairs was a complete break with the previous three hundred years, when the ground-floor hall had been the dominant entertaining room.

Often, in bigger terraced houses, there were two interconnecting drawing rooms on the *piano nobile*. These new terraced houses were almost as grand as a country house; or so Elizabeth Elliot – who had just moved to a terraced house in Bath – thought in Jane Austen's *Persuasion* (1818):

> She must sigh, and smile, and wonder too, as Elizabeth threw open the folding doors, and walked with exultation from one drawing room to the other, boasting of their space, at the possibility of that woman, who had been mistress of Kellynch Hall, finding extent to be proud of between two walls, perhaps 30 feet asunder.

Note the use of 'drawing room' here – it's no longer called the withdrawing room. And it's striking that several rooms were called drawing rooms, so the idea that you withdrew into the drawing room from another room was already dying out. Among television style experts, though, it still hasn't: Laurence Llewelyn-Bowen insisted in the BBC's *The Grumpy Guide to Class* (2007) that you could only have a drawing room if you also had a sitting room to withdraw from in the first place.

It was also around Austen's time that the idea gradually emerged of having a bathroom and a lavatory *inside* the house. As late as 1751, grand Felbrigg Hall, Norfolk, had a garden lavatory designed with care by the architect William Windham, whose thoughts survive: 'Should not the inside be stuccoed? Or how do you do it? How many holes? There must be one for the child; and I would have it light as possible. There must be a good place to set a candle on, and a place to keep paper.'

And a ledge for a good book?

Most privies were swept away under later plumbing improvements. A few Georgian examples survived, though, like a weatherboarded three-seater from 1775 outside a farmhouse in Benenden, Kent, given Grade II listing in April 2008.

How much better, by the way, to have lavatories that look like grand buildings, rather than the other way round. When the University of Melbourne's hideous Grainger Museum – with its unnerving resemblance to a public convenience – was built in 1938, the vice-chancellor Sir John Medley wrote:

> Pass on, impatient stranger;
> This is not for your affair.
> Pray for the soul of Percy Grainger,
> But pray relieve yourself elsewhere.

Eighteenth-century garden privies were much praised by Jonathan Swift, and 'to pluck a rose' became a popular euphemism: 167

The bashful maid, to hide her blush;
Shall creep no more behind a bush;
Here unobserved, she boldly goes,
As who should say, to pluck a rose.

Still, the garden privy didn't stop lazy people sticking to their chamber pots. In 1810, a French American, Louis Simond, showed himself more American than French in his shock at British manners:

Will it be credited, that in the corner of the very dining room there is a certain convenient piece of furniture to be used by anybody who wants it? The operation is performed very deliberately and undisguisedly, as a matter of course, and occasions no interruption of conversation.

It wasn't until the late nineteenth century that bathrooms became a standard feature of middle-class houses. Staff, who used to bring water to bedrooms, were in short supply, and improved drainage and water pressure made it easier to get running water to upper floors. In poorer households, the bath – and often a bed, too – stayed in the kitchen until the 1920s.

The palazzo prototype applied to the humblest terraces in Britain. The only difference was that there was no room for the grand drawing room on the first floor – its space was taken by another bedroom.

On the ground floor, though, the plan was similar to that of smart terraced houses and palazzi. The front room or parlour, leading off a small hall, was a formal entertaining space open to the view of the street. Families spent most of their time in the back room – the equivalent of the dining room in grander houses. Behind was the kitchen, with the washhouse and scullery behind that.

The parlour became the Victorian family knick-knack repository, like this one in Kitchener Road, East Dulwich, south London, described in P.G. Wodehouse's *Indian Summer of an Uncle* (1925):

> Barring a dentist's waiting-room, which it rather resembles, there isn't anything that quells the spirit much more than one of these suburban parlours. They are extremely apt to have stuffed birds in glass cases standing about on small tables, and if there is one thing which gives the man of sensibility that sinking feeling it is the cold, accusing eye of a ptarmigan or whatever it may be that has had its interior organs removed and sawdust substituted.

The Invisible Pillars on a Terraced House

The next stage in the development of the terraced house came in around 1730 and lasted until the 1830s. Those pillars or pilasters on the façade were no longer added to new houses – for reasons of economy, but also of style. Still, the proportions of the windows and the spaces

Robert Adam's 61 Portland Place (1773), first with pilasters and then, hey presto!, they're gone. The window proportions and the cornice remain as they were.

169

between them, and the ceiling heights, were dictated by the dimensions of the pillars or pilasters – even though they were no longer there. And those bits that accompanied the pilasters – the cornices and string courses which showed the classical divisions of the façade – remained behind.

This pattern – palaces without pilasters, you might call it – continued in most terraced houses in Britain, like the one owned by Charles Pooter of the Laurels, Brickfield Terrace, Holloway, north London, in George and Weedon Grossmith's *The Diary of a Nobody* (1892):

> A nice, six-roomed residence, not counting basement, with a front breakfast-parlour. We have a little front garden, and there is a flight of ten steps up to the front door, which, by the by, we keep locked with the chain up . . .
>
> We have a nice little back garden which runs down to the railway. We were rather afraid of the noise of the trains at first, but the landlord said we should not notice them after a bit, and took £2 off the

170   Mr Pooter's inspiration: The Laurels and 62 Pemberton Gardens (both 1865).

rent. He was certainly right; and beyond the cracking of the garden wall at the bottom, we have suffered no inconvenience.

Following the late-Georgian and Victorian pattern, the Laurels had no pillars or pilasters, but its proportions were still dictated by those absent pilasters. You can see the cornice running along the roofline and the basement standing in for the pedestal of the invisible order.

The only house in Holloway that matches the Grossmiths' description is 62 Pemberton Gardens, a cut-through from Holloway Road to Junction Road, built in 1865 by George Truefitt, surveyor to Henry Tufnell, owner of the Tufnell Park Estate. Not much has changed. There are still ten steps leading up to the front door. Just as in the book, a pair of handsome posts mark the entrance. The little side door that the Pooters liked to use was open on the day I had a nose around the place.

The back garden was admittedly a little more overgrown than the Pooters'. Charles Pooter was proud of his garden. In the diary entry for Sunday 8 April he wrote, 'Took a walk round the garden, and discovered a beautiful spot for sowing mustard-and-cress and radishes.'

Sadly, one thing is no longer there – the scraper that Cummings, a work friend of Pooter's, fell over after coming round to show him the Meerschaum pipe he'd won in a raffle in the City.

'Must get the scraper removed or else I shall get into a scrape. I don't often make jokes,' said Pooter.

When Pooter bought the Laurels in the 1890s (the diary first appeared as a serial in *Punch* and came out as a book in 1892), it's not clear how much he earns. But he did get terribly excited when his boss, Mr Perkupp, gives him a £100 rise. Today Holloway is banker land – you won't get into the Laurels for much under £1 million.

DATING TIP

Another seventeenth-century triumph, alongside the invention of the terraced house, was the town square – not only a pretty burst of green among the bricks and stucco, but also a useful sort of roundabout.

Bloomsbury Square and St James's Square in London, built in the 1660s, were the first squares. Now, as then, these were not much more than a series of terraced houses formed into four ranges at right angles to each other.

In 1727 Edward Shepherd built Grosvenor Square. Though made up of individual houses, the four sides of the square, when viewed together, look like four Palladian palaces, with great pediments and pilasters in the middle – something Jules Hardouin-Mansart (1646–1708) had done in the Place Vendôme, Paris, in 1690. Also in 1727, over in Bath, John Wood pulled off the same illusion of a series of palaces in Queen Square.

The Roof Over Your Head

There's one problem with the terraced house's imitation of an Italian palace: the British climate doesn't do the decent thing and imitate the Italian weather. So the terrace ended up as a row of Italian palaces with heavy-duty British roofs and chimneys slapped on top of them.

Because we get more rain than the Italians, we need steeper roofs to throw the stuff off. The need was particularly acute in the seventeenth and early eighteenth centuries. Before the easy and cheap transport of lightweight slate from Lord Penrhyn's Caernarvonshire mines in 1765 – by 1800 he was sending twelve thousand tons a year to London – tiles covered British roofs. Heavier than slates, tiles had to be hung at a steeper angle to reduce the pressure on roofs. So that meant steeper roofs spanning shorter distances.

Tiles were made from what was handy – stone in the Cotswolds and, where stone was hard to get, clay. They were often bedded in limestone mortar, mixed with calf's hair to stop the tiles breaking when you walked on them.

Nowadays you still find tiles in rural Britain. One street in Hythe, Kent – built in the 1920s by Herbert Deedes, owner of Saltwood Castle and father of the previously mentioned Bill Deedes – was nicknamed Lobster Row because of the lurid red of the new tiles. In Lancashire in around 1900 they reversed the trend and replaced the slates with smooth red or pink tiles. Tiles have mostly gone from the cities, but the old steep roofs remain.

Slate, too, came in different colours. The deep-black slates used to roof most of Glasgow came from quarries in Easdale and Ballachulish; other parts of the city have red, grey and green slates from Luss.

Because slate roofs were shallower, they could be hidden behind the parapet to give a more convincing Italianate palazzo front. Houses often had several shallow slate roofs separated by a lead-lined gutter in a central valley – sadly prone to heavy leaking these days.

When the roof span was too wide to accommodate a steeply pitched roof, early Georgians went for the M roof – a double-pitched roof with an M-shaped profile, which allowed the pitch to be that much steeper.

The problem was that the M roof, with its small, squeezed internal spaces, didn't allow for much human activity inside. A mansard, or kirb, roof was the answer: a hipped roof, steeply pitched to begin with, before breaking into a shallow, hipped roof further up. A hipped roof looks like it sounds – a normal sloping roof with 'hips' on either side – that is, a roof that slopes on all four sides.

The mansard roof was named, with a slight change in spelling, after François Mansart (1598–1666), the French architect who popularised it. That initial steep pitch could accommodate even the tallest Frenchman or Englishman without cracking his head. Christopher

'Last night I dreamt I went to Manderley again – to admire its hipped roof' – Daphne du Maurier's Menabilly (c. 1600, rebuilt 1715), Cornwall, the inspiration for Manderley in *Rebecca* (1938).

Wren introduced the first British mansard roofs in an unexecuted 1665 design for a pair of staircases at Trinity College, Oxford.

Mansard roofs were lit with dormer windows – windows let into the roof. The combination of mansard roof and dormers made for a particularly French look.

If you have a row of mansard roofs in a terrace, the sides are usually joined together – that is, they're no longer hipped. You then end up with a series of what are called gambrel roofs.

King of the Terraces

Thomas Cubitt (1788–1855) was the king of the terraced house. In 1815 he invented a terraced-house factory, with a single all-in-one contractor who supplied the building trade with every single fanlight, shoe-scraper and door-knocker your heart could desire. Bloomsbury,

Camden, Islington and Belgravia in London, and much of Brighton – they were all covered with great stretches of Cubitt's mass-produced houses; then within the budget of City clerks, now only within the budget of City bankers.

While these terraces simplified Palladio's prototype, a later set of buildings became more, and not less, ornate, following an Italian palazzo style based on Roman and Florentine sixteenth-century palaces.

Charles Barry introduced the palazzo to Britain in his Travellers' Club (1831), an adaptation of Raphael's Pandolfini Palace in Florence. He perfected the style twelve years later at the Reform Club, modelled on the Palazzo Farnese in Rome.

The palazzo was championed by Prince Albert. With Cubitt, the Prince designed the royal retreat at Osborne in 1851 in the style of a high-Renaissance Italian villa.

Urban palazzi became indelibly associated with town institutions, from clubs to banks, from the Foreign Office to numerous town halls.

Italianate elements were defining features of the London terrace and square of the mid and late nineteenth century. However great the Gothic Revival, in sheer volume alone Italianate could be called the Victorian style. Gothic Revival terraces were thin on the ground.

Italianate stucco lapped in creamy-white waves through the British suburbs. You can see the semicircular stucco tideline running across the city close to the North London Line, the cross-city railway built in 1869.

This Italianate 'Villa Line' runs from Hackney in the east, through Canonbury, Highbury, Camden, Kentish Town, Hampstead Heath, Kensal Rise, Acton and Kew, to Richmond. Take the train, look out of the window at Canonbury Station – right if you're heading west – and you'll see the streets round St Saviour's, Aberdeen Park, where John Betjeman's parents courted. 'Solid Italianate houses for the solid commercial mind,' he wrote in 1948 of these great big double villas, built in 1853.

Herr-Doktor-Professor Pevsner Dates Your Terraced House

For anyone wanting to date their house, the starting point is the Buildings of England series by Sir Nikolaus Pevsner, later extended to Wales, Scotland and Ireland.

Your house or flat is unlikely to have its own entry in Pevsner – unless you are the Duke of Devonshire or the Queen, or staying at Her Majesty's Pleasure in an architecturally alluring jail like Pentonville (which gets three pages and two illustrations in *London 4: North* (1998) by Pevsner and Bridget Cherry). But it might figure as part of a larger development of terraced houses.

Pevsner's county architecture guides are such an institution among building obsessives that they are referred to simply by his name.

'Have you packed for your trip to Much Guilding in the Marsh?'

'Yup – oh no, bloody hell. Forgot my Pevsner.'

Pevsner's ambition – to record every building of note in Britain – was so vast that the guides are still coming out, a quarter of a century after he died. It also meant that the stern German-born scholar – nicknamed Herr Doktor Professor Sir Nikolaus Pevsner by John Betjeman – was necessarily a bit of a skimmer.

John Newman was one of his drivers in the sixties, using the 1933 Wolseley Hornet that Pevsner borrowed from his publishers, Penguin. The good Herr Doktor rode shotgun and wrote notes. '"Early English windows, Norman porch," he would say as we swept past some church in East Anglia at thirty miles per hour,' Newman told me.

Pevsner was in such a hurry that he liked to eat spaghetti – it slipped down easily and didn't take long to eat.

176   The series was started in 1951 by Allen Lane, Penguin's presiding

mind. The full team was two German refugee art historians, a secretary and Pevsner. One of the art historians would work for a year on a county and then Pevsner would get into the Hornet, covering two counties in the Easter and summer university holidays.

At the end of each day Pevsner wrote up the first draft. He dedicated one volume to 'those publicans and hoteliers of England who provide me with a table in my bedroom to scribble on'. (*Bedfordshire* (1968) was dedicated to the inventor of the ice lolly.) Once the Hornet was garaged, he wrote the long introduction to each guide in a week.

First came *Cornwall* (1951); the last by Pevsner alone was *Staffordshire* (1974). Since then most of the English counties have been revised and Scotland, Wales and the beginnings of Ireland have been written. They're expensive – the updated *Essex* (2007) by James Bettley and Pevsner costs £29.95 – but you can pick up the earlier, not so comprehensive but equally addictive, 1954 edition for less than a tenner.

Betjeman was rather scornful of Pevsner for being too dry. His own Shell guides to the counties (1933–84), on which he collaborated with the artist John Piper, were altogether jollier things. In a 1963 letter to Juliet Smith, the author of the *Shell Guide to Northamptonshire and the Soke of Peterborough* (1968), he said that Pevsner

> does not tell you what the place is really like, i.e. whether it is strung with poles and wires, overshadowed by factories or ruined army huts, whether it is suburban or a real village, nor whether it is a place of weekend hide-outs and carriage-lamp folk with wrought-iron front gates by the local smith . . . whether there are trees in the village, nor what sort, if they are remarkable for size and planting.

Pevsner rarely risked jokes, although in one volume he does refer to a Victorian designer of town halls as 'widely unknown'.

17

Change and Decay in All Around I See

Eighteenth-Century Ruins and the Picturesque

In the drawing room of Aberglasney – a fine 1720 house, twenty miles north-west of Swansea – high up by the cornice an elaborate chunk of plasterwork is missing. It's a fine early-eighteenth-century console, carved with honeysuckle and acanthus – touches much favoured by the Greeks.

To my deep and lasting shame, I know where to find the missing bit of plaster. In fact I can see it now, some ten feet from where I'm writing this. It's sitting on a tall mahogany stand next to my desk in my north London sitting room. Its protuberant plaster leaves are a nice prominent perch for my keys where I won't forget them. Still, the console would probably look better glued back to the cornice in Aberglasney's drawing room. I will return it, I promise.

Aberglasney has now been restored, and its rare Tudor cloister garden is a honeypot for Carmarthenshire tourists. Fifteen years ago, though, when I stole the console, on the way to my parents' cottage in Pembrokeshire, the house was in a terrible state.

I climbed over a gate choked with nettles and rhododendrons as high as the gateposts. The roof of the house had fallen in. Its portico

Stolen goods – a 1720 console from Aberglasney, Carmarthenshire, currently resting in Kentish Town, north London.

had been stolen and was about to be flogged at Christie's. (An eagle-eyed Welsh antiquarian spotted the distinctive Ionic pillars in a sales catalogue and the portico has now been restored to its original site.)

Just in front of the house there was a six-foot-deep pile of plaster and wood. The plaster console lay on top of the pile. If I didn't take it, someone else would – that was my wicked logic, anyway.

Now that most of those consoles have been returned to Aberglasney's ceiling, my despicable excuse hardly carries much weight. Neither is it helped by a recent article in which another man admitted to pillaging Aberglasney twenty years before me – Neil Hamilton, the disgraced Tory MP, who grew up in nearby Ammanford.

I made several further trips to Aberglasney. I never took anything else, though I was sorely tempted by a pale-oak bedhead with Doric pilasters. It was too big to fit in the boot. But I didn't go to Aberglasney just for criminal reasons. I was enchanted by the feeling of decay and emptiness where once there had been life and grandness. I had been touched by the hypnotic, macabre, nostalgic pleasure of ruins.

My pleasure was literally nostalgic. The Greek roots of the word 'nostalgia' mean 'the pain of going back', and the pleasure in ruins is also pain – pain at the encroaching extinction of something you love.

How odd that I was first touched by the pleasure of ruins in this obscure – then unvisited – Welsh valley. It was here, 280 years earlier, that a Welsh poet wrote about that same pleasure for the first time in British history.

The Beginning of the Heritage Industry

John Dyer (1699–1757) was brought up at Aberglasney, where his father built that charming Ionic façade. Rejecting his father's plans for him to become a lawyer, he took up painting in London and Rome.

But it was as a poet, back at home in Aberglasney, that he achieved fame, writing about the domed hill opposite the house – Grongar Hill, which gave its name to his poem of 1716.

If you visit Grongar Hill today, beware of the furious sheepdog that guards the gate leading from Aberglasney. The dog is as devoted to the hill as Dyer, but less happy to share its joys with the world.

In 'Grongar Hill', Dyer was the first poet to write in a picturesque way about ruins and landscapes. The very idea that ruins might be attractive was revolutionary. Dyer's spark later fired the first late-eighteenth-century romantic poets to write odes to buildings. Thomas Gray's *Elegy Written in a Country Churchyard* (1751), was a tribute to St Giles, Stoke Poges, Buckinghamshire: 'From yonder ivy-mantled tower the moping owl does to the moon complain.'

Dyer's poem described not just Grongar Hill, but also the view from Aberglasney down the valley, with a series of crumbling castles perched on crags above the meandering River Towy:

> The pleasant seat, the ruin'd tower,
> The naked rock, the shady bow'r,
> The town and village, dome and farm,
> Each gives each a double charm.

Just before Dyer unearthed the poetic charm of ruins, Sir John Vanbrugh became the first man to try to save a ruin for posterity. Before Dyer and Vanbrugh, ruins were merely buildings that had fallen apart and needed to be replaced. Afterwards, they gradually began to be prized as heart-stirring relics of fading, fragile beauty.

In 1709 the Duke and Duchess of Marlborough – when they were building Blenheim – demanded that Woodstock Manor, the decayed medieval pile opposite the new palace, must be swept away. Woodstock was where Henry II hid his girlfriend Rosamond from his wife Eleanor of Aquitaine in an impenetrable maze – Fair Rosamond's

Bower, as writers from John Aubrey to Tennyson called it. Tennyson wrote in 'A Dream of Fair Women' (1833):

> 'Alas! alas!' a low voice, full of care,
> > Murmur'd beside me: 'Turn and look on me:
> I am that Rosamond, whom men call fair,
> > If what I was I be.
> 'Would I had been some maiden coarse and poor!
> > O me, that I should ever see the light!
> Those dragon eyes of anger'd Eleanor
> > Do hunt me, day and night.'

Vanbrugh desperately tried to save the old manor at Woodstock, in what became the first-ever British preservation drive. Old buildings, he said, 'move more lively and pleasing reflections than history without their aid can do'. They also increased the 'paintability' of a place in conjunction with nature. If trees were planted next to the ruins of Woodstock Manor, 'It would make one of the most agreeable objects that the best of landskip painters can invent.'

'Landskip' wasn't really the Duchess of Marlborough's thing. 'I morally hate all gardens and architecture,' she once said. A contemporary described her as 'at warfare with the whole world'.

It didn't help that Vanbrugh had already done up a couple of rooms in the old manor at the duchess's expense for his own use. She ordered that the place be torn down. The first attempt to save a British ruin had been an abject failure.

Vanbrugh's dealings with the duchess got worse. Once Blenheim Palace was finished, he wasn't even allowed inside the wall that skirted the park. When he visited Blenheim with the Earl of Carlisle in 1725, he had to walk around the outside of the estate, occasionally jumping up to get a glimpse over the wall at the thing to which he'd devoted twenty years of his life.

Still, he and Dyer had laid the ground for the cult worship of old buildings. Soon after, the first follies emerged – a sham church at Fawley Court, Henley, and a pretend hermitage, King Alfred's Hall, Cirencester Park – both built in 1729.

By the time Elizabeth Bennet, in Jane Austen's *Pride and Prejudice* (1813), went on a tour of Derbyshire (including Chatsworth) with her aunt and uncle a century or so later, the habit of appreciating great houses and their surrounding landscape was taken as read. When the three of them get to Pemberley, they are shown round the house by the housekeeper:

> Every disposition of the ground was good; and she looked on the whole scene – the river, the trees scattered on its banks, and the winding of the valley, as far as she could trace it – with delight. As they passed into other rooms, these objects were taking different positions; but from every window there were beauties to be seen. The rooms were lofty and handsome, and their furniture suitable to the fortune of their proprietor; but Elizabeth saw, with admiration of his taste, that it was neither gaudy nor uselessly fine; with less of splendour, and more real elegance.

Two centuries on, the Dyer-Vanbrugh old-buildings cult now has millions of paid-up acolytes. The National Trust, with 3.5 million subscribers, has far more members than any other organisation in Britain.

Lancelot Brown Gets a Nickname – The Landscape Gardener is Born

Whenever a Palladian house met a landscaped garden, Lancelot 'Capability' Brown (1716–83) usually arranged the introduction.

He got the nickname from telling clients that their land had great 'capability' of improvement – and that the best way to improve things was, funnily enough, by employing him. The flattery worked – Brown landscaped over 170 great estates. His commissions read like a gazetteer of the leading country houses of England: Longleat, Blenheim, Alnwick, Althorp, Chatsworth, Badminton, Stowe, Wilton, Woburn – all of them eminently capable of improvement.

Brown's trademarks included closely cropped, smooth, undulating terrain that came right up to the house. In his desire to bring on the sensation of nature all around, he wasn't averse to clearing whole villages to open up the view. Clumps and belts of trees dotted and lined the near and distant landscape, ideally around a lake, like at Blenheim.

One of Brown's chief capabilities was the creation of water features from dammed streams; once you'd built some great big pile, it couldn't just lord it over some tiny puddle.

At Blenheim, the River Glyme wasn't much more than a brook until first Vanbrugh, and then Brown, came along, dammed it and produced a satisfyingly thick stretch of water just outside the front gates of the palace. Now it was big enough to deserve a bridge with the longest span in Britain.

So, although Brown was sweeping away the formal, patterned gardens that had come before, his landscapes were still intensely planned ones. Artifice, pure artifice, designed to look like nature, pure nature.

Brown was happy to admit to this tight control of things. At Hampton Court in 1782, he summed up his skills to the writer Hannah More:

'Now there,' said he, pointing his finger, 'I make a comma, and there,' pointing to another spot, 'where a more decided turn is proper, I make a colon; at another part, where an interruption is desirable to break the view, a parenthesis; now a full stop, and then I begin another subject.'

Picturesque Goes Wild in the Country

The Dyer-Vanbrugh idea – that nature and ruins sparked off an artistic thrill – was elaborated on and written down almost a century later in the Picturesque movement. Roughly translated, this meant the romantic setting of buildings in the landscape. One of its chief proponents, William Gilpin, described the picturesque as 'that kind of beauty which is agreeable in a picture' – not unlike Vanbrugh's idea of paintability.

In 1794 and 1795 the three founders of the Picturesque movement – Humphry Repton, Uvedale Price and Richard Payne Knight – all wrote books that helped to launch the movement. Repton's great innovation was his 'red books' – you flipped the pages to show the 'before' and 'after' effect of the Repton treatment on your landscaped park.

All three men had different views, but Price and Payne Knight were broadly against the formal tricks Capability Brown used to make an informal landscape. Nature should be left in its wild state and only tamed to enhance the natural look – 'the wild and shaggy genius' of a place, as Repton put it.

Jane Austen was an early convert to the Picturesque movement. In *The History of England by a Partial, Prejudiced and Ignorant Historian* (1791), she said that the only silver lining to Henry VIII's barbarism was, 'that his abolishing religious houses and leaving them to the ruinous depredations of time had been of infinite use to the landscape of England'.

18

Strawberry Hill for Ever

An Eighteenth-Century Gothick Romance

Stephen Potter (1900–69) was the academic turned comic writer who invented the term 'gamesmanship' – 'the art of winning games without actually cheating'. He applied this bluffing art to all sorts of things – Well Readship, Winesmanship and Writership among them. He then parlayed the art into several international bestsellers, including *Gamesmanship* (1948), *Lifemanship* (1950) and *One-Upmanship* (1952).

One of Potter's gambits was the perfect stock answer for when somebody talks about something you know nothing about.

'"Yes, but not in the South," with slight adjustments, will do for any argument about any place, if not about any person. It is an impossible comment to answer,' he wrote in *Potter on Lifemanship* (1950):

> EXPERT: (Who has just come back from a fortnight in Florence) And I was glad to see with my own eyes that this Left-wing Catholicism is definitely on the increase in Tuscany.
> YOU: Yes, but not in the South.

The equivalent response, when it comes to the history of British buildings, is, 'Oh, around the second half of the eighteenth century.'

More turning points happened then than in any period before or since.

Among the questions it answers are: when did Gothick and Indian buildings get going? Oh, and what about Chinoiserie/neo-classicism/the Greek Revival and the use of cast iron? And circuses and crescents? And what about the Picturesque movement? And when was the first association of British architects set up?

To answer that last one first: in 1791, the Architects' Club – the first professional association of English architects, with members including Robert Adam and Sir William Chambers – was founded to deal with the new commissions in all these different styles.

Despite this proliferation of new styles, Palladian palaces remained popular until the late eighteenth century. Too popular in fact. As early as 1731, Alexander Pope took against gimcrack Palladian imitations in 'Epistle to Burlington', a poem of 1731 addressed to Lord Burlington, the leading Palladian architect:

> Yet shall (my Lord) your just, your noble rules,
> Fill half the land with imitating fools.

The reaction to the correct classical severity of Palladianism was its opposite: a playful Gothic style, or, as it's also called, Gothick or Georgian Gothick. Architects picked and mixed the most decorative, recognisable and frothy Gothic features – ogee arches, quatrefoils, heavy crocketing, pointed and traceried windows, particularly Y-shaped glazing bars (as in the Carew Methodist chapel on page 249).

This new freestyle Gothic was used a lot from the mid-eighteenth century onwards, particularly for follies in the shape of sham ruins – not that surprising, really, since most real ruins at the time were Gothic.

The great Gothic building of the age was Strawberry Hill in Twickenham (1766), built by Horace Walpole (1717–97), son of Sir Robert Walpole, Britain's first Prime Minister. Walpole was determined that the house should be asymmetrical, in its plan and its roofline. Back in 1750 he had written, 'I am almost as fond of the Sharawaggi, or Chinese want of symmetry, in buildings, as in grounds or gardens.'

Strawberry Hill's pair of round towers – one with a crenellated crust – had no defensive role. They were there to evoke a medieval romantic feel – the sort of towers that Rapunzel let down her hair from.

Inside, the playful, childlike romance of the place deepened. There were fan-vault ceilings made out of papier mâché, gilt fretwork and mirrored glass – the height of Rococo Gothic to match anything on the Continent.

Gothic fantasy reached giddy heights – real and metaphorical – in James Wyatt's Fonthill Abbey (1807), Wiltshire. The house was built for William Beckford (1760–1844), an MP who learnt music from Mozart and wrote the first Gothic novel, *Vathek,* at twenty-one.

Beckford took risqué flights of fancy in his writing – and in his life. After a gay affair with a fellow young grandee in his twenties, he lived on the loucher fringes of society. Among his staff he retained the services of a personal dwarf.

Fonthill, built with the millions Beckford inherited from his family's Jamaican sugar plantations, reflected his artistic and self-indulgent character. His mammoth Gothic palace was gathered round a 315-foot-tall tower on an octagonal design inspired by Ely Cathedral. The tower was so broad that a coach and six could be comfortably driven within its inner wall. Among the treasures was Beckford's ornate Gothic library at the foot of the tower, at the heart of which was Edward Gibbon's book collection.

For all the fortune spent on it, Fonthill was fatally weak – it fell twice before finally collapsing in 1825. Beckford was so keen to see his house go up that it was built at lightning pace – by six hundred builders camped round the site, working by the light of enormous bonfires. It didn't help that Wyatt used flimsy cement and timber instead of stone and brick for the tower.

Ever since the Normans, builders had had little idea of what kept buildings up, and had played it pretty much by ear. Churches and cathedrals regularly fell down – from the 1180 abbey at Malmesbury, Wiltshire, whose tower collapsed in a storm in 1500, to the cathedral at Beauvais, just north of Paris, once the tallest in the world. Beauvais collapsed not once, but twice – in 1284 and 1573.

In the nineteenth century the church at Oxburgh, Norfolk, caved in.

The next morning the butler said gleefully to the lord of the manor, whose Bedingfield family chapel was part of the church, 'The spire has collapsed and demolished the church, sir, but *your* chapel is perfectly unharmed.'

Britain's Eighteenth-Century Chinese Takeaway

The first bluestocking was a man. Benjamin Stillingfleet (1702–71) was an eccentric scholar who appeared in 1756 at the salon of Elizabeth Montagu, the literary lioness, in a pair of blue worsted stockings. These were worn by the poor; smart people like Stillingfleet usually wore white silk. He caused such a shock that everyone at the gathering – including a bunch of clever women – got the nickname 'bluestocking'. In his *Life of Johnson* (1791), Boswell said of Stillingfleet's absence at some bookish bunfight, 'We can do nothing without the bluestockings.'

These bluestockings gathered at Mrs Montagu's house in Hill Street, Mayfair. It was appropriate that such a fashionable woman would want her house to be designed by Robert Adam; appropriate too that he should design a room in *the* style of the day – the Chinese style. The room was thick with pagodas and mandarins with bobbing heads. In the middle of all this, Adam designed an elaborate Chinese circular carpet decorated with wispy-bearded Chinamen at work in the fields.

The earliest Chinese buildings in Britain were erected at Wroxton, Oxfordshire, in 1753. But there had been earlier glimpses – at Stonyhurst, the Lancashire school, there's a Chinaman's face on the main keystone of the 1699 building.

When it came to textiles and porcelain the Chinese fashion had been around since the late seventeenth century. The *Treatise of Japanning and Varnishing* (1688) by John Stalker and George Parker was the first pattern book for British craftsmen copying Chinese motifs in lacquer, silver, ceramic and textiles. In Hogarth's *Tête à Tête*, from his series *Marriage à la Mode* (1743), you can see, behind the dissipated couple, a Chinese firescreen and clock and several smiling Pu-Tai figures – take-offs of the Chinese god of happiness.

Buildings caught on to the trend half a century after textiles, partly in reaction to the ever-tightening straitjacket of Palladianism.

In 1750 Horace Walpole wrote to Sir Horace Mann in Florence, 'I am sure whenever you come to England, you will be pleased with the liberty of taste into which we are struck,' and said of the new Chinese buildings that they brought 'a whimsical air of novelty that is very pleasing'.

Just as Chinese food in Chinatown bears little relation to Chinese food in China, early Chinese buildings were hardly authentic, borrowing and exaggerating the most comic Chinese features. An early home-grown Chinese takeaway was the pagoda at Kew, built by Sir William Chambers in 1762; at 163 feet it was the tallest Chinese building in Europe. Purists, though, object to it – traditional Chinese towers had an odd number of floors; the Kew pagoda has ten.

Nearly two centuries later, chinoiserie makes a cameo appearance in *Brideshead Revisited*. The Chinese drawing room at Brideshead is 'adazzle with gilt pagodas and nodding mandarins, painted paper and Chippendale fretwork'. It is in this 'splendid, uninhabitable museum' that Lord Marchmain chose to die.

Woods, Circuses and Crescents

It's no surprise that Bath produced some crucial firsts – the first circus and the first crescent. Bath, Buxton and Dublin were the only places in the British Isles to have a thoroughgoing town-planning scheme in the eighteenth century.

To our modern, experienced eyes, the circus – a round range of buildings – seems the most obvious thing on earth. Actually, until

1754, when John Wood (1704–54) built the first circus, the idea wasn't at all logical. Well, not in Britain anyway – Mansart pulled off a similar trick in the Place des Victoires, Paris, in 1685.

Before, round buildings looked outwards – and so, when Tobias Smollett first saw the Bath Circus, he called it a little Colosseum 'turned outside in'. Smollett apart, the Circus was immediately fashionable – William Pitt the Elder moved straight into number seven; his next-door neighbour at number eight was Thomas Gainsborough. Thackeray later moved into number seventeen.

In an astonishing father-and-son double act, while John Wood the Elder invented the circus, John Wood the Younger (1728–82) invented the crescent – again in Bath, where in 1767 the Royal Crescent was built on a hill above the city. This is really a street of terraced houses with an Ionic order set above the ground floor as a podium; a street bent into a stately curve.

Brighton, Hastings, Buxton and Edinburgh went crazy for the crescent. And, in 1789 another Bath architect, John Palmer (1738–1817), took the idea further in Lansdowne Crescent. This was really four crescents joined together – a stone-and-slate snake wriggling around the Bath hills in a concave-convex-concave-convex quadruple curve.

19

Neo-classicism

Anthony Blunt, MI5 Vandals and the
Two Courtauld Institutes

Now a private members' club popular with Sir Tom Jones and Sir Elton John, Robert Adam's Home House was, until recently, literally scarred with the memories of another artistic knight – Sir Anthony Blunt (1907–83), world expert on Poussin and double agent recruited by the Russians in 1934. Well, he was a knight until he was stripped of the honour in 1979.

Adam was particularly popular in London – Marchmain House in *Brideshead Revisited* had 'a long elaborate, symmetrical Adam room, with two bays of windows opening into Green Park', which Charles Ryder paints just before it is demolished.

Home House in Portman Square, built in 1776 for Elizabeth, Countess of Home, was a rare escapee from the wrecking ball. Even so, when I toured the place in 1996, it was in a worrying state. Shortly to be converted into the members' club, it still showed signs of fifty-eight years of housing the Courtauld Institute.

More precisely, Home House still held memories of its old director from 1947 to 1974 – Anthony Blunt. Up on the second floor, where Blunt's office was, I spotted some rough holes gouged deep into the plasterwork – where MI5 cut into the wall to retrieve listening devices used to monitor Blunt.

There also used to be an enormous mural in the students' common room in the basement. The mural showed members of staff posing with their favourite objects. In an interview before his exposure as a Russian spy, Blunt cheerfully admitted that he was painted with a bottle of wine in one hand and a copy of Karl Marx in the other. The painting was done in 1937. It took MI5 only another twenty-six years to work out that Blunt had Communist sympathies.

Anyway, back to the original builder of Home House. There, in the Etruscan Room, you'll see what people are getting at when they talk about the Adam style. The Etruscans were the civilisation that came before the Romans, but you could, a few quibbles apart, call the Etruscan Room the Roman Room.

Discoveries of Roman frescoes at Herculaneum in 1709 and Pompeii in 1748 deepened the craze for all things classical. Adam was an early groupie. He was keen on all sorts of ancient influences – from Greece, Dalmatia and Syria among others – but Italy was the most powerful. And not just ancient Italy – the masters of the Renaissance and later Adam's friend Piranesi (1720–78), the master of drawings of eighteenth-century Rome, also affected him deeply.

The distinctive mark of the Roman-Etruscan-Adam style was ultra-delicate, spare plasterwork with strings of white plaster, often on a bright-green or pink background, strewn across ceilings, walls and façades. The decoration itself was elegant and spare in detail; but there was lots of it and rarely any panelling. Instead, narrow moulded bands marked out the division of the walls. On the ceiling, lunettes and ovals were painted with classical scenes by the likes of Angelica Kauffmann.

Date Your Ceiling

Copies of Adam ceilings, with profuse yet delicate ornament, remained popular until 1790, particularly as refinements in plastering technique developed.

Ceilings then began to get a little simpler. Look at ceilings in post-1790 houses – which means most surviving Georgian and Victorian terraces in Britain – and you'll usually see a plain ceiling rose in the middle, an ornate cornice, often in a floral design, around the edge, and a blank expanse of plaster in between.

Adam's characteristic spareness extended to the architectural framework of the rooms. In the music room at Home House, the pilasters are anorexic – as they are at Adam's Kenwood House, Hampstead (1774). It made sense, because the pillars had to look like they supported hardly anything – there's barely an architrave or cornice resting on those capitals.

All this broke the rules of Palladio and Vitruvius that dictated precise dimensions for columns and entablatures. This was pretty revolutionary; and Adam's profusion of spare detail got up people's noses. Sir William Chambers called it 'filigrane toy-work'. Horace Walpole said in 1785, 'How sick one shall be . . . of Mr Adam's ginger-bread and sippets of embroidery'.

There were other distinct aspects of the Adam style – the neo-classical, eighteenth-century French taste for a series of differently sized rooms running into one another, as at Syon House (1762), Middlesex; and the non-stop movement of façades and skylines. In his book *Ruins of the Palace of the Emperor Diocletian at Spalatro* (1764), Adam put all this down to the ancient Romans, the masters of 'diversity of form, as well as of dimensions', as opposed to modern architects who went for 'a dull succession of similar apartments'.

The neo-classical watchwords were restraint and pared-down plainness, in emulation of the purity of ancient Greek art. This new minimalism didn't always go down well: Sir John Soane was attacked for his 'pilasters scored like loins of pork'.

This stripped-down look took on a different form with Sir William Chambers, particularly in his masterpiece, Somerset House (1780) – London's greatest square. Although Somerset House was built on an enormous scale, with four ranges around a central courtyard and a grand façade to the Thames, it doesn't loom large to the passer-by in the Strand front – pictured to the right of St Mary-le-Strand on page 132.

Until 1996, when I studied at the Courtauld Institute, which fills that front range on the Strand, I barely noticed the existence of Somerset House. This is partly because that façade was squeezed into a narrow site facing the street. It's also because of that neo-classical restraint exercised by Chambers, who had none of the bombast and conscientious grandness that puffed up a lot of his

Palladian predecessors. The building borrowed from Inigo Jones and Palladio with a touch of Louis XVI, but always in a low-key, unflashy way.

Chambers's basic unit remained the house – Somerset House certainly felt more like a series of houses than one vast palace when I mooched around the place in breaks from my Courtauld thesis. The Inland Revenue building seemed detached from the Courtauld Gallery, which in turn seemed separate from the Gilbert Collection.

This effect of a series of houses also appeals to location scouts working on BBC period dramas. Whenever you see a costume drama with what looks like a row of late-eighteenth-century houses, the chances are it's Somerset House. The building is so varied that directors use its plainer subterranean streets for pox-and-prostitutes London, and its upstairs show rooms for gavotte-and-chandelier, upmarket eighteenth-century London. Somerset House features heavily in *The Duchess* (2008), the biopic about Georgiana, Duchess of Devonshire (1757–1806).

Upstairs, Downstairs – Somerset House, London (1780).

20

The Empire Style Strikes Back

India Comes to Gloucestershire

Sequestered among trees, a noble pile,
Baronial and Colonial in its style
Gables and dormer-windows everywhere,
And stacks of chimneys rising high in air.
Henry Wadsworth Longfellow, Lady Wentworth (1871)

Longfellow (1807–82) was writing about the house in Portsmouth, New Hampshire, America, belonging to the British governor, Sir Benning Wentworth. In 1760, in a celebrated scandal, the sixty-four-year-old Wentworth married his twenty-year-old housekeeper, Martha Hilton.

When British grandees like Sir Benning returned home, with or without their young brides, they brought back that baronial and colonial style. In the late eighteenth and early nineteenth centuries, colonial themes loomed large in Britain. India, the Empire's new powerhouse, was a leading influence.

The first great house influenced by Indian or 'Hindoo' – or, strictly speaking, Indo-Saracenic – style, was Sezincote (1803), Gloucestershire, built for Sir Charles Cockerell by his brother Samuel Pepys Cockerell, Surveyor to the East India Company. The family had deep colonial roots – another brother, Colonel John Cockerell, had returned from Bengal in 1795 to buy the Sezincote Estate.

Sezincote was a light, airy skit of a house. Its jigger-jagger arches, minarets, peacock-tail windows, jali-work railings and daringly deep cornices were in the so-called Moghul style outside, Greek Revival within.

John Betjeman stayed there in the 1920s with a friend, John Dugdale, whose father owned the house. Betjeman wrote about Sezincote in his blank-verse autobiography, *Summoned by Bells* (1960):

And there they burst on us, the onion domes,
Chajjahs and chattris made of amber stone . . .
Stately and strange it stood, the Nabob's house,
Indian without and coolest Greek within.

John Betjeman's first taste of country houses – Sezincote, Gloucestershire (1803).

Chattris are the slim minarets on the corners of the building, and chajjahs those projecting cornices with their deep brackets. Like the dome, these were Muslim devices. Above the front door, an iwan, or arch, reaches right up to the roof, as in the mosques of Bokhara and Samarkand, the ancient Moghul homeland.

This powerful cocktail of stone and glass resonated in Brighton Pavilion's dome, built by John Nash fifteen years after Sezincote. The pavilion jumped all over the place for inspiration, from Hindoo domes to dragons snaking round bulging chandeliers and glaring at fake-bamboo furniture and luridly coloured Chinese vases.

The look caught on across Britain – front parlours bulged with decorative fire-irons, frosted glass, china knick-knacks, bamboo chairs and pot plants. P.G. Wodehouse evoked the Royal Pavilion at Brighton when disparaging the fictitious Ashby Hall, in the same county of Sussex, in *Company for Henry* (1967):

A hideous pile that looked partly like the Prince Regent's establishment at Brighton and partly like a medieval fortress. Local humourists were accustomed to speak derisively of it as The Castle. It's not a thing you want to come on suddenly, particularly to be avoided by nervous people and invalids, designed by an architect steeped to the tonsils in spirituous liquor as so many architects were in the days of the Regency.

Whenever the Empire boomed, its echoes were felt back home on British building sites. So, in Royal York Crescent, Bristol – a city built on slavers' fortunes – there was a strong plantation feel to the umbrella-roofed balconies of 1820, even if the sun never gets

Alexander 'Greek' Thomson (1817–75), a magpie of an architect, might just as well have been known as Alexander 'Greek, Egyptian, Assyrian and Indian' Thomson for his St Vincent Street church, Glasgow (1859). A tower inspired by a Hindu temple, with Assyrian details, soars up one side of a Greek temple on an Egyptian base.

Indian Takeaways – Verandahs and Bungalows

After their creation in Bath, circuses and crescents took off throughout Britain in the late eighteenth century, notably in Brighton's Royal Crescent in 1798. This crescent also sported one of the first British verandahs. The idea was brought back from India by nabobs – 'verandah' comes from the Hindi *varanda*, itself originally Spanish or Portuguese, meaning railing, balustrade or balcony.

Bungalows took their name from the Hindi *bangla*, meaning Bengali and, in this context, a house in the Bengal style – one-storey thatched houses with verandahs. The word caught on during colonial days, as a 1676 entry in the diary of Streynsham Master, working in the India Office, showed: 'It was thought fitt to sett up Bungales or Hovells for all such English in the Company's service.'

Since the dawn of time, shortage of funds had dictated that most humble houses in Britain were inevitably one-storey; the modern concept of the bungalow as a positive style choice took off in the late nineteenth century. The first British bungalows were built at Westgate-on-Sea and Birchington, both on the Kent coast, in 1869. That seaside connection gave them a healthy holiday air. The artist Dante Gabriel Rossetti came to Birchington to recover from illness in a bungalow. He died there in 1882.

---

quite as hot in the West Country as in the steamy plantations of Jamaica.

Egyptian motifs became popular after Nelson won the Battle of the Nile against Napoleon Bonaparte's navy in 1798. Over a decade later, in Maria Edgeworth's novel *The Absentee* (1812), Egyptian themes were still all the rage. An early professional interior decorator, Mr Soho, advises Lady Clonbrony, married to a dreary Irish peer, to deck her ballroom out in the prevailing fashion: 'If your la'ship prefers it, you

The view the Blairs lost, along with £1.18 million. Richmond Avenue, Islington, London (1841).

can have the Egyptian hieroglyphic paper, with the ibis border to match! The only objection is, one sees it everywhere – quite antediluvian – gone to the hotels even.'

The Egyptian style lasted long into the nineteenth century. It accounted for the quirky set of sphinxes and obelisks that greet visitors to the handsome villas of Richmond Avenue, Islington, just opposite Tony Blair's old house in Richmond Crescent – the one that Cherie Blair was so cross at having to sell in 1997 for £615,000. It's now worth £1.8 million.

Nelson's fame was so great that these lovely little sphinxes and obelisks were inscribed with the word 'Nile' in 1841, forty-three years after the battle, by Joseph Kay, surveyor to Islington's Thornhill Estate.

21

It's All Greek to Me in 1803

When it came to the development of the gentleman's club, the BBC TV series *Blackadder* was spot on, as it was on so many historical questions. In *Blackadder the Third* (1987) – the Regency episodes – much of the action took place in Mrs Miggins's architecturally correct coffee house:

Shelley: Oh, Love, oh ecstasy that is Mrs Miggins, wilt thou bring me but one cup of the browned juicings of that naughty bean we call 'coffee', ere I die . . .

Mrs Miggins: (swoons) Ooohhhh, you do have a way of words with you, Mr Shelley! . . . Don't you worry about my poets, Mr Blackadder . . . they're just being 'intellectual'.

Edmund: Mrs Miggins, there's nothing intellectual about wandering around Italy in a big shirt, trying to get laid.

Ben Elton and Richard Curtis, the writers of this series, were right about the importance of the coffee house to high society. The earliest gentleman's clubs grew out of coffee houses and several in St James's – like White's (originally a chocolate house) – owed their names to the first owners of these early cafés.

White's was opened by Francis White in 1693, although its current home is a 1788 rebuilding of a 1674 mansion in St James's Street. Its members-only policy is so strict that not even Simon Bradley, author of the 2003 Pevsner guide to Westminster, was allowed through the door – 'A visit was not permitted, so the description is from published sources.'

The real boom in clubmen, and the boom in clubhouses, came later, with the expansion of the professional classes after the Industrial Revolution and the victory at Waterloo. New clubs were built on a vast, splendid scale. 'There is something exhilarating about the extravagance of space in these older clubs,' the late Hugh Massingberd said. 'We can all walk tall in well-proportioned rooms.'

This economic boom coincided with the Greek Revival, so the style proved popular on the burgeoning club scene. Accordingly, Decimus Burton's Athenaeum (1830) sports a copy of the Parthenon frieze.

The most famous Greek Revival building is the British Museum, built by Sir Robert Smirke (1780–1867). Smirke was responsible for an exhausting list of institutions, lots of them Greek Revival, from 1808 to 1836: the Royal College of Physicians, barristers' chambers in the Inner Temple, King's College, London, the General Post Office, the Custom House, the Royal Mint, Covent Garden Theatre and no fewer than three clubs – the Oxford and Cambridge Club, the United Service Club and the Union Club.

The Greekest Building in Britain

The Greek Revival reached a peak in 1822, in St Pancras New Church. Built by William Inwood (1771–1843) and his son Henry Inwood (1794–1843), it was, at £89,296, the most expensive church in London since St Paul's Cathedral. It was also the Greekest church in Britain.

Although St Pancras had that classic shape of St Martin-in-the-Fields – tower blasting up and out of the middle of a great big portico – it was all wrapped up in Greek clothes. Every single detail came from ancient Athens. The three-stage tower was a copy of the Athenian Tower of the Winds of 50 BC (the two lower bits) and the Choragic Monument of Lysicrates of 335 BC (the top bit).

But the most exciting parts of St Pancras New Church were the transepts – you get a close-up as you head west on the Euston Road. You'll see four caryatids – butch maidens – taken straight from the Erechtheum, one of the side temples of the Parthenon.

It's hard to say exactly when the Greek Revival began. Some say 1803, when Stratton Park, Hampshire, was the first country house in Britain to be given a Doric portico. But, for several decades before this, architects had been visiting Greece to find the source of pure Greek architecture and inject it into British buildings. Thus the nickname of James 'Athenian'   209

Greek lighting – caryatids and their torches, St Pancras
New Church, London (1822).

Stuart, who used the same inspiration as the Inwoods – the Tower of
the Winds – for his Temple of the Winds (1782) at Mount Stewart,
County Down.

The First Interior Decorator

If you've had enough of *Changing Rooms,* Laurence Llewelyn-Bowen
and all that, you have one man to blame – Thomas Hope (1769–1831),
a Dutchman who wore Turkish fancy dress and invented the term

The Athens of the North. Dugald Stewart's Monument, Calton Hill, Edinburgh (1831), by William Playfair, a copy of the Choragic Monument of Lysicrates in Athens.

'interior decoration'. In his mid-twenties Hope moved from Holland to London, where he designed a house in Duchess Street that had a huge effect on Regency style.

His rooms, broadly neo-classical, were full of all sorts of influences, but they were mostly Greek, Egyptian and Roman. The overall effect was Caesar's Palace-meets-Elton John high camp. The later slightly over-the-top Regency style – sulphur-yellow curtains, royal-blue and crimson lyres, plenty of sphinxes and cornucopias – owed a lot to Hope.

Attitudes to interior decorators were just as sniffy then. After Hope's 1807 hit, *Household Furniture and Interior Decoration* – the first mention of interior decoration in the English language – Byron called 211 him a mere 'house-finisher'. But the difference from many of today's interior decorators – women called Araminta who do a bit of stippling and kilim-sourcing in Ankara – is that Hope knew his stuff. He spent eight years studying ruins in Europe and Egypt, and later commissioned the great sculptors John Flaxman, Sir Francis Chantrey and Antonio Canova.

Even Byron finally admitted defeat – he wept when he read Hope's last book, because he hadn't written it and Hope had.

22

Sven-Göran Eriksson and the Birth of the Urban Villa

Keen students of the life and works of Ulrika Jonsson will remember the precise details of her affair with the England football manager, Sven-Göran Eriksson. They will recall how he two-timed her with the busty secretary Faria Alam, who worked at the Football Association. Miss Alam had also been involved with Mark Palios, the FA's chief executive. They will also know that Sven was supposed to be attached, engaged even, to the Italian firecracker Nancy Dell'Olio.

They probably know, too, that Sven and Nancy shared a house at the northern tip of Regent's Park. What they are unlikely to know is quite how crucial that house is to British architecture.

Number twenty-six Park Village East – the love-nest in question – belongs to the first street of purpose-built semi-detached villas in the country, designed in 1824 by John Nash (1752–1835), an exceptionally inventive Welsh wizard of an architect.

There had been semi-detached houses in London as early as 1700, but they were isolated examples. In Park Village West and Park Village East, he designed a series of ground-breaking villas – from Greek, through Italian, Gothic, gabled Tudor and French – each

Can you hear the crockery breaking? The former love-nest of Sven-Göran Eriksson and Nancy Dell'Olio (John Nash, 1824).

of which looked like one grand house but was in fact two. With this high-profile development, Nash brought the country villa to town.

Sven-Göran's villa is half of an identical pair in a playful classical style, with deep eaves and depressed arches springing from a thick cornice band – these depressed arches were popular from the 1820s onwards.

Calling a semi-detached house a villa gave it a lot of cachet. Villas had had grand connotations ever since their ancient birth, the Latin *villa* meaning 'country house' or 'seat'. Cicero used the word to mean a residence for foreign ambassadors.

Before Nash, the British villa retained this Roman feel of rural splendour, particularly in provincial cities, where there was more building room. Bath – Britain's most Roman city – was full of generously proportioned villas; Cheltenham, Worthing and Brighton too. A villa was, in Evelyn Waugh's phrase, the sort of 'lovely house where an aged colonel plays wireless music to an obese retriever'.

After Nash the word was used of small, suburban houses with rural aspirations. With his Park Villages, the idea of *rus in urbe* – the country in the town – took off, a trend commented on in this suburban ode to Barnsbury, north London, from *Hone's Table Book* (1827):

> You who are anxious for a country seat
> Pure air, green meadows and suburban views;
> Rooms snug and light – not overlarge but neat,
> And gardens water'd with refreshing dews,
> May find a spot adapted to your taste,
> Near Barnsbury Park, or rather Barnsbury Town
> Where everything looks elegant and chaste,
> And Wealth reposes on a bed of down.

And in Charles Morris's (1745–1838) poem, 'Country and Town':   215

Some mocked the idea of a villa in the heart of the city.
Then in town let me live and in town let me die,
For in truth I can't relish the country, not I.
If one must have a villa in summer to dwell,
O give me the sweet shady side of Pall Mall.

These first villas were semi-detached – a quality which, in among the terraces crawling all over the country, had considerable snob value, as an anonymous Islington clerk testified of his new house in *How I Managed My House on £200 a Year* (1864):

It is only three miles from London, perhaps a little more to the office, but that does not signify . . . We shall have no neighbours yet, and I have observed very common people do not live in semi-detached houses; they like to congregate near a market, and so ought we . . . but I think fresh air better than very cheap food. So, little wife, it is settled.

The Park Villages were part of Nash's Regent's Park development of the 1810s and 1820s. Outside the park, two streams of clotted cream-coloured terraces flowed down both its sides before draining in a kinking, swerving line down Regent Street into Nash's Carlton House Terrace at the bottom. This, by the way, was where the Prince Regent's palace – Carlton House, built by Henry Holland (1745–1806) in 1795 – stood, before it was demolished in 1826. The Whig taste of the time was much influenced by France – Carlton House was a mixture of Adam style and French neo-classicism on a grand scale.

Inside the park, Nash harnessed nature to architecture in line with Picturesque ideals. He intended 'that no villa should see any other but each should appear to possess the whole of the Park'. This aim was achieved with the grandest villa in the park, St John's Lodge

(1817) – actually built by John Raffield – which perches, alone, on a small hill by the Inner Circle.

The house now belongs to Prince Jefri of Brunei, the younger brother of the Sultan of Brunei. In 2000 the Sultan sued his brother over his alleged splurging of state funds on pointless baubles, including his fifty-metre yacht *Tits* and its tenders, *Nipple 1* and *Nipple 2*. In June 2008 it was reported that Prince Jefri went on the run, unwilling to face court demands to hand over the money. He has, though, been allowed to keep St John's Lodge – money spent on such a lovely house could surely never be considered indulgent.

Regent's Park so delighted its inspiration, the Prince Regent, that when he first saw the plans in 1811 he said, 'It will quite eclipse Napoleon.' Napoleon would certainly have been jealous of the scheme; if only so much of it hadn't been demolished over the past two hundred years.

The original plan envisaged that tide of cream stucco flooding all the way down to Pall Mall. At the bottom of the park, Nash funnelled the tide into Park Crescent – a bewitching semicircle of buildings – before it straightened out into the broad thoroughfare of Portland Place. When this thoroughfare hit a big cross street – at Oxford Street and Piccadilly – Nash installed circuses.

And where the road made a little left-hand, then right-hand, swivel, Nash built the perfect eye-catcher – the church of All Souls, Langham Place, a needle rising out of a colonnade which turns the axis of the road with you hardly noticing. Betjeman called this little conjuring trick one of the 'easy theatricalities' that Nash was so good at.

All Souls is V.S. Naipaul's favourite church. In his memoir of how he fell out with Naipaul, *Sir Vidia's Shadow* (1998), Paul Theroux described how he walked down Portland Place with him and came across the church. All Souls is opposite the Langham Hotel, once a BBC building where Naipaul worked in the Overseas Service. In the Freelance Room there, with its ochre walls and pea-green dado, he began his writing career.

The eye-catcher that caught V.S. Naipaul's eye – John Nash's All Souls, Langham Place (1824). In the background, Broadcasting House (1931) by G.Val Myers, with a sculpture of Ariel by Eric Gill over the entrance.

'Such a lovely church,' he said as we entered Langham Place.

'All Souls,' I said. 'Thomas [sic] Nash.'

'It is Nash's only church,' Vidia said. 'So strong. Look what he does with the simplest lines. They ridiculed it when it was built in the 1820s. No one approved.'

'Kipling got married here,' I said.

Vidia smiled. He loved sparring.

'That was just before he went to America,' he said. 'Of course, his wife was American.'

'Henry James was his best man,' I said.

'And then Kipling came back to England, moved into a grand house, and wrote nothing,' Vidia said.

A Roman Legacy – The Triumphal Arch

If you're ever walking down the eastern edge of Regent's Park, it's worth taking in Nash's Chester Terrace (1825), a good example of a triumphal arch. This shape – a big central arch, with two smaller subsidiary arches on either side – had an ancient lineage going back to the second century BC, when the Romans set them up to commemorate great events.

They became known as triumphal arches later on – the *arcus triumphalis* is first mentioned in the third century AD. Some celebrated military triumphs but others recorded more peaceful activities – the achievements of republican aristocrats or, later, members of the imperial family.

The most familiar example is the Arch of Constantine, in the shadow of the Colosseum. It was built in AD 315 to commemorate the Emperor Constantine's victory in the Battle of the Milvian Bridge three years earlier. It was on the night before this battle that Constantine saw a cross in a dream and converted to Christianity.

These Roman arches often had triumphal chariots on top of them – as do some modern copies, like Decimus Burton's Wellington Arch (1830) at Hyde Park Corner, with its whacking great 1912 sculpture of Victory in a chariot, then the biggest bronze in Europe – 'Like a vast paperweight or capital ornament of an Empire clock, the Quadriga's horses, against a sky of indigo and silver, pranced desperately towards the abyss' (Anthony Powell, *A Buyer's Market* (1952)).

The Italian Renaissance revived the triumphal arch and it caught on all over Europe – notably with the Arc de Triomphe in Paris (1806) and, in Britain, Marble Arch (1828) – originally built by Nash as the entrance gate to his newly revamped Buckingham Palace.

Modern triumphal arches allowed cars to pass through the central arch and pedestrians through the little side arches. Sadly, the only British triumphal arch where this aim is properly achieved today is at Chester Terrace.

Theatrical Architecture – Chester Terrace, Regent's Park, north London (1825). The actor Sir Ralph Richardson (1902–83) lived in the house on the right.

Marble Arch is stranded in the middle of Speakers' Corner, with traffic forbidden to go through it; ditto Wellington Arch, although bicycles are allowed through both and it lifts the spirits to freewheel through them. How much more beautiful buildings are when they become incorporated into everyday life.

While we're on the subject, another Roman building deserves special mention – the second-century BC Temple of Hercules in Rome, which inspired not only St Peter's in the same city, St Paul's Cathedral, Hawksmoor's mausoleum at Castle Howard and the Radcliffe Camera in Oxford but every dome on a colonnaded drum in the world.

The Radcliffe Camera, Oxford (1749), after the fall of civilisation, by Jonathan Wateridge.

Georgian Malls – the Prettiest Shops in the World

After the Great Fire of London, shop fronts were the only buildings still given permission to bulge out dangerously into the street.

The 1667 Act for Rebuilding the City of London declared:

No bulks, jetties, windows, posts, seats shall be erected in any streets to extend beyond the ancient foundation of houses ... saving only that in the high and principal streets it shall be lawful for inhabitants to suffer their stall boards to extend 11 inches from their houses into the streets for the better convenience of their shop windows.

221

Through the Georgian period, shop fronts grew more inventive and ornate – barrel-shaped, bowed, arched, often with gold lettering on a black background.

Shopping took off in the post-Waterloo economic boom, and John Nash was quick to move in on the trend. The first shopping arcade in London was the Royal Opera Arcade, built by Nash in 1818. This is just off Pall Mall, which took its name from a sixteenth-century game – a sort of croquet; in turn, the street bequeathed its name to that other leisure hotspot – the shopping mall.

Georgian, and even Victorian, shop fronts that have their original glass are rare survivals. Shops, often desperate to court new trends, are particularly prey to modernisation. Keith Waterhouse noticed the process in the Leeds undertakers he worked for in the late 1940s, fictionalised as Shadrack and Duxbury's Tasteful Funerals of Stradhoughton, an industrial northern town. He wrote in *Billy Liar* (1959):

222

The first shopping mall – the Royal Opera Arcade, Pall Mall, built by John Nash in 1818.

Young Shadrack, taking advantage of Duxbury's only trip abroad, a reciprocal visit by the town council to Lyons (described by Man o' the Dales as the Stradhoughton of France), had pulled out the Dickensian windows, bottle-glass and all, and substituted modern plate-glass and a shop sign of raised stainless-steel lettering. Thus another piece of old Stradhoughton bit the dust and the new effect was of a chip shop on a suburban housing estate.

23

Please, Sir, Can I Have Some More Prisons

The Nineteenth-Century Hunger for Porridge

A friend recently told me about her grandfather, who only died in 2001 but remembered shooting pheasant as a boy in Holland Park just before the First World War. The park was then Lord Ilchester's five-hundred-acre estate, surrounding his Jacobean seat, Holland House. The house was badly bombed in the war but it remained in the family until 1952, when it was handed over to Kensington and Chelsea council, its current owners.

Large tracts of British cities were – like this estate in the heart of London – still country three hundred years ago. Through the eighteenth and nineteenth centuries, rural parishes on the edges of those cities met and melded into a mass of brick, mortar and tile, with new terraces filling up the fields between them.

In *Barnaby Rudge* (1841), Dickens described rural eighteenth-century Islington during the Gordon Riots, the anti-Catholic disturbances of 1780. It's the night after the riots and Barnaby Rudge has been sprung from Newgate Prison where he'd been sent for unwittingly helping the rioters. He fled with his father:

> The two fugitives made towards Clerkenwell, and passing thence to Islington, as the nearest point of egress, were quickly in the fields. After wandering about for a long time, they found in a pasture near Finchley a poor shed, with walls of mud, and roof of grass and brambles, built for some cowherd, but now deserted. Here, they lay down for the rest of the night.
>
> They wandered to and fro when it was day, and once Barnaby went off alone to a cluster of little cottages two or three miles away, to purchase some bread and milk.

This is quite a walk – Smithfield to Finchley is around ten miles. Now every inch of the route the Rudges took is covered in concrete, tarmac and brick either side of the road. Certainly it's been a long time since you could find pasture in Finchley. During their journey, the two

London, a collection of villages. In around 1825 Little Nell, like Barnaby Rudge, made for the suburbs. She rested on Parliament Hill with her grandfather, looking towards St Paul's. From *The Old Curiosity Shop* (1841), picture by Phiz. This vista remains one of London's viewing corridors, protected by law since 1991.

men would have passed through Holloway, just a village in 1780. By the time Dickens was writing, sixty years later, Holloway was swelling into the rows of terraced houses that survive today.

From 1810 to 1830, in the post-Trafalgar boom, London's development outward from the City was strung along the main arteries to the country – still where you'll find some of the older houses in the suburbs. J.F. Murray in *The World of London* (1840) described suburban villages connected by arterial roads stretching out into the countryside as 'onions on a rope'.

This random, organic growth of British cities explains their disorderly plans, in contrast with the grids of New York. Only cities built in planned stages at precise times allowed for such neat geometrical development.

The nature of British cities – of ancient origin with sudden spurts of growth – militates against urban planning like this. So Manchester – originally the Roman fort of Mamucium, occupied from the first century AD – had a tremendous spurt in the late Middle Ages, particularly when Edward III imported a colony of Flemish weavers in 1375. John Leland (1506–52), the English antiquary, called the city 'the fairest, best builded, quikkest and most populus tounne of al Lancastreshire'.

And, of course, Manchester had a much bigger spurt during the Industrial Revolution. Karl Friedrich Schinkel (1781–1841), the German architect, said of Manchester in 1826, 'Since the [Napoleonic] war, 400 large new factories for cotton spinning have been built, several of them the size of the Royal Palace in Berlin, and thousands of smoking obelisks of the steam engines 80 to 180 foot high destroy all impression of church steeples.'

There were admittedly many planned *areas* in cities, but they tended to be piecemeal developments begun long after the essential shape of the place had been set in stone – or brick. Birmingham got its market charter in 1166; its first planned development, Old Square, wasn't begun until 1697.

It was really only in smaller towns that any proper planning could work on an overall scale. In the county of Powys, for example, there are several thirteenth-century grid-planned towns – Knighton, New Radnor, Presteigne and Rhayader.

The Architecture of Punishment

Old Newgate, which stood near the Old Bailey, was the prison Barnaby Rudge escaped from. Built by George Dance in 1769 and demolished in 1902, Newgate was a study in prison architecture. Like many prisons, it had a rusticated basement to give an impression of solidity and security. Most prisons had forbidding castellated fronts, too. The old 1852 gatehouse at Holloway Prison – home to Oswald and Diana Mosley during the Second World War – was based on Caesar's Tower at Warwick Castle, and got the nickname Camden Castle.

For obvious reasons, Newgate didn't have many outside windows, except in its entrance block. Despite its austerity and strength – and the unusual requirement that it should keep residents in and minimise windows and doors – it was also beautiful; a Florentine palazzo for crooks.

Still, the real golden days of prison building came seventy years after Newgate was built, when Victorian cities – and Victorian crime – mushroomed.

In the TV series *Porridge* (1973–7), Slade Prison was home to Ronnie Barker's Norman Stanley Fletcher, sentenced to five years for stealing an articulated lorry and driving it through several back gardens. He was convicted for robbery and dangerous driving, and 'several other fences were taken into consideration'.

Because the Home Office refused permission to film in a real prison for fear of negative publicity, the BBC built their own mock-up in a big metal tank – previously used for underwater filming at Elstree Studios – fitted out with the familiar iron staircases of Victorian prisons. For exterior shots they used the gloomy gatehouse of the former St Alban's Prison (1866), Hertfordshire. Other external scenes in the series, like the football match and the rooftop strike, were filmed at various Gothic Revival psychiatric hospitals in London.

Porridge (1979), the feature film, was shot at a real Victorian jail – Chelmsford Prison in Essex, built in 1828. The BBC sneaked in while the prison was refurbished after a fire.

The archetypal Victorian prison behind the *Porridge* look is Pentonville Prison in Islington, north London. Built in 1842 by Colonel Joshua Jebb, in its time it has hosted Oscar Wilde, George Best, the *Spectator* columnist Taki Theodoracopulos and Pete Doherty.

On a sunny day, Pentonville's classical façade – regularly repainted a creamy white to cover fresh graffiti by former or aspiring inmates – is as handsome as a Nash terrace.

Look round the back and sides, and all is not so picture-postcard pretty. The prisoners are squeezed into small cells built out of dirty, plain, London stock brick. The windows are necessarily tiny and barred, just big enough – as I saw one afternoon on my way home from school – to allow the Birdman of Pentonville to feed a pigeon on the window sill.

A series of wings were laid out like spokes in a bicycle wheel around a central control tower. This design was known as the Separate System – the prisoners are separated by these radiating wings. The idea came from the Eastern State Penitentiary in Philadelphia, built in 1829.

Pentonville's hub design was the template for British prisons for the next thirty years – fifty-four were built over the next six years, and hundreds more across the Empire.

The classic Pentonville prison plan was not quite a panopticon (Greek for 'see everything'). This was the prison design invented in 1791 by Jeremy Bentham, who coined the term 'utilitarianism' and founded University College London. In this great big cake of a building, a warder sat in the hub and, using a series of Venetian blinds, saw into every cell without being seen himself.

24

The Victorians Get Medieval on Your Apse

The Gothic Revival

Whatever may be said in favour of the Victorians, it is pretty generally admitted that few of them were to be trusted within reach of a
trowel and a pile of bricks.

P.G. Wodehouse, Summer Moonshine *(1938)*

When Wodehouse wrote this, the reputation of Victorian buildings was
at a low ebb. That ebb stayed low for another half-century. By the time
John Betjeman helped found the Victorian Society in 1958, Victorian
buildings were a lost, ugly cause.

The rehabilitation of Victoriana is still a relatively recent thing.
Betjeman's chief victory over the bulldozer – St Pancras Station and its
hotel – only received its deserved praise in St Pancras's reincarnation
as the new Eurostar rail terminal at the end of 2007. There's a stirring
statue of the poet gazing with joy at W.H. Barlow's heavenly train-shed
roof, at the point where its blue iron girders meet like crab claws clash-
ing between dazzling great sheets of glass.

Despite all this Victorian splendour, P.G. Wodehouse had a point.
The Victorians took a freer approach to buildings than any of their
predecessors, dipping into a ragbag of historic and foreign styles with
abandon. 'Victorian' encompassed a multitude of styles, including
the house in the Wodehouse quote above, Sir Buckstone Abbott's
Walsingford Hall:

> Built in the time of Queen Elizabeth on an eminence overlooking
> the silvery Thames, it must, for two centuries and more, have been
> a lovely place. The fact that it now caused sensitive oarsmen, round-
> ing the bend of the river and seeing it suddenly, to wince and catch
> crabs was due to the unfortunate circumstance of the big fire, which
> sooner or later, seems to come to all English country houses . . .
>
> What Sir Buckstone was now looking at, accordingly, was a vast
> edifice constructed of glazed red brick, in some respects resembling
> a French château, but, on the whole, perhaps, having more the

appearance of one of those model dwellings in which a certain number of working-class families are assured of a certain number of cubic feet of air. It had a huge leaden roof, tapering to a point and topped by a weathervane, and from one side of it, like some unpleasant growth, there protruded a large conservatory. There were also a dome and some minarets.

Victorian villagers gazing up at it had named it Abbott's Folly, and they had been about right.

What the Victorians mostly scooped out of the ragbag, particularly from 1840 until 1870, were old Gothic styles – thus the Gothic Revival.

After reaching a peak in the late nineteenth century, the Gothic Revival had a tragic collapse. By the time of Evelyn Waugh's *A Handful of Dust* (1934), Gothic was another word for hideous. To live in a Gothic house seemed utterly mad; only schools and convents were still built in the style. Hetton Abbey, the building loved by the novel's tragic hero, Tony Last, is loathed by everybody else, especially his wife Brenda: 'I detest it . . . at least I don't mean that really, but I do wish sometimes that it wasn't all, every bit of it, so appallingly ugly.'

Chateau Impney, Droitwich Spa, Worcestershire (1875), the inspiration for Walsingford Hall and now a hotel, on offer for £17 million in June 2008. P.G. Wodehouse often stayed there.

Hetton's critics joked that it was the only building built by Mr Pecksniff, the conman architect in Charles Dickens's *Martin Chuzzlewit* (1843), who never built anything but embezzled his students' fees.

For half a century after *A Handful of Dust*, whenever a writer described something archetypally hideous it was always Victorian. In Tom Sharpe's *Blott on the Landscape* (1975), the blot in question was a Victorian rebuilding of a classical house, Handyman Hall (1899):

> An amalgam in stone and brick, timber and tile and turret, a monument to all that was most eclectic and least attractive in English architecture . . . It was a nightmare. Ruskin and Morris, Gilbert Scott, Vanbrugh, Inigo Jones and Wren, to name but a few, had all lent their influence to a building that combined the utility of a watertower with the homeliness of Wormwood Scrubs.

Mr Pecksniff, his daughters and Martin Chuzzlewit. His unbuilt projects are on the wall. Picture by Phiz.

These hideous fictional houses were always Gothic Revival, never original Gothic; no one was suggesting that you should knock down Westminster Abbey.

This revulsion against Gothic Revival in the early twentieth century was extreme, given how all-pervading the style had once been – seven thousand of England's sixteen thousand parish churches were restored in the mid-nineteenth century in a Victorian vision of the Gothic ideal.

Betjeman, in 'The Church's Restoration' (1928), described these churches – in much the same state today – under the hand of an unnamed restorer:

> He gave the brass for burnishing,
> He gave the thick red baize;
> He gave the new addition
> Pulled down the dull old aisle,
> To pave the sweet transition,
> He gave th' encaustic tile!
> Of marble brown and veinéd
> He did the pulpit make,
> He ordered windows stainéd
> Light red and crimson lake.

Sir George Gilbert Scott (1810–77) – not to be confused with his grandson, Sir Giles Gilbert Scott, designer of the red phone box – was the king of the restorers. He built and restored over 730 buildings, including 476 churches; among his new buildings were the Midland Grand Hotel at St Pancras (1876) and the Albert Memorial (1872). He was so overwhelmed by commissions that, during one restoring trip, he telegraphed an assistant to ask, 'Why am I here?'

There were two waves of new churches in the nineteenth century. The first wave – of three hundred, built between 1819 and 1830 – came with the 1818 Million Act, when Parliament approved a £1m grant for churches in Britain's booming towns. Known as Commissioners' Churches or Waterloo Churches, these were mostly classical. Look out for them wherever there are street names with early-nineteenth-century, Regency echoes – Brunswick Square, Regent Square, Hanover Terrace, Nelson Street, Adelaide Square. Any address with Gloucester in it was usually built after 1816, when Princess Mary married the Duke of Gloucester.

The churches were everywhere in Regency boom towns like Cheltenham, Bristol, Leamington, Harrogate, stretches of Liverpool and London, and every cathedral city and town. These towns' Regency terraces and crescents were built on the fringe of their medieval heart. Another few hundred yards out, the later Gothic Revival suburbs begin.

The second wave of church-building came in the mid-nineteenth century – all Gothic this time; hardly any classical churches were built between 1840 and 1900.

So you get a strange new combination across Britain in the mid-Victorian years: rows and rows of classical terraces clustered round an imitation Gothic church, as in Aberdeen Park, Highbury, north London. There the Gothic church is St Saviour's (1865), where Betjeman's parents were married in 1902. The Betjeman family firm – which made tantaluses, lockable drinks cabinets to keep servants and younger sons from the sherry – was down the road, near the Angel, Islington.

This church was packed with Gothic devices: buttresses, a broach spire with an octagonal lantern and an iron flèche – literally an arrow, but in fact a mini-spire or spirelet. In 'St Saviour's, Aberdeen Park, Highbury, London' (1948), Betjeman wrote:

> Great red church of my parents, cruciform crossing they knew.
> Over these same encaustics they and their parents trod
> Round, through a red brick transept, for a once familiar pew.

DATING TIP

Encaustic tiles were cult objects in Victorian churches. See any brightly coloured, new-looking tiles in a church, particularly in red and yellow, and they're probably encaustics from the mid-nineteenth century onwards. They are also known as Minton tiles. After digging around in medieval kilns, Herbert Minton (1793–1858) of Stoke revived the ancient practice of firing coloured tiles in the 1840s. They weren't painted but fired in their different colours. Encaustic colours were particularly robust because the colour was burnt in (which is what 'encaustic' means).

The forerunners of the round blue plaques on famous people's houses were originally encaustic. These first plaques, set up by the Royal Society of Arts in 1867, were chocolate brown and made by the Minton factory. The oldest surviving plaques are those to John Dryden and Napoleon III, both erected in 1875.

In 1901 the London County Council took over the scheme, changing the colour to blue from 1903, and to cheaper glazed Doulton ware from 1921. The Greater London Council took over the plaques in 1965, and English Heritage in 1986. Different authorities like different colours – the Corporation of the City of London uses rectangular blue plaques; Westminster City Council goes for green ones.

Augustus Welby Pugin (1812–52), the greatest Gothic Revival architect, was particularly keen on encaustic tiles. He is most famous for the Houses of Parliament, built with Sir Charles Barry (1795–1860). His real obsession, though, was a return to the perfect Gothic style of the pre-Reformation Catholic Church.

A Catholic convert at eighteen, Pugin wrote ferocious pamphlets arguing that Gothic was *the* style of the true faith. He became so obsessed with the Middle Ages that he ate off Gothic plates and made his wife wear medieval dresses. An eccentric thread ran through his life, to put it mildly – widowered, imprisoned for debt and ship-wrecked by twenty-one, he spent his last ten years on the verge of insanity and ended up in Bedlam.

If you see a Pugin church, it's probably early-fourteenth-century Decorated Revival work; he thought it was the most authentically medieval period. Most Victorians agreed; they considered Early English too primitive, Perpendicular too decadent. If you want to sound impressive, call it Middle Pointed instead of Decorated, like Betjeman in 'A Lincolnshire Church': 'A tower silver and brown in the sunlight, worn by sea-wind and shower, Lincolnshire Middle Pointed.'

> **DATING TIP**
>
> A Victorian principle held that the closer a church gets to Heaven, the more Gothic it should get. Or, in other words, the taller the tower, the more ornate the details.

Pugin proudly admitted to being a Gothic plagiarist. At the opening of his St Chad's, Birmingham, in 1841 – the first English cathedral since St Paul's – he boasted, 'There is not a single detail which has not been faithfully imitated.' His church of St Giles, Cheadle, completed five years later, was, he said, the 'complete parish church of the time of Edward I'.

Not only Catholicism, but a studied medieval pageantry, was at the heart of Pugin's buildings. At Alton Castle – as in neighbouring Alton Towers, and Princess Diana, Princes William and Harry going down the log flume – Pugin built a Gothic palace for the ultra-Catholic Earl of Shrewsbury in 1851, equipped with stained-glass windows, armoury and blind harpist. Even then Alton Castle was quite an attraction, receiving twelve thousand visitors a year.

Pugin's guiding doctrine was, 'First, that there should be no features about a building which are not necessary for convenience, construction, or propriety; second, that all ornament should consist of enrichment of the essential construction of the building.'

This was a little disingenuous. Lots of medieval buildings used materials to trick the eye – like that fourteenth-century octagon crossing spire at Ely Cathedral, where joiners imitated stone in sham wooden vaults and hid the supports that held up the building.

The Gothic Age of the Train

Railway station designers agreed with Pugin that Decorated was best, so the style chosen for buildings inspired by the greatest innovation of the nineteenth century was that of the thirteenth and fourteenth centuries. Pugin even sketched out Gothic trains hurtling over Gothic viaducts.

The religious influence over the railways was strong. Great Western locomotives, built in Swindon in 1902, were called Saint Agatha, Saint Augustine and Saint Helena.

Stations were often designed like churches. Betjeman pointed out that Liverpool Street Station, completed by Edward Wilson in 1875, divided into a nave with aisles, transepts and a choir, and clustered columns just like those that support the roofs of medieval cathedrals. A footbridge stood in for the rood screen and there were steps to the first-floor buffet where the pulpit should be.

It was because of an incident in Liverpool Street's pulpit-like buffet in 1981 that the writer and full-time eccentric Quentin Crisp (1908–99) decided he must leave Britain for ever.

A friend of his, waiting for a Colchester train, bought a KitKat at the station café. The place was full, so she shared a table with a young man eating an orange. Without saying anything the young man broke off two fingers of her KitKat and stuffed them in his mouth. Outraged, she leant over, took two segments from his orange and ate them. A few minutes later she got on her train. Only on settling into her carriage did she open her handbag and see an intact KitKat – she had eaten the man's KitKat and his orange.

This, said Crisp, was the reason why he left Britain. In America someone would complain immediately if you stole their KitKat, and the quiet resentments dictated by politeness would never have been allowed to fester.

Not all railway stations were Gothic. Philip Hardwick's Euston Arch (1837, demolished 1962) was the greatest Doric arch ever built – more precisely, it was a propylaeum, the ancient Greek word for the entrance to a temple.

But we really prefer our railway stations to be Gothic. When the Hogwarts Express left platform 9½ at King's Cross in *Harry Potter and the Philosopher's Stone* (2002), W.H. Barlow's spikily Gothic St Pancras railway shed was used for filming instead of classical King's Cross.

St Pancras has been a popular film set for some time. The Spice Girls' video for 'Wannabe' (1996) was filmed there, and earlier it starred in *The Ladykillers* (1955), where Mrs Wilberforce, the lady in question, has a direct view of the station and the Midland Grand Hotel from her front door.

The Midland Grand (1876) was the quintessential Victorian Gothic building. It borrowed from the town halls and cloth halls of the Low Countries for the rows of pointed windows and square towers; from thirteenth-century England for its plain tracery, oriel windows and capitals; from northern Italy for the pale stone alternating with red brick in the arches standing on polished stone shafts.

But the greatest contribution of railways to architecture was the train shed. Barlow's 243-foot-wide shed at St Pancras covered the world's biggest enclosed space in 1868. Though dependent on recently invented cast iron to span such a great gap, the shed was still medieval in origin – imitating the late-Gothic, four-centred arch shape.

Certain railway companies followed certain styles. The Great Western Railway designers, for example, liked Tudor, after its Bristol Temple Meads Station was designed in the style by Isambard Kingdom Brunel in 1840.

The view from Mrs Wilberforce's House of the Midland Grand Hotel (1876) at St Pancras Station, star of *The Ladykillers*.

How do you distinguish between original medieval Gothic and its nineteenth-century imitations? The most obvious difference was the material – nineteenth-century copies were usually built in brick and rubble, as against the stone of the originals.

Copies often looked like they've been done on the cheap, too, with a few Gothic features slapped on to a brick box – like flimsy St Mary's, Euston (1826), built by the Inwoods, the father-and-son team responsible for that utterly Greek church at nearby St Pancras. It's yet to be confirmed whether that flimsiness was behind the decision to make St Mary's the official church for British Rail. It's also the official taxi-drivers' church because it's so close to their haunts at Euston, St Pancras and King's Cross.

An enraged Pugin said of St Mary's:

The architect has endeavoured to give the shell the appearance of an ancient pointed church, but when the interior is seen the whole   241 illusion vanishes, and we discover that what had somewhat the appearance of an old Catholic church, is, in reality, nothing but a modern preaching house, with all its galleries, pews, and other fittings.

Another way to tell the difference between old and new Gothic is the location. By the end of the original Gothic period – around 1530 – most modern settlements in Britain had already been founded. Milton Keynes and a handful of new towns may have been built later – they tend not to have any Gothic churches. But otherwise, in even the smallest village, an ancient church was already present by 1530, although many have been replaced. So the church in the centre of town is usually the real thing – old Gothic. Victorian Gothic Revival churches were scattered among newer suburbs built in rings around this old centre.

Yet another way is to look for new materials – among them concrete, cast iron and corrugated iron.

A Concrete Dating Tip

For all the concrete eyesores of recent years, concrete is not a modern invention. The Romans used an early sort, made from quicklime, ash and pumice stone. The roof of the Pantheon in Rome, built by the Emperor Hadrian in AD 126, was made of two types: a heavy mix of brick and travertine (a white Italian limestone) for the lower parts, and a lighter combination of tufa and pumice (volcanic stones) for the upper bits.

In 1756 the stuff made a comeback when the British engineer John Smeaton mixed lime with powdered brick and pebbles as the aggregate. The mass use of concrete came with the patenting of Portland Cement in 1824, made by heating limestone with clay, and grinding it up with gypsum. Gypsum is properly called hydrous calcium sulphate, the stuff you use to make plaster of Paris – the original source was the gypsum bed under Montmartre. Mixed with water and sand, gravel or crushed stones, the combination became concrete.

Britain gets Irony

Wrought iron – beautifully forged into scrolls and acanthus shapes on a nationwide scale – has been around since the late seventeenth century. The use of iron cast into great structural shapes dated from only 1779, and Thomas Pritchard's and Abraham Darby III's iron bridge at Coalbrookdale, Shropshire.

The arrival of cast iron in the late eighteenth century is sadly not that useful as a dating tip – it's often disguised as the brick, stone and timber of earlier buildings. Sometimes you'll tap the apparent limestone of a Gothic pillar and, only when you're answered with a high metallic ring, do you know what you're dealing with.

So, the dome of John Nash's Royal Pavilion of 1818 was built to imitate sixteenth-century Moghul buildings. In fact it was made of thoroughly modern materials: an iron armature with a timber cage wrapped in sheet iron and the latest stucco – Hamlin's Mastic.

In Nash's Carlton House Terrace (1827), the stately Doric columns – most ancient of the Greek orders – are iron; a long way from the tree trunks that the original orders are said to have been based on.

Iron's strength meant you could carry more weight on thinner supports. As a result, the iron Gothic pillars in the nave of St George, Merseyside (1812), could be ultra-flimsy. If those had been limestone, or even granite, the thing couldn't have supported itself.

In the mid-nineteenth century, cast iron was used to great effect in conjunction with another recent invention, sheet glass. The mammoth greenhouse took off, notably in the form of Sir Joseph Paxton's Crystal Palace, built for the Great Exhibition of 1851.

Builders of railway stations, too, took to the combination. High girders covered in glass allowed smoke to rise above passengers and disperse, while letting in fat shafts of light.

Regency Britain also saw an explosion in mass-manufactured decorative iron features, particularly in railings, skylights and sashes.

Ironwork technology was vastly improved after the Napoleonic Wars, allowing for greater intricacy and elaboration.

Cast iron catered to the Regency taste for balconies, particularly in spa towns like Cheltenham – home to the most intricate trellis work – and seaside resorts like Brighton. Balconies – and bay windows – were crucial vantage points for watching people take their daily promenades. French windows on first-floor balconies took off from the 1830s.

Robert Adam, and his brother John, were keen on cast iron – often mixed with copper and brass – for their ornate fanlights. Earlier fanlights were rectangular; later ones semicircular.

Strong meant slim. A lot of iron features imitated wood, but could be thinner and more delicate because of the metal's greater strength. Joseph Bottomley, a fanlight manufacturer from Cheapside, London, boasted in 1793 that his fanlights let in 50 per cent more light than the old wooden ones; a crucial advantage when the fanlight had to illuminate a long, dark, narrow hall.

Iron stair balusters with mahogany handrails also took off in the late eighteenth century.

Iron gets Corrugated

In 1829 Henry Palmer, an English engineer, patented 'indented or corrugated metallic sheets'. Corrugated iron – the light, strong, hideous stuff that covers Brunel's Paddington Station, every refugee camp and every tramp's jerry-built shelter – was born.

Corrugation was done by running flat, cold iron sheets through fluted rollers. The first corrugated-iron building was Palmer's Turpentine Shed, near the Tower of London, which, Palmer said, had 'the lightest and strongest roof constructed by man since the days of Adam'.

Nissen huts were invented by Peter Nissen, a Canadian. He spotted the potential of those corrugated-iron Swiss rolls cut in half while serving at Ypres in 1916 with the Royal Engineers. By the end of the war 100,000 had been built.

Corrugated iron has suffered for, if anything, being too robust. Charities now house refugees in tents – corrugated-iron refugee camps all too often become permanent.

The Sight of the Eternal Life Church (1858), Hackney, east London, the oldest 'tin tabernacle' in the world, built in ten weeks as a Presbyterian chapel.

Walt Disney goes Victorian

A vogue for more-medieval-than-medieval castles – *Citizen Kane* meets Walt Disney – hit Britain in the 1810s and 1820s. Eastnor Castle (1815), Herefordshire, and Lowther Castle (1811), Cumbria, were two of the most notable. They were eclipsed only by the genuine article – Windsor Castle, given a mock medieval makeover by Jeffry Wyatville (1766–1840) in 1824.

In the same way that lots of apparently ancient Coronation rituals were in fact cooked up by Queen Victoria, royal buildings were often a reheat – on a high flame – of older themes.

Windsor Castle retains much of its earliest stonework from Henry II's 1179 building. But it has also been mock-medievalised several times – once under Wyatville, once as early as 1675 by Hugh May.

This neo-Gothic castellar style came under attack in the twentieth century. Anthony Powell, in his *The Valley of Bones* (1964), wasn't very keen on Castlemallock, the neo-Gothic Victorian pile based on Tullynally Castle, County Westmeath, Ireland, the childhood home of his wife, Lady Violet Powell. In the novel the castle has become the Corps School of Chemical Warfare where Nicholas Jenkins, the narrator of the whole *A Dance to the Music of Time* cycle, was stationed during the war:

> There was an undoubted aptness in this sham fortress, monument to a tasteless, half-baked romanticism, becoming now, in truth, a military stronghold, its stone walls and vaulted ceilings echoing at last to the clatter of arms and oaths of soldiery. It was as if its perpetrators had recreated the tedium, as well as the architecture, of medieval times.

Church and Chapel

In the mining villages of Wales, the suburbs of British cities and Cornish mining towns, somewhere you'll find a plain Gothic or classical box. These boxes are an unusual size – smaller than Anglican churches, bigger than terraced houses. Inside, the materials are simple but fetching: stencilled texts from the Bible, pine pews, brass lighting brackets.

These are the chapels and the meeting houses of the nonconformists and dissenters, the Christian groups that broke away from the Church of England: the Puritans and Presbyterians of the late sixteenth century, the Congregationalists, Baptists and Quakers of the seventeenth century, the Methodists of the eighteenth.

With all these strands of Christian thought, it's difficult to nail a particular type of building to each one. Think of chapels as elephants – difficult to describe, but you know one when you see one. To make things trickier, there were many more different types of nonconformism than there are types of elephants. And they all had their idiosyncrasies. The Unitarians weren't allowed spires or towers; Congregational churches were classical until 1860, Gothic afterwards; Baptists were keen on big, plain, classical chapels; Presbyterians were closest to Anglicans, with their liking for Decorated Gothic.

A unifying feature of all these eclectic buildings was their location. Built long after the medieval parish church, chapels were further from the ancient heart of town.

Although they were Gothic and classical, chapels didn't look much like churches, which was half the point, really. They were specifically built to be different from the grand edifices of the faith their founders had broken away from. They were simple, four-square buildings of one period, with none of the deep layers of styles, statues and monuments you get in Anglican churches. Often their architects had no formal knowledge of the rules of classical architecture.

247

Their main priority was that a single voice – and, particularly in Wales, choirs – could be heard by a large congregation; and that they shouldn't cost much. There were exceptions in areas where chapel was more popular than church, where fortunes were spent on the buildings – like in Wales; more precisely, at the Tabernacl Welsh Chapel in Morriston, just north of Swansea – a beguiling mix of classical, Romanesque and Gothic. As well as being the biggest Congregational chapel in Wales, it is home to the world's most famous Welsh male-voice choir, the Morriston Orpheus Choir.

Some of the earliest nonconformist places of worship were Quaker meeting houses. Built after 1650, they looked exactly like that – houses, and houses that matched Quaker demands for no worldly ornamentation: white walls, clear glass windows, simple oak seating and plain stone floors.

The real boom in nonconformist building came with the boom in John Wesley's Methodists during the late eighteenth century. This boom was particularly powerful in Wales, effectively a nonconformist country by the mid-nineteenth century. But not just in Wales – the 1851 religious census showed there were almost as many nonconformists in Britain as there were Anglicans.

Methodist chapels were usually cheap versions of Greek Revival and Perpendicular Gothic models – often not much more than decorated barns, with simple Gothic ceilings, plain oak pews, clear glass windows and mahogany pulpits.

The Nonconformist Valhalla was John Wesley's chapel in City Road, London. Wesley's handsome 1778 chapel, by George Dance, stands on one side of the road, with his tomb in front of it. On the other side is Bunhill Fields, the greatest nonconformist graveyard in the country. Among its residents are William Blake, John Bunyan and Daniel Defoe.

Their tombstones were particularly handsome. When the *Independent* was set up in 1986, Nicholas Garland, now the *Daily Telegraph*'s cartoonist and then one of the new paper's founding fathers, was asked for stylish typefaces. He suggested looking around in the graveyard next to the *Independent*'s offices – Bunhill Fields – jam-packed with fine examples of eighteenth-century writing.

Incidentally, it was also the fashion in the eighteenth century to carve figures around the top edge of the stone – putti (Italianate cherubs) if you were in an optimistic mood, death's heads and cross-bones if you weren't.

One of John Wesley's classical barns – Methodist chapel, Carew, Pembrokeshire (1852).

25

Elementary Schools, My Dear Watson

Sherlock Holmes's Favourite Style

Holmes was sunk in profound thought, and hardly opened his mouth until we had passed Clapham Junction.

'It's a very cheering thing to come into London by any of these lines which run high and allow you to look down upon the houses like this.'

I thought he was joking, for the view was sordid enough, but he soon explained himself.

'Look at those big, isolated clumps of building rising up above the slates, like brick islands in a lead-coloured sea.'

'The Board schools.'

'Lighthouses, my boy! Beacons of the future! Capsules with hundreds of bright little seeds in each, out of which will spring the wise, better England of the future.'

Arthur Conan Doyle, The Naval Treaty *(1893)*

Sherlock Holmes's excitement on the Woking-to-Waterloo line has been mocked for its Victorian liberal optimism and the misguided faith that the stranglehold of public schools, Oxford and Cambridge over the Establishment would be toppled.

Well, even if Holmes was wrong about the political result, he was right about the stirring beauty of the board schools – the great red-brick soaring things that went up across Britain from the 1870s until the 1890s. They were set up under the Foster Act of 1870, under which School Boards ran non-compulsory state schools, paid for by a local school rate.

Holmes was right about their being beacons and lighthouses, too. One of their distinguishing features was their huge windows – sash and casement – to light up enormous classrooms. While the frames were big, the panes were kept small to minimise replacement costs. Jealous vandals took to smashing the windows of the prominent new schools with their soaring Flemish gables and chunky chimney stacks.

Board regulations demanded thirty square inches of light for every

The girls' entrance to the Board School, Offord Road, north London. Lots of board schools have been converted into flats, but they still retain their distinctive features – such as separate entrances for boys and girls, who were originally segregated.

square foot of floor, and that ceilings should be at least fourteen feet high. Big dormer windows were slotted into the roof, so that attics – normally dark, dingy, unused rooms – could provide light-filled class-rooms.

Alongside these smaller classrooms, there was one big, high-ceilinged central classroom where all the children could be taught together. To accommodate these generous proportions, space else-where was rationed – there were no corridors in board schools.

The multi-coloured schools were a mixture of brown stock brick, red-brick dressings and white woodwork. Variety was achieved at low cost – the only designed ornament was the odd panel of terracotta. A favourite was a picture of Knowledge strangling Ignorance. Board

253

schools were just one symptom of a new style sweeping across Britain in the late nineteenth century.

A Window on the Homeless

Window shapes are vital clues to the purpose of a building. At Arlington House, a 1905 red-brick Gothic down-and-outs' hostel in Camden, north London, there are hundreds of very small windows in the façade. Arlington House was one of the first such places to provide a single room for each resident. The architect decided the residents would have greater independence if they got their own window too.

By the 1870s the Gothic Revival was petering out. The colossal Gothic Royal Courts of Justice, commonly known as the Law Courts, dating from 1871, were the last significant national building in the style. The so-called Queen Anne Revival followed, even if there were few details in common with the buildings of that queen's reign from 1702 to 1714. A better name for it was Sweetness and Light, which neatly captured its jaunty, multi-coloured, rules-free air.

Let's Go Pont Street Dutch

The Queen Anne Revival blossomed all over the place – seaside resorts, Oxford dons' houses and Cambridge colleges. Because it borrowed from lots of styles – the seventeenth and eighteenth centuries, Elizabethan, Old English, Japanese, Dutch, farmhouse vernacular, Palladian – it's hard to pin down any ruling credo behind the style. If anything, the most important elements were its lack of rules and its eclecticism.

The 1840s had seen an obsession with Decorated Gothic architecture; the 1850s and 1860s turned towards Early French Gothic. How slavish all this imitation was, thought the architects of the Queen Anne Revival. Why follow the French, when you had inspirational native

Early English features on your doorstep? Half-timbered, tile-hung and weather-boarded houses flourished in the late nineteenth century, so the movement also got called 'Olde English'. The style suited the new breed of commuter heading home from a day's work in London to his rural retreat in the Home Counties.

Further additions came from the early and mid-seventeenth century – jutting timber-framed oriel windows, gables, brick pilasters, pediments and those great big chimney stacks on the board schools. The later seventeenth century and the eighteenth century were also useful sources, for railings, cupolas, hipped roofs, sash windows and scrollwork.

Throw in a curious taste for sunflowers sculpted out of terracotta and all you can say to identify Queen Anne is that it's a bit of everything and a lot of red brick.

Thackeray sparked the fashion for redness in the house he designed in 1862 at 2 Palace Green, Kensington. It survives, even if it's hard to get close to it because 2 Palace Green is now the Israeli Embassy.

The sweetest and lightest spot in the country was the area behind Harrods in Knightsbridge. This was the heartland of the nineteenth-century red-brick house with Dutch gables – christened Pont Street Dutch by Osbert Lancaster.

Lord Cadogan – as in the Cadogan Estate, which still owns much of Chelsea – plumped for the style in 1876–8, cutting a red-brick swath through the white-stucco acres of west London.

It took off in the country, too, in places like P.G. Wodehouse's village of King's Deverill, Hampshire, described in *The Mating Season* (1949):

> The village hall stood in the middle of the High Street, just above the duck pond. Erected in the year 1881 by Sir Quentin Deverill, Bart, a man who didn't know much about architecture but knew what he liked, it was one of those mid-Victorian jobs in glazed red brick which always seem to bob up in these olde-worlde hamlets and do so much to encourage the drift to the towns.

Pont Street Dutch, by Osbert
Lancaster, in *Pillar to Post* (1938).

Home, Sweet and Light Home

Next time you see a row of dingly-dell, red-brick, suburban cottages,
you have one man to thank – Norman Shaw (1831–1912). Shaw did
more than anyone else to create the image of the new British house in
the late nineteenth century. 'I'm a house man not a church man,' he
said, 'and soil pipes are my speciality.'

The workaholic Shaw had his shirts tailored with outsized cuffs so he
could sketch plans for houses on them for clients he sat next to at grand
dinner parties. (In another sign of the growing grandness of architects,
William Butterfield (1814–1900), the man behind All Saints, Margaret
Street, insisted that scaffolding was dusted before he arrived on site.)

Shaw also founded the higgledy-piggledy, Olde English, ever so
slightly twee, commuter's cottage school of architecture.

You can see it best in Bedford Park, begun in 1875, his development beyond Shepherd's Bush, west London – thick with Dutch gables, tile-hanging and oceans of red brick. A contemporary satire said:

> With red and blue and sagest green
> Were walls and dado dyed,
> Friezes of Morris there were seen
> And oaken wainscot wide.
> Now he who loves aesthetic cheer
> And does not mind the damp
> May come and read Rossetti here
> By a Japanesey lamp.

G.K. Chesterton based Saffron Park, in *The Man Who Was Thursday: A Nightmare* (1908), on Bedford Park: 'The stranger who looked for the first time at the quaint red houses could only think how very oddly shaped the people must be who could fit in them ... Even if the people were not "artists", the whole was nevertheless artistic.'

Drinking, Olde English style – the Tabard Inn (1880), Bedford Park, London, by Norman Shaw with tile-hung gables and shallow curved bay windows.

Marchmain Arts and Crafts

To get a feel for Arts and Crafts, visit the Catholic chapel at Brideshead, decorated at the turn of the nineteenth century.

> Angels in printed cotton smocks, rambler-roses, flower-spangled meadows, frisking lambs, texts in Celtic script, saints in armour, covered the walls in an intricate pattern of clear, bright colours. There was a triptych of pale oak, carved so as to give it the peculiar property of seeming to have been moulded in Plasticine. The sanctuary lamp and all the metal furniture of bronze, hand-beaten to the patina of a pock-marked skin; the altar steps had a carpet of grassgreen, strewn with white and gold daisies.
> 'Golly,' I said.
> 'It was papa's wedding present to mama. Now, if you've seen enough, we'll go.'
>
> *Evelyn Waugh,* Brideshead Revisited *(1945)*

The chapel was the only bit of Brideshead to be drawn from Madresfield Court, Worcestershire, where Waugh often stayed with the Lygons, the family that owned the place for nearly a thousand years. Its walls were painted by a leading Arts and Crafts artist, Henry Payne (1868–1940), in 1902 to celebrate the marriage of Lord and Lady Beauchamp. The figure of Lady Beauchamp was whitewashed in 1937 at the orders of Lord Beauchamp when she didn't support him after the exposure of a gay affair six years earlier.

John Ruskin (1819–1900) inspired the Arts and Crafts movement, particularly in *The Stones of Venice* (1851–3) and *Unto This Last* (1860). The principles were pretty amorphous – the general idea was to connect the country's moral and social health to the qualities of its architecture and design. The answer came, Ruskin thought, from a society full of creative, skilful workers. The closest architectural embodiment of this was the Red House, Bexleyheath, Kent, built by Philip Webb (1831–1915) in 1859 for William Morris (1834–96), artist, writer and another founder of the Arts and Crafts movement.

The watchwords of the movement were there: the desire to expose the natural surfaces of ordinary materials, such as stone and hanging tiles; and all then thrown together into an asymmetrical, jumbled composition. Where materials were manufactured – like William Morris's floral wallpapers – they were made by hand.

Utopia Meets Suburbia

The Norman Shaw spirit of the eclectic suburban terraced villa continued into the twentieth century – most strikingly in London's Hampstead Garden Suburb (1907) and Welwyn Garden City (1920), Hertfordshire.

Garden cities were dreamt up by the social reformer Ebenezer Howard (1850–1928) in *Tomorrow: the Peaceful Path to Real Reform* (1898). He wanted to build suburban, mid-sized towns, surrounded by a permanent belt of agricultural land. This was realised in the first garden city: Letchworth (1903), Hertfordshire. Later offshoots of the garden cities were the new towns, built after the New Towns Act of 1946, notable among them Stevenage, Hertfordshire, and Milton Keynes, Buckinghamshire.

Garden suburbs were different things: new developments with a rural feel, attached to ancient cities. The movement had its roots in Bedford Park. Other inspirations included Port Sunlight, Merseyside, an Arts and Crafts town begun in 1899 by Lord Leverhulme for workers at his Lever Brothers soap factory; and Bournville, the Birmingham model town built by the Cadburys in 1893 for their chocolate factory employees.

Hampstead Garden Suburb was the most successful example,

micro-managed by Dame Henrietta Barnett (1851–1936), whose father had made a fortune out of Macassar oil for men's hair. The building density was low – eight houses or fewer per acre. Every house had a private garden and there were no walls, only hedges – a popular idea in American gated communities from the early twentieth century onwards.

Dame Henrietta picked leading architects to produce wildly differing looks in line with Sweetness and Light: tile-hanging, half-timbering and low eaves were combined with casement windows. Neo-Georgian mansions proliferated, too, and Sir Edwin Lutyens produced his own Romantic-Byzantine-cum-Nedi style (his nickname was Nedi) for St Jude's, the suburb's Gothic church. Like Pugin before her, Dame Henrietta thought Gothic was the style of the true Christian religion. Evelyn Waugh attended St Jude's as a child and was confirmed there in 1921.

These detailed, varied developments, though, were at the expensive, hand-tooled end of the market. Sweetness and Light caught on in a big way in the British suburbs in a mass-manufactured way, as described by P.G. Wodehouse in *Leave it to Psmith* (1923):

It was a peculiarly beastly little street. Situated in the middle of one of those districts where London breaks out into an eczema of red brick, it consists of two parallel rows of semi-detached villas, all exactly alike, each guarded by a ragged evergreen hedge, each with coloured glass of an extremely regrettable nature let into the panels of the front door; and sensitive young impressionists from the artists' colony up Holland Park way may sometimes be seen stumbling through it with hands over their eyes, muttering between clenched teeth, 'How long? How long?'

The First Flat-Warmings

Hermann Muthesius, author of *The English House* (1904), said that by the end of the nineteenth century Britain was the only advanced country in which the majority of the population still lived in houses.

Houses may have been divided up for centuries – in 1911 40 per cent of all London families shared a house with others. But those houses had not been designed with multiple occupancy in mind. Purpose-built flats – of varying sizes for different classes – only appeared on a nationwide scale in the mid-nineteenth century, a long time after the Continent.

Scotland got there first. Where English houses tended to be owned outright, individual ownership of Scottish flats was common even in the eighteenth century. Tenements in Glasgow, on the edge of the medieval city in Gallowgate, survive from as early as 1771. They were rather upmarket, elegant buildings – palace-fronted, neo-classical and more spacious than those put up by the City Improvement Trust in Glasgow from 1866 onwards. These included the notorious, minuscule 'single ends', which combined a sitting room with a kitchen and four tiny bedrooms.

Edinburgh got there even earlier. John Knox House, with two tenements on top of a ground-floor shop, dates from the sixteenth century. Each flat had a hall and bedroom, with little rooms in the attic and projecting timber galleries.

The first flats in England that were expressly designed to alleviate the plight of the working classes weren't built until 1849. They survive today in Streatham Street, Holborn, London. They were built for the Society for Improving the Conditions for the Labouring Classes by Henry Roberts. This evangelical Christian and adviser to Prince Albert on social housing was shocked by the overcrowding and disease in poor areas:

A leading feature of the plan should be the preservation of the domestic privacy and independence of each distinct family; and the disconnection of their apartments, so as effectually to prevent the communication of contagious disease.

This is accomplished by adopting one common open staircase, open on one side to a spacious quadrangle, and on the other side having the outer doors of the several tenements, the rooms of which are protected from draught by a small entrance lobby.

Parents were given separate bedrooms from their children. There were separate kitchens and lavatories for each flat, too, with communal baths and coal and potato stores in the basement.

Large concentrations of mid- and late-nineteenth-century flats were found in London and Tyneside – perhaps, in the latter case, because of the proximity of Scotland. The steep hills of Gateshead and Newcastle lent themselves to multi-storey buildings where the upper levels were accessible from the back.

By the 1870s large numbers of two-storey Tyneside flats were going up – with a flat to each storey. In the classic Tyneside flat, each dwelling had its own yard with its own bin, coal shed and lavatory, and its own back door to the back lane.

Still, these looked much like terraced houses, apart from a profusion of front doors for each household, and a rear exterior staircase leading to the upper floor.

The London cottage flat (also called a maisonette) looked pretty similar – two-storey, purpose-built buildings with a separate front entrance for the upper flat, like the Victoria and Albert Cottages in Woodseer Street and Deal Street, Spitalfields.

By 1890 each floor of the cottage flat had two bedrooms, a kitchen, lavatory and, later, a bathroom. To begin with, the lavatories were placed at the back of the houses, reached by an outdoor passage, in line with the idea that the working classes should only have an outside lavatory.

Queen Anne's Mansions (1873, demolished 1973) in Queen Anne's Gate, by St James's Park tube station, was the first big block of upmarket London flats for the middle classes – Sir Edward Elgar was a tenant. It was also the first domestic building in the country with a hydraulic lift. The classic flat in the block consisted of a living room of about twenty-three feet by fourteen feet, with a bedroom and bathroom.

This historic block wasn't in the Queen Anne style, despite the name. Most residential blocks that followed in the late 1870s and 1880s were – in a style copied across London and Britain for blocks of flats, both private and council-owned.

Popular features on the new upmarket blocks of flats included those familiar huge Flemish gables, lots of red brick and large, many-paned windows with white frames.

Yet in 1911 still only around 3 per cent of all English and Welsh dwellings were flats; 10 per cent were detached or semi-detached; and the vast majority were terraced houses.

The real expansion of flats came after the First World War, with the collapse in the supply of servants and – after the huge hike in tax – the inability to pay for them. In 1851 there were 115,000 women between fifteen and twenty years old in London and the suburbs; forty thousand of them were in domestic service. Between 1911 and 1921 the number of servants in London's commuter belt fell by half.

The size of households began its downward slide, too – in 1842 the average Victorian household was 5.8 people, compared with 1.9 now. They all had to find somewhere to live – and to drink.

26

Den and Ange Victorian, and Other Pub Styles

In 1393 Richard II ordered that signs must go up outside drinking places, not just to help illiterate drunks but also to make it easier for inspectors checking ale quality to spot a pub. The legislation stated, 'Whosoever shall brew ale in the town with intention of selling it must hang out a sign, otherwise he shall forfeit his ale.'

The pub sign had arrived. And so began the journey towards juke boxes, quiz machines and little white disinfectant dice rolling along gents' urinals. The pub sign was the first bit of drinking paraphernalia to distinguish the pub from those neighbouring cottages that looked so similar.

Pub customisation was a slow process. Smaller inns were accommodated in unremarkable premises until the Georgian period. Coaching inns were different – from the 1660s, the expansion of coaching services had led to an expansion of appropriate premises. They were set up like monasteries – with a dormitory and dining room ranged around a courtyard entered by a central gateway. Late-eighteenth-century coaching inns even had ballrooms, thick with ornate plaster sphinxes, goats and Greek muses.

Very few pre-eighteenth-century coaching inns survive. But their memory lives on in countless pubs called the Coach and Horses, like the one in Soho that was the local of the late Jeffrey Bernard (1932–97), the *Spectator*'s Low Life correspondent. *Private Eye*'s weekly lunches are still held there. Former editor Richard Ingrams and the current incumbent, Ian Hislop, preside over three long, Formica-topped tables placed in a U-shape and set with school cutlery. The simple lunch – steak and chips, ice cream, red wine in Duralex tumblers – is served in the handsome first-floor dining room. You sing for your lunch, providing fodder for the magazine's gossip columns – principally 'Street of Shame', the column devoted to Fleet Street.

With an explosion in drinking came an explosion in drinking places. Ever since the Dutch introduced gin after the Glorious Revolution of 1688, its consumption had soared. By 1740 six times as much gin as beer was drunk in Britain; half of London's fifteen thousand drinking places were gin shops.

Damned Cup! that on the vitals preys,
That liquid fire contains,
Which Madness to the heart conveys,
And rolls it thro' the veins
From the original caption to Hogarth's Gin Lane, *1751*
(Getty Images)

The gin shop in Hogarth's *Gin Lane* is that plain building distinguished only by a jug hanging from the façade, like the one hanging from the bridge in the foreground. Lots of street signs were originally hanging objects – like the coffin and the pawnbrokers' balls elsewhere in the picture. Pawnbrokers' balls are one of the few shop symbols to survive today.

When the painting was done, in 1751, a quarter of the shops in St Giles's parish – where it was set – were gin shops. There was a full-blown gin craze on, after the Government cut gin prices to encourage distilling and prop up the grain price.

In the picture you can also see the spire of Hawksmoor's St George's, Bloomsbury (1731). In his characteristic way he plundered an exotic source for the stepped spire – the tomb of Mausolus (hence 'mausoleum') at Halicarnassus (now Bodrum, Turkey), one of the Seven Wonders of the World.

King George I took Mausolus's place on top of the spire. And a supersized heraldic lion and unicorn have stepped off the royal coat of arms to prowl round the spire's lower steps and protect their king. The Victorians thought the stone animals were so over the top that they chiselled them off in 1871. They were only put back in 2006.

In Hogarth's *Beer Street*, painted at the same time, everything looked healthier. The pawnbroker's has closed down; the drinkers are plump and well, and flirting with each other.

Note the alluring terraced houses in the background – with their first-floor windows taller than those on the second, in correct *piano nobile* fashion. Above them soars the pretty tower of a Wrenesque spire.

Alehouse premises expanded in the fightback against the gin craze. In the late eighteenth century, a saloon was added to lots of them. There, for an admission fee – or for more expensive drinks – song-and-dance shows were performed and table service provided. The saloon, or lounge bar, retained some cachet into the twentieth century, while the taproom or public bar sold cheaper drinks to a supposedly cheaper clientele.

Despite the promotion of beer, gin remained popular into the nineteenth century. In the late 1820s, the first gin palaces were built in Holborn and Old Street. The expansion came on the back of an 1825 cut in the duty on spirits from eleven shillings and eightpence farthing a gallon to seven shillings.

Gin palaces were based on the late-Georgian shopping arcades – gleaming temples to retail. Gaslights, gleaming expanses of wood and etched glass were fitted. Dickens, in *Sketches by Boz* (1836), said the gin

Beer, happy Produce of our Isle –
Labour and art upheld by thee
Successfully advance,
We quaff thy balmy Juice with Glee
And Water leave to France.
From the original caption to William Hogarth's Beer Street *(1751)*
(Mary Evans Picture Library)

palaces were 'perfectly dazzling when contrasted with the darkness and dirt we have just left'. And they had a powerful effect on the modern pub. The broad, long pub bar – ideal for quick service and attaching beer pumps – was borrowed from the gin palace, as were etched glass and ornate mirrors.

Throughout the nineteenth and early twentieth century the number of pubs rocketed, to cater to the flourishing heavy industries and their

269

workers in the new stretches of terraced houses springing up across the country.

Once Wellington's 1830 Beer Act removed beer duty, gin lost pace. Within a year, thirty-one thousand new beer licences were issued. Today there are sixty thousand pubs in Britain – and no gin palaces. The exhaustion, misery and dehydration brought on by manual jobs in factories, mills and mines had encouraged beer drinking. And, as British industry has shrunk, so beer has given way to wine, cocktails and the alcopop. Fourteen million pints of beer are now sold every day – the lowest level since the Great Depression. At the height of the market in 1979, sales were 50 per cent higher.

In reaction to this drinking epidemic, the British Association for the Promotion of Temperance was founded in 1835; worries about binge drinking are nothing new. Still, the teetotallers couldn't stop the building of thousands of pubs.

The pub was the biggest, most architecturally distinguished house in the new terraces. When a builder put up a terrace, he often built the pub first and became its landlord. The Churchill Arms, on Campden Street in Holland Park, west London, was built in 1849 by Henry Gilbert, 'builder and victualler', who went on to build another seven houses next door.

Builders drank and ate in the pub while they finished a terrace. Then, towards the end of the project, the developer sold the licence to raise the funds to finish the work.

The pub was a crucial outrider in the spreading British suburbs, as noted in an article on north London in *The Builder* magazine in 1854:

> On the pastures lately set out for building you may see a double line of trenches with excavation either side . . . and a tavern of imposing elevation is standing alone and quite complete, waiting for the approaching row of houses. The propinquity of these palaces to each other in Camden and Kentish Towns is quite ridiculous. At a distance of 200 paces in every direction, they glitter in sham splendour.

In BBC TV's *EastEnders* (1985–), the Queen Vic, at 46 Albert Square, Walford, is a quintessential Victorian pub. The fake premises are accurate in every detail – a generously proportioned, three-bay, late-Victorian building, taller and wider than the houses on the square.

The Queen Vic's first-floor windows have attractive Gibbs surrounds. On the ground floor, the Corinthian pilasters are connected by a subtle cornice with a string of dentils below. This cornice skirts the full length of the pub, tying the façade neatly together around that awkward corner site.

A second, deeper cornice runs along the top of the first floor beneath the roof – a nod to the pilasters that appeared on the first terraced houses and were left off later ones.

The London Borough of Walford, E20, was invented by one of *EastEnders'* creators, the late Tony Holland (1940–2007), who took the name from Walford Street, a handsome late-Victorian road in Hackney. Walford's fictional tube station, Walford East, is shown on the *EastEnders* tube map on the same spot as Bromley-by-Bow tube station. The set of Walford Square was in fact based on Fassett Square, E8, further west – a typical mid-Victorian city square, built in the early 1860s.

Victorian pubs went through several stages: robust Den and Ange Classical in the 1840s and 1850s; Gothic Revival up until around 1870; high-Victorian in the 1850s and 1860s; French classical in the 1860s and 1870s; in the 1870s and 1880s, a mixture of Queen Anne and Flemish brick and terracotta; and Art Nouveau by around 1900.

Still, relatively few Victorian pubs were built in the Gothic style. John Ruskin was wrongly pleased with himself when he showed off in 1872 about popularising Gothic style:

> I have had indirect influence on nearly every cheap villa-builder between Denmark Hill and Bromley; and there is scarcely a public house near the Crystal Palace but sells its gin and bitters under pseudo-Venetian capitals copied from the Church of the Madonna of Health or Miracles.

271

Most landlords, like Den and Ange, in fact sold their gin and bitters under classical capitals.

The swaggering confidence of the mid-Victorian Queen Vic style wasn't approved of in genteel circles. Pubs were still considered down-market joints with all the gimcrack sleaziness of gin palaces. In reaction, 'good' and 'improved' pubs were set up by philanthropists, along with public houses which served only coffee and other non-alcoholic drinks. They didn't last long.

The style chosen for good pubs was Queen Anne Revival, thought to be more sophisticated. Out went the mirrors, etched glass, overblown gas lamps and over-the-top stucco decoration. In came small panes of plate glass, tiles, red brick and tile-hanging – an altogether more sober and Olde English rural look like in Norman Shaw's Tabard Inn in Bedford Park (1880), pictured earlier.

There was a problem for the morality police, though. Commercial publicans also liked Queen Anne. To the untutored eye, the two sorts of pub melded into one. These publicans of the 1890s took elements of Queen Anne – imitation Jacobean plasterwork, tiles on the walls, Flemish gables, terracotta panels – and drenched them with the dazzle of the gin palaces.

They went for enormous mirrors and hinged glass panels engraved with swirly rococo patterns and Japanese birds. Curved stretches of glass were incorporated into front doors; the joys of drinking were made crystal clear to passers-by. Back came the broad shafts of light from gas – and, now, electric – lights. Carpenters found ingenious ways of holding glasses on island centrepieces and wall shelves, or 'wagons' and 'back fittings'. Twisted balusters and broken pediments were squeezed into the packed space between drinkers' heads and lincrusta ceilings.

Edwardian streets – and their pubs – were more humble affairs. Witness the Rovers Return. Opened in 1902, it was originally called the Coronation in honour of Edward VII's coronation that year. The street kept the name, but the pub was renamed The Rover's Return in honour

A high Victorian temple to the swift one: the Crown Liquor Saloon (1885), Belfast.

of a local soldier, Lieutenant Philip Ridley, who came home safely from the Boer War. After more local soldiers came back from the First World War in 1918, the two singular nouns were replaced by a noun and verb – The Rovers Return. The definite article was dropped in the 1960s.

T't Rovers, the corner shop and seven houses together made up Coronation Street.

The houses on Coronation Street are the classic, simple, two-up, two-down terraced Edwardian cottages popular across Britain, particularly in expanding industrial areas. Built of red brick, with sash windows (two-over-two panes on the first floor), their most handsome feature is the bow window to one side of the front door.

They are not, though, back-to-back houses – the hated terraces built to accommodate workers in furnaces, mills and mines from the 273

Where's the cat? Edwardian Coronation Street, Manchester. (Rex)

early nineteenth century onwards. These had two storeys, with one room upstairs and one downstairs. Because the houses were joined at the back, they had no through ventilation. Every ten houses there was a tiny breathing space – a courtyard with a pump and lavatory. Their horrors were recognised almost as soon as they were built, and Sheffield banned their construction in 1864. Still, they went on being built elsewhere. In Bradford, 65 per cent of all houses built in the 1880s were back-to-backs; they weren't outlawed there until 1900. Back-to-backs were still being built in Leeds in the 1930s.

Pubs were more sophisticated buildings than the cottages they abutted. Special attention was given to a complex series of drinking rooms in the Rovers – a notional building, of course, but one based precisely on real life. Before the pub was knocked into one big room after a fire in 1986 – lots of pubs across Britain opened up like this in the eighties – the Rovers had three separate rooms.

274

First came the main room – the public bar. Then the select, the equivalent of the old saloon bar. Then came the snug – up until the First World War this was the only place where women could be served. Even in 1960, there was a sign in the Rovers' snug saying women shouldn't linger at the bar. Paul Johnson, writing in the *Spectator* on 19 January 2008, looked back fondly at the snug:

The term is nautical: a ship was made snug against stormy weather, or in harbour, everything tied down or tidied up. It went on shore to become the cosiest part of a multi-room port tavern, and so spread inland. In the snug you were private, protected from the bustle and noise of the 'public' or saloon bar, and you had a coal fire to warm your hands at.

Social divisions in pubs continued into the 1950s. X Trapnel, the bohemian writer in Anthony Powell's *A Dance to the Music of Time*, drank himself to death in the Hero of Acre in Fitzrovia, just north of Soho, as related in *Books Do Furnish a Room* (1971):

The Hero, one of those old-fashioned pubs in grained pitchpine with engraved looking-glass (what Mr Deacon used to call a gin palace) was atomised into half a dozen or more separate compartments, subtly differentiating, in the traditional British manner, social divisions of its clientele, according to temperament or means: saloon bar; public bar; private bar; ladies' bar; wine bar; off-licence; possibly others too.

Roadside pubs had a coffee room as well, like the one in the Goose and Gherkin in P.G. Wodehouse's *Ring for Jeeves* (1953):

[The coffee room] had the usual dim religious light, the customary pictures of *The Stag at Bay* and *The Huguenot's Farewell* over the mantelpieces, the same cruets and bottles of sauce and the traditional

275

ozone-like smell of mixed pickles, gravy soup, boiled potatoes, waiters and old cheese.

Theatrical Style

Just as heavy Victorian drinking brought a boom in pub building, heavy Victorian theatre-going brought a boom in theatres. These, of course, had been around for centuries, but they were on the whole pretty unremarkable buildings. Because the theatre wasn't subsidised in Britain – unlike in France and Italy in the eighteenth and nine-teenth centuries – seating capacity was more crucial than a pretty façade. Lots of eighteenth-century theatres were built behind ordinary terraced house fronts, with the cheap land behind the terrace taking up the auditorium.

A few Georgian theatres remain, notably the Theatre Royal, Drury Lane (1812), the Theatre Royal, Haymarket (1821), the Old Vic (1818) and the most complete survival, the Theatre Royal in Bristol (1766) – also the oldest continuously working theatre in Britain, although now under threat of closure due to lack of funds.

Most theatres today, though, belong to the peak late-Victorian years of theatre and music hall – from the 1880s to the end of Edward VII's reign in 1910. Every style under the sun was nabbed for these fantasy buildings: Neo-Baroque with Indian plasterwork, free classical and rococo, Moorish Alhambra. Those with imperial themes were often called the Empire.

The master of these blowsy, international influences was Frank Matcham (1854–1920). Between 1879 and 1912 he designed some 150 theatres – nearly a quarter of all theatres built then. The Hackney Empire, the London Hippodrome, the Coliseum, the Palladium, the Victoria Palace Theatre, the Shepherd's Bush Empire and the Grand Opera House in Belfast were just a few of his triumphs.

Matcham was one of the first theatre architects to use steel instead of timber and cast iron. He could then carry deep balconies across the full width of the theatre without columns, and so cut down on restricted-view tickets.

Lillie Langtry, the music-hall singer, hailed these sightlines when she unveiled Matcham's Cheltenham Theatre and Opera House in 1891:

> Nay, where (within this house you'll all agree)
> Not all can sit, but all can see –
> The Architect's arrangements if you'll watch 'em,
> (Like these two rhymes), 'tis hard to Match 'em.

Oriental Ulster – the Grand Opera House (1895), Belfast, by Frank Matcham.

Putting on the Ritz – Edwardian Imperial style

If you see a bank – more likely a bar, now – it's probably built in the Edwardian style that Edwin Lutyens called Wrenaissance: a cruder, overblown version of the Wren buildings of two centuries before. Town councils and government offices also liked the look, and the city halls of Belfast and Cardiff (both 1906) are fine examples.

Hotels, too, were drenched in this grandiose style – Edwardian Imperial, as it was also known – borrowing from sources as rich and varied as Viennese Baroque and Louis XIV (for extra points, say 'quatorze').

Louis XVI was the inspiration for the Ritz in Piccadilly (1906), built for the hotelier César Ritz by Charles Mewès and Arthur J. Davis. With its bank of Portland stone upper floors resting on Norwegian granite arcades, the Parisian look is straight out of the Rue de Rivoli.

The Ritz was built on an extravagant scale – then the biggest steel-framed building in London, not including industrial structures. In those days the steel frame was concealed by stone, as this super-strong steel was too thin to meet the minimum wall thickness regulations that still applied.

You'll need a strong disposition to stomach the Louis XVI tea room, with its gilt trellis cornice and nymphaeum. And a strong stomach, too – the first chef was the gastronome Auguste Escoffier.

The Ritz was the Queen Mother's favourite restaurant. She was cheered to the bronze-garlanded chandeliers and the ceiling, frescoed with fluffy clouds, every time she sat down to her prawn cocktail washed down with gin and Dubonnet.

Art Nouveau Crosses La Manche

Art Nouveau is familiar enough – water lilies twisting towards a ceiling illuminated by Tiffany lamps, and trim, flowing, curving lines drawn by Aubrey Beardsley; stretched furniture punctured with heart-shaped holes and Japanese print designs.

Still, for all its familiarity, the style never really took off here, flaming only for a brief moment in the early twentieth century. Taking its name from a Parisian shop, La Maison de l'Art Nouveau, the fashion first blossomed on the Continent between 1890 and 1905.

It was in Scotland that Art Nouveau reached its British heights, chiefly through Charles Rennie Mackintosh (1868–1928), who pioneered a sort of Beardsleyesque Scottish Baronial style. His brave modernity was so influential that in Germany, until the First World War, the new style had its own name – Mackintoshismus.

A rocket ship straight out of Dan Dare. Futuristic oriel windows on Charles Rennie Mackintosh's Glasgow School of Art (1910) emphasise its soaring lines. The zigzagging round the basement door even looks forward to Art Deco ziggurats of twenty years later.

Symbolist artists like Whistler, Beardsley and Munch were the inspirations for Mackintosh's repoussé – raised or beaten – metalwork, his decorative panels and that distinctive, stripped-down, elongated, Japanese style.

The most striking Mackintosh building was the Glasgow School of Art (1910), which shows how Arts and Crafts overlapped with Art Nouveau, particularly in the sculptures of sinuous, anorexic women over the front door. Its library was rich with quintessential Mackintosh touches – circular and rectangular perforations alongside bright little coloured squares, and all on a dark stained timber background with a Japanese feel to it.

These Mackintosh trademarks cropped up elsewhere in Glasgow in his Willow Tea Rooms (1904), and later in a thousand table lamps and promotional pencil cases.

27

Ginger Rogers Goes to Arsenal

Art Deco, the Architecture of Entertainment

It has now become par excellence the style of the arterial highroads, the cinema studios, the face-cream factories, the Tube stations of the farther suburbs, the radio-ridden villas of the Sussex coast.

Evelyn Waugh, A Call to the Orders*, 1938*

Those villas, white Art Deco houses inspired by ocean liners, with their flat roofs, polished parquet floors and metal windows, are now rather prized.

Those face-cream factories have aged handsomely, too. Well, the household cleaning appliance factories, in any case, if the Hoover factory at Perivale by the A40 – now a Tesco – is anything to go by (pictured on the back of this book). Built in 1938 by Wallis, Gilbert & Partners, this Art Deco Leviathan retained classical proportions beneath its white skin; a skin brightened with a few splashes of primary colour, inspired by the Aztec fashions of the Paris Exposition des Arts Décoratifs (1925).

Alive to the Hoover factory's classical influences, John Betjeman called it an Art Deco Wentworth Woodhouse – that mammoth Palladian palace in Yorkshire.

It's on passing a similar Art Deco building – the Jensen swimwear factory, beyond Chiswick, on the A30, the Great West Road – that Nick Jenkins first kissed Jean Templer in Anthony Powell's novel *The Acceptance World* (1955):

On either side of the highway, grotesque buildings, which in daytime resembled the temples of some shoddy, utterly unsympathetic Atlantis, now assumed the appearance of an Arctic city's frontier forts. Veiled in snow, these hideous monuments of a lost world bordered a river of black, foaming slush . . .

The exact spot must have been a few hundred yards beyond the point where the electrically illuminated young lady in a bathing dress dives eternally through the petrol-tainted air; night and day, winter and summer, never reaching the water of the pool to which she endlessly glides. Like some image of arrested development, she returns forever, voluntarily, to the springboard from which she started her leap. A few seconds after I had seen this bathing belle journeying, as usual, imperturbably through the frozen air, I took Jean in my arms.

Art Deco was the entertainment style of the 1920s and 1930s. Just look at William Binnie's 1936 East Stand in Arsenal's old Highbury Stadium – the only Grade II listed football stadium in the country, designed by Binnie and Claude Waterlow Ferrier.

It was the style of the retail temple, too. Peter Jones in Sloane Square (1936), Barkers in Kensington High Street (1935) and Simpsons in Piccadilly (1936) – this last the inspiration for the Grace Brothers' department store in the BBC TV series *Are You Being Served?* (1972–85) – were all followers.

The Savoy Hotel was given an Art Deco full metal jacket in 1930 – wrapped in chromium and mirrored stainless steel, and covered in aluminium, set off with Chinese, jazz and Aztec motifs. The metal is being buffed up at the moment – the hotel is due to reopen in May 2009 after a £100-million refurbishment.

As for the familiar Art Deco cinema look, that was thanks to Oscar Deutsch, as in 'Oscar Deutsch Entertains Our Nation', or Odeon (also the ancient Greek word for a musical theatre). Deutsch (1893–1941), born in Birmingham to Jewish immigrant parents, opened his first cinema in Brierley Hill, Dudley, in 1928, and nine years later could boast: 'Our buildings express the fact that they are specially erected as the houses of the latest, most progressive enlightenment in the world today.' That distinctive maritime Art Deco Odeon look – cream tiles, thin, coloured bands, fins, neon tubing, slab towers and very few windows – was the brainchild of a designer called Harry Weedon. The Weedon Partnership survives today, with more than three hundred Odeons to its name.

Art Deco has confused origins – indeed it only got the name in a *Times* headline in 1966. The style has also been called Jazz Age, Moderne and Jazz Modern. That Paris Exposition in 1925 was the initial spark of the style. Cubism, the Ballets Russes, Austrian Arts and Crafts and Exoticism were fellow midwives at the birth. It reached its architectural heights in crowstepped skyscrapers – modern Mayan ziggurats like the Empire State Building and the Chrysler Building – and the curved and geometric, chrome Hollywood backdrops to the dancing feet of Fred Astaire and Ginger Rogers.

The British version of Art Deco was more muted; a moderate form even got the name Restrained Jazz. Battersea Power Station (1934) by Sir Giles Gilbert Scott was classic Restrained Jazz, with its modest Art Deco tiles, subtle stepped towers and delicately striated walls. It also breathed a few last gasps of the classical age in the fluting of its four distinctive towers. The biggest brick building in the world, the cathedral of the electrons, it has just begun a ten-year restoration programme.

Art Deco touches could also be applied cheaply on a mass scale. Thirties suburban semis used the style's distinctive sunray pattern in door frames, alongside white rendered walls, flat concrete porches and metal-framed curved windows decorated with small chevrons – often Crittall windows, named after the manufacturer, based in Braintree, Essex. Metal windows were frequently on the corner of a house – a spot that, with earlier building materials, would have been structurally dangerous.

There were, though, moments of unrestrained genius on British Art Deco buildings, particularly when it came to sculpture – like the figures on London Underground Headquarters, designed in 1929 by Charles Holden (1875–1960). Among the sculptors were Eric Gill, Henry Moore and Jacob Epstein, whose *Night and Day* has the look of a pre-Columbian *pietà*.

Frank Pick (1878–1941), head of London Underground, employed Holden to design the stations on the extensions to the Central and

Piccadilly lines. These Art Deco classics were distinguished by circular drums (Arnos Grove, 1932, and St John's Wood, 1939) and distinctive towers (notably the glazed slab of Boston Manor, 1933, and the glass obelisk of Osterley, 1934). Holden and Pick visited Holland together in 1930, and their station work owed a lot to Dutch Modernism.

It's hard to define a style born of so many different sources which grew into such different animals. Michael Dugdale's satirical poem on the Hoover factory, 'Ornamentia Praecox', did rather a good job when it appeared in the *Architectural Review* in July 1932:

> Leave no space undecorated:
> Hide those ugly wheels and pipes.
> Cover them with noughts and crosses,
> Mess them up with stars and stripes.
> Now for curves and now for colour
> Swags and friezes, urns and jars.
> Now for little bits of faience
> Now for giddy glazing bars.

The Estate Agent and the Council House Are Born

If an estate agent were transported back in his decal-plastered Mini to the First World War, his commission would barely cover a bottle of Chablis.

In 1914 the pattern of house ownership in Britain had barely changed since feudal times, and hardly anyone owned – or could buy or sell – their own home. Only 10 per cent of the 7.75 million households belonged to owner-occupiers; the rest were owned by private landlords. By 1938 the number of owner-occupiers had rocketed to 3.75 million out of 11.75 million households.

The First World War kicked off an unprecedented building programme. There had been council houses since the 1890 Housing of the

Working Classes Act, when local authorities began to improve housing. But the real impetus came with the 'Homes Fit for Heroes' election of December 1918. The Liberals were re-elected on a pledge to build half a million new houses in three years, let at subsidised rents by local authority landlords. As a result of the 1919 Housing Act, a million council houses were built over the next twenty years – mostly two-storey cottages planned in fours and sixes, and built of brick with hipped roofs and sash windows. This cheap Georgian look was so basic that they became known as 'boxes with lids'.

On top of the council house building programme, rent control in private houses – with rents often frozen at 1914 levels – meant private landlords were desperate to offload their properties. Between the wars they sold three million houses to owner-occupiers.

The typical 1930s council house was built on a relatively generous scale, with a living room and kitchen on the ground floor and three bedrooms and a bathroom on the first floor. Outside decoration on these council houses was limited to a bare minimum by local authority budgets.

Private houses in the housing estates of the burgeoning suburbs had more money thrown at them. Helped by cheap land, government incentives and expanding building companies, they were laid out in space-devouring cul-de-sacs and crescents. The 1930s semis could be bought for between £400 and £1500. Detached houses cost around £100 more.

They had more elaborate features, applied to a standard semi-detached or detached plain box. Ambitious estate architects borrowed Arts and Crafts features and wrapped houses in elaborate neo-Georgian, mock-Elizabethan and mock-Tudor skins – mockingly called 'Tudorbethan'. As well as the leaded windows and mock-timber panels, pebble-dash was added to give a taste of rustic life – this is what Osbert Lancaster called the By-Pass Variegated style of the between-the-war suburb. More expensive houses had a full-height bow window and a garage to one side of the property.

Suburban expansion was particularly marked outside London. Between 1921 and 1937, the inner London population fell by half a million; Greater London increased by a million and a half. The Second World War brought an even bigger public housing boom. Four hundred and fifty thousand houses were destroyed, and another three million damaged, by bombing. The Attlee government of 1945–51 built a million local authority houses, among them 170,000 'prefabs'. These, prefabricated in factories, were ultra-simple in design and made of steel, aluminium, timber and asbestos. Still, the combination of an entrance hall, two bedrooms, a bathroom, lavatory, sitting room and kitchen was a vast improvement on pre-war slum housing. The former Labour Party leader Neil Kinnock recalled his prefab in Tredegar, Wales, in 'When I Was a Child' in the *Daily Mail* of 26 September 1986: 'It had a fitted fridge, a kitchen table that folded into the wall and a bathroom. Family and friends came visiting to view the wonders. It seemed like living in a spaceship.'

The other beneficiaries of these revolutionary changes in home ownership were estate agents. They hadn't got their upmarket job title until the early twentieth century; their origins had been rather murkier. They began life in medieval times as stewards – disreputable figures whose sharp practices were reined in during the eighteenth century, when they were replaced by land agents and surveyors. The Surveyors Club, founded in 1792, was chaired by John Clutton, ancestor to the modern firm of Cluttons.

Surveyors were generally more admired – Daniel Defoe's Robinson Crusoe was named after a King's Lynn surveyor – with the odd exception: Richard Adams, one of London's first surveyors, was dismissed for malpractice over a Mayfair property deal in 1720 for the Grosvenor Estate. The reputation of estate agents still had some way to fall over the next three centuries.

28

A Thousand Years
in an Hour

A Stroll through the Architectural
History of London

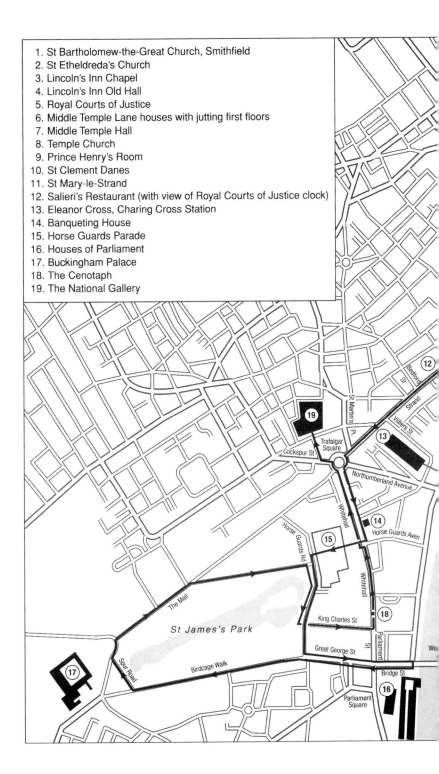

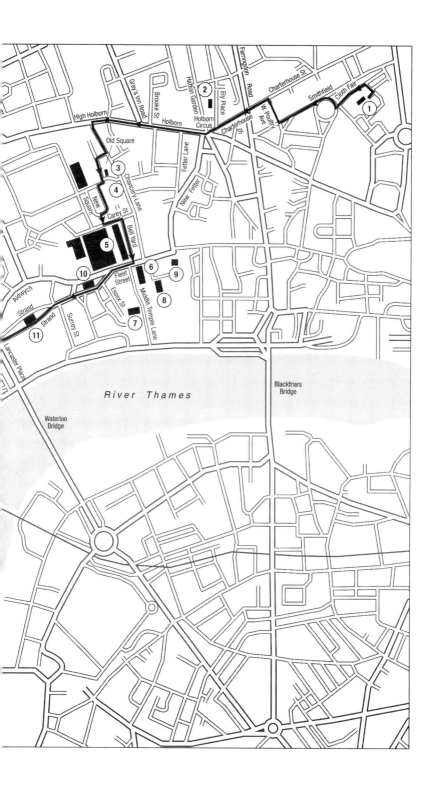

Map labels:

- Cloth Fair
- Smithfield
- Charterhouse St
- Farringdon Road
- Ely Place
- Hatton Garden
- Gray's Inn Road
- Brooke St
- High Holborn
- Holborn
- Holborn Circus
- Charterhouse St.
- W. Poultry Ave
- Old Square
- Chancery Lane
- Fetter Lane
- New Fetter
- New Square
- Carey St
- Bell Yard
- Fleet Street
- Essex St
- Middle Temple Lane
- Aldwych
- Strand
- Strand
- Surrey St
- Lancaster Place
- River Thames
- Waterloo Bridge
- Blackfriars Bridge

1
2
3
4
5
6
7
8
9
10
11

This walk takes you through the essential three periods of British buildings: the spread of Norman architecture through Britain after 1066, the development of Gothic architecture from the late twelfth century, and the growing sophistication of British classicism from the late sixteenth century onwards.

The three-mile chronological walk takes the reader from the Norman chancel of St Bartholomew-the-Great in Smithfield (1123) to the classical 1833 National Gallery with its modern addition, the 1991 Sainsbury Wing.

Begin at St Bartholomew's, where the first gay wedding in an Anglican church was held in June 2008. Next time you're watching *Four Weddings and a Funeral* (1994), look for the bit where Hugh Grant ditches Duckface at the altar. It's a good scene, and not just because of the acting of Grant and Anna Chancellor. In the background of the wedding – or jilting – scene, you get luscious shots of that early-twelfth-century chancel, in the shadow of the ancient Smithfield meat market.

Those massive pillars that run either side of the nave, with their

The best Norman columns in London, St Bartholomew-the-Great, Smithfield (1123). Plus Hugh Grant and Anna Chancellor. (Photos12.com – Collection Cinema)

simple scalloped capitals, are the best Norman columns in London. While you're standing in front of the altar, look right and left and you'll see the typical three-floored walls of British cathedrals and large churches: an arcade with a triforium and clerestory above.

On your right, you'll see an oriel window, jutting out from the first floor. The Tudors and Stuarts loved them; this one's Tudor, from the early sixteenth century.

Take a few steps to the right as you look at the altar, and you stride forward 450 years. In the big tomb of Sir Walter Mildmay, Chancellor of the Exchequer and founder of Emmanuel College, Cambridge, who died in 1589, English classicism was beginning to stir. The simple columns were a good bash at classicism, but they're still pretty far from the precise dimensions dictated by Italian rules. Those would have to wait two decades for the buildings of Inigo Jones.

Now leave the church and head west towards St Etheldreda's Church in Ely Place, Holborn. As you walk through the City of London, look at the course you're forced to take – it's almost impossible to walk in a straight line.

A charming chaos prevails today in the City of London. The place might now be filled with uniform glass-and-steel tower blocks, but they are still happily squeezed into the curving, squiggly lines of the asymmetrical plan of London before the Great Fire of 1666.

The odd shape of those streets has been made even odder by the IRA. The checkpoints on roads into the City introduced in the 1990s to cut down on terrorist attacks have gone. But the imprint of the ring of steel remains, with roads narrowing to chicanes where those checkpoints once were; and sudden dead ends in the middle of streets where gaps in the defensive ring were plugged with bollards, marked with mid-90s dates.

If Christopher Wren had had his way, these streets you're walking along would have been as straight as a die. But he didn't, so your walk goes along streets that barely run for fifty yards in a straight line before they climb or dip, swerve or zigzag, swing round an ancient church site or plunge towards the course of the old River Fleet, which runs beneath you as you cross Farringdon Road towards St Etheldreda's church.

Built in 1290, St Etheldreda's is the oldest Catholic church in London. It is in Ely Place, once part of the Bishop of Ely's palace, with a garden known to Shakespeare. In *Richard III* the king says to the Bishop of Ely, 'When I was last in Holborn, I saw good strawberries in your garden there. I do beseech you, send for some of them.'

The enormous Gothic window over the altar, depicting the sixteenth-century Catholic martyrs, can only be so big and support the roof above because it is pointed at the top – the big giveaway that we have moved into the Gothic world.

Look closely at the tracery. Already, in the late thirteenth century, windows have become pretty complicated. The style is on a turning point between Geometrical tracery of around 1250–1310 and the overlapping, Decorated tracery of 1290–1350. Geometrical tracery was restrained, even and, as the name would suggest, symmetrical. This window was on the cusp of the more complex, ornate Decorated style, where tracery weaved in and out, criss-crossing, forming little jagged-edged lozenges in the shape of daggers, teardrops and a thousand other things you last saw at the bottom of a kaleidoscope.

A short stroll to the Inns of Court leads to Lincoln's Inn Hall, built in 1489. This was the Court of Chancery in the opening pages of *Bleak House* (see page 49). Look out for not one, but four oriel windows.

On the other side of the hall is the 1518 gatehouse, built in classic Tudor gatehouse style, familiar from Hampton Court, Eton and St James's Palace. Among the coats of arms over the gateway are Henry VIII's.

Next door is Lincoln's Inn Chapel. Go inside and up the stairs. There, on the wall of the ante-chapel, you'll see a portrait of Spencer Perceval, a barrister of Lincoln's Inn and the Prime Minister assassinated on his way to the Commons in 1812 by a madman.

When the chapel was built in 1623, the main east window (pictured on page 52) would have looked pretty old-fashioned. Just across town at St James's Palace, Inigo Jones was already erecting the classically proportioned Queen's Chapel, and here were the benchers of Lincoln's Inn still sticking to medieval Gothic styles.

Look carefully at this window. This style, Perpendicular, is the last of the three Gothic movements, after Early English and Decorated. In traditional Perpendicular style, those mullions soar straight to the top without diverting into the twirly-whirly curls and circles you saw at St Etheldreda's.

Walk on through Lincoln's Inn, heading south, until you leave through a covered passage with Wildy's bookshop – of pleasingly Dickensian aspect – on either side.

Ahead lies the last gasp of the Gothic Revival – G.E. Street's Royal Courts of Justice of 1871 – inspiration for the Palace of Justice in George Orwell's *1984*. Its more familiar elevation is on the other side, where you'll see the main doorway and steps favoured by the late George Carman QC, Michael Mansfield QC and Heather Mills after great victories and embarrassing divorces.

As always, look at the windows – pointed, yes, but not complicated pointed. The tracery is very simple, so you're dealing with something early and Gothic – in this case, a copy of French and English styles from the mid-thirteenth century.

If you're standing outside the Royal Courts of Justice impersonating Heather Mills, look to your left and you'll see a plinth with a dragon on it in the middle of the road. This marks the site of the Temple Bar, the old division between the Cities of London and Westminster.

The original Temple Bar is a bit further east – in the shadow of St Paul's. It was returned to London in 2001 after more than a century in the grounds of a country house in Enfield owned by a brewer, Sir Henry Meux. Built in 1672, less than half a century after that window in Lincoln's Inn Chapel, Christopher Wren's classical Temple Bar is several lifetimes ahead in style.

Scrubbed clean now, Temple Bar bears little resemblance to the decaying old edifice described by Dickens in *Bleak House* (1853): 'The raw afternoon is rawest, and the dense fog is densest, and the muddy streets are muddiest near that leaden-headed old obstruction, appropriate ornament for the threshold of a leaden-headed old corporation, Temple Bar.'

Look across to the other side of the road and you'll see a lovely example of early British classicism – the Middle Temple gateway, built by Roger North in 1684. North was a gentleman architect rather than a professional. Still, the correctness of his giant Ionic pilasters with that pediment and rusticated basement show how thoroughly he had absorbed the proportions of Renaissance Italy.

Compare the neat lines and subtle colours of the red brick and white Portland stone with the garish clumsiness of the Mildmay tomb in St Bartholomew's, and you'll see how well the British had absorbed the classical rules by the late seventeenth century.

Go through the little door in the bottom-left corner of Middle Temple gateway (open during the week in office hours), and you'll find yourself in a cobbled lane.

Look up to your left at numbers two and three Middle Temple Lane as you go down the hill. You'll see some timber-fronted houses with upper floors jutting out over the street.

'Pre-Fire,' you purr to yourself with confidence after reading the immensely enjoyable opening pages of Harry Mount's *A Lust for Window Sills* (2008). I'm afraid not. These were actually built in 1694, in the old pre-Fire style, breaking the 1667 Act requiring rebuilding of the City to be done in brick and stone. The Act also outlawed those teetering wooden storeys that spread fire across and along streets so well. I'm afraid people, lawyers included, sometimes break the law – and my dating tips, too.

296   Follow this cobbled lane south until you get to Middle Temple

dining hall on the right, built in 1570 and the finest Elizabethan building in central London. You're not allowed in unless you're with a barrister but, if you're wearing a suit and can pull off a swaggering, entitled enough air, you should be able to walk straight in between 12.30 and 1.45 on a weekday. The trick is not to look in the porter's eyes; even better, if you're with someone, dissolve into laughter and look *them* in the eyes as you walk past the porter.

This is where, in 1602, Shakespeare held the premiere of *Twelfth Night* on 2 February, or Candlemas, the culmination of the long winter feast. Middle Temple Hall is also the perfect spot to see a crucial turning point in British architecture – when Gothic gave way to classical.

Walk along the screens passage and take a right through the screen into the middle of the hall. Above you is the double hammerbeam roof built in 1570 by John Lewis, Sir John Thynne's chief carpenter at Longleat.

DATING TIP

The hammerbeam roof depended on a series of arches and braces supported by rows of horizontal brackets projecting from the walls. If it's a double hammerbeam roof, like Middle Temple's, there are two rows of brackets and arches.

Pilgrims' Hall, Winchester, built in the mid-fourteenth century, is the earliest surviving hammerbeam roof in Britain. Given the lack of good stone quarries and the expense of stone, hammerbeam roofs were popular in parish churches, too. There was a glut of them in the Perpendicular period, particularly in East Anglia.

The biggest hammerbeam roof in Britain is the 660-ton one built in 1401 by Henry Yevele at Westminster Hall in the Palace of Westminster.

So, the Middle Temple roof wouldn't have looked out of place a century earlier in a medieval manor house. Within a few decades of going up here, it looked distinctly dated.

Turn around now, look back at the screen you walked through, and you'll see pretty good classical columns set into a screen built in the 1570s.

Those classical details were nearly right – Roman Doric columns with a metope frieze below, and Ionic capitals supported by sombre-looking elderly men above. Back on the passage side of the screen, the classical theme continues with fluted Doric pilasters.

The hall side of the screen was lavished with strapwork. This mixture of classical columns with ornate decoration sprayed on in spades was typical. With this proliferation of detail, Elizabethan architecture ended up more ornate than the pure classical architecture that followed.

If you don't con your way into the hall, you'll still find the exterior has some good sixteenth-century features.

Those windows with their mullions and transoms are typical of the time. Look how the building bulges out into a bay window at the right-hand end. That marked the high table, where benchers of the Inns of Court dine. When I was a miserable barrister eating my lunch

298   First night of *Twelfth Night* – Middle Temple Hall (1570), the Temple, London.

on the lower tables, a puce-faced bencher at high table once ordered a waiter to tell me to stop reading my newspaper – reading is banned in the halls of the Inns of Court.

Just around the corner from Middle Temple Hall, you'll find the Temple Church, one of the earliest Gothic churches in England. The church was founded by the Knights Templar in 1160 and built on a circular plan – the design favoured by Crusaders all over Europe and the East in homage to the round Sepulchre of Christ.

From the fourth century, pilgrims travelled to Jerusalem to see the church of the Holy Sepulchre, and the circular plan caught on in Norman churches. Several of those Knights Templar were buried in tombs radiating off the centre of the circular nave in the Temple church.

Dan Brown was quite wrong, then, in his architectural analysis in *The Da Vinci Code* (2003): 'The Templars ignored the traditional Christian cruciform layout and built a perfectly circular church in honour of the sun. A not so subtle howdy-do to the boys in Rome. They might as well have resurrected Stonehenge in central London.' Despite the mistake, the church remains a pilgrimage site for Brown's fans. It also rejoices in the name of a Peculiar – a place of worship that falls directly under the control of the monarch, not the diocese. Those with royal connections, like Westminster Abbey, are Royal Peculiars.

Look at the windows on the round nave – they're round-headed in the Norman style. Then look at those windows on the outside of the right-hand bit of the church – and the inside, if the place is open. Yes, they're *pointed*! We have arrived at the beginning of the Gothic age. The porch you go through was built between 1160 and 1185, as was the round nave on your left. The nave was consecrated in 1185 by the Patriarch Heraclitus of Jerusalem. The outsized chancel on your right was built a little later, in 1220–40.

So, the Temple Church was perfectly pitched between the Romanesque era and the Early English period – the first Gothic, pointed period, from around 1190 to 1250. Well, strictly we're in something called the

Transitional phase between Norman and Gothic, which lasted for a mere quarter of a century, from 1175 to 1200.

The locked door on the far side of the circular chapel is still late Norman, with its round arch and three orders of elaborate colonnettes – that is, little columns. But go back to the entrance porch, and there the Gothic touches begin. The porch has Gothic rib vaults. Inside the circular nave, the arches have pointed arcades – all absolutely revolutionary. The chancel, built almost half a century later, is more purely Gothic – those windows, with triplets of lancets, are classic Early English.

Leave the church, turn right and right again, hugging the church and you're on the way to Fleet Street, but before you reach it, you'll pass under a rare pre-Fire survivor – the 1611 Inner Temple Gateway, built in a cocktail of styles. Those two oriel windows are quintessentially Jacobean; the bulging first and second floors oversailing the ground floor are typically Elizabethan. Those Ionic pilasters above Doric ones were another game attempt at correct classical work. The dimensions were still not quite right but soon, soon . . .

Inside, on the first floor, is Prince Henry's Room, named after the initials P and H and the Prince of Wales's feathers in the classic Jacobean plaster ceiling, though there's no evidence that the real Prince Henry, James I's son, ever lived here.

Again, we are on the cusp of the classical revolution: those four Doric pilasters on the west wall looked forward to the approaching classical age; but, with all that strapwork, they also looked back to the sixteenth century.

Go back down the stairs and on to Fleet Street. Head left and you'll come across Christopher Wren's St Clement Danes, built in 1682 and now the RAF church; as in '"Oranges and lemons," say the bells of St Clement's.' The church's bells – 22–3 per cent tin, the rest copper, incidentally, like most church bells – play the tune regularly. The 1719 tower, above the clock stage, is by James Gibbs – look for those distinctive Gibbs surrounds.

St Clement Danes sits on an island in the middle of the Strand, flanked by a statue of Arthur 'Bomber' Harris – the one daubed in paint by fans of Dresden's architecture a day after it was unveiled in 1992.

Keep on walking, leaving Sir William Chambers's neo-classical masterpiece, Somerset House (1780), to your left and another Gibbs work, St Mary-le-Strand (1717), to your right (as pictured on page 132).

Surefire Bet Number Two

This was the one thing Bertie Wooster could remember when he gave a speech to Miss Tomlinson's School for Young Ladies near Brighton. The episode comes in the only story ever narrated by Jeeves, 'Bertie Changes His Mind', in P.G. Wodehouse's *Carry On, Jeeves* (1925):

'My old Uncle Henry gave me the tip when I first came to London. "Never forget, my boy," he said, "that, if you stand outside Romano's in the Strand, you can see the clock on the wall of the Law Courts down in Fleet Street. Most people who don't know don't believe it's possible, because there are a couple of churches in the middle of the road, and you would think they would be in the way. But you can . . ." And, by Jove, he was perfectly right, and it's a thing to remember. Many a quid have I . . .'

Miss Tomlinson gave a hard, dry cough, and he stopped in the middle of a sentence.

'Romano's was a real night-clubby type of restaurant,' Tony Ring, President of the International Wodehouse Association and former editor of *Wooster Sauce*, tells me. Romano's has now been replaced by a joint called Salieri's, but Bertie Wooster's advice still holds true. If you stand on the pavement outside the restaurant – looking past St Mary-le-Strand and St Clement Danes – you can just make out the clock to their right.

When you get to Charing Cross Station you'll see the eponymous Charing Cross, an 1863 mock-up of the late-thirteenth-century Eleanor Crosses (see page 71). Look at the intricate masonry on this cross – classic Decorated Gothic work from 1290–1350.

Walk on, via Trafalgar Square, down Whitehall and you will see, on your left, one of the first classical buildings in England and the first in central London: Inigo Jones's Banqueting House (1622), where Charles I was executed.

Bear in mind that the Banqueting House was built barely a decade after the charming but clumsy Prince Henry's Room. How ordered, how balanced, how correct Jones's dimensions are, compared with what went before; and how Italian – the Banqueting House owes much to Palladio's palaces built in Vicenza half a century earlier.

One crucial Palladian rule the Banqueting House observed was the seniority of the orders. Composite columns framed the first floor windows, through one of which Charles I climbed on his way to the scaffold. So, following the hierarchy of the orders, the ground floor had Ionic columns.

Look across the road to where the tourists gather to watch the Changing of the Guard, and you'll see what happened in the next century and a half of classical architecture after Inigo Jones.

There, behind the familiar sentry boxes, is Horse Guards, built in 1759, apparently to designs by the Palladian architect William Kent. Walk between the sentry boxes and on to the parade ground beyond.

Turn round and look at the Horse Guards building. You can see this is a classical building, with lots of the same features as the Banqueting House – the absolute symmetry, the little pediments over the principal windows of the first floor. But how much more complicated the language has become, with such rapid movement of surfaces, backwards and forwards, up and down. Those squarish towers on either side were classic Palladian features. Even more typical were the seven Venetian windows – short, flat-headed one, tall, arched one, short, flat-headed one.

Now turn left when the gravel of Horse Guards runs out, then left again at Birdcage Walk, and straight ahead you'll see the Houses of Parliament, the best-known Gothic Revival building in the world. After Horse Guards went up in 1759, various forms of classical architecture – notably Greek Revival and neo-classical – flourished for the next seventy or so years. But by 1840, when the Houses of Parliament were begun, a Gothic Revival had taken hold of the country. The revival lasted until the 1870s.

The terms of the competition to see who would design the new Parliament dictated that the most important new building in British history must be either Elizabethan or Gothic – how outdated classical work had become! Even though the Houses of Parliament took thirty years to build, its Perpendicular style never went out of fashion in all those decades. How outdated classical work remained!

As we've seen, Augustus Welby Pugin was the Gothic Revival architect *par excellence.* In 1998 it was Pugin's devotion to exact Gothic detail at the Houses of Parliament that got Lord Irvine, then Lord Chancellor, in such unfair trouble when he did up his parliamentary quarters. £59,000 was spent on wallpaper that matched up to Pugin's exacting Gothic standards.

Pugin's partner, Sir Charles Barry (1795–1860), was really a classical architect. So he yielded to Pugin when it came to the exact Gothic detailing; things like the right sort of twirly-whirly leaves and heart shapes to use for Lord Irvine's wallpaper. Or those great outer walls of honey-coloured panels, made of magnesian limestone from Anston, Yorkshire, piled high on top of one another – soaring, straight, Perpendicular lines that sprout out of true into a thousand finials and crockets when they hit the roofline.

But when it came to the general shape of the building, Barry's son, Alfred Barry, the Bishop of Sydney, said that his father preferred a Renaissance model; and that's why the river front of Parliament was utterly symmetrical.

By the way, the most famous bit of the most famous Gothic building in the world – the Clock Tower, aka Big Ben, voted Britain's greatest landmark in 2008 – was pure fantasy Gothic; a figment of Pugin's imagination. He cooked up the idea in an earlier design for Scarisbrick Hall, Lancashire.

It's easy enough to find your way to Buckingham Palace. Just head back to St James's Park and any itinerant tourist in a comically undersized bobby's helmet will point you in the right direction.

Buckingham Palace has gone through several incarnations since it was built in 1705 for the first Duke of Buckingham by William Winde, the man who built Wotton House, next to the South Pavilion – Tony Blair's new country cottage. The original Buckingham House was distinguished by giant pilasters, a distinctive attic and those concave wings that Inigo Jones conjured up seventy years before at Stoke Bruerne, Northamptonshire.

Queen Charlotte brought the house into the Royal Family in 1762 and it soon became a real Russian doll of a place, wrapped in multiple layers of stone by eminent architects. Winde's work still lies at the heart of the main house; to get to see it, you'd have to take a few tips from Michael Fagan – the man who broke into the Queen's bedroom in 1982. You have to go through the famous front range, sneak across the courtyard and burrow into the garden side of the palace.

Sir William Chambers made changes to the place in 1780. George IV had it encased by John Nash in 1828. Next time you're invited to a garden party, it's Nash's work you'll see from the tea tent.

Edward Blore (1787–1879) changed the palace even more in 1850 and Thomas Cubitt made further alterations in 1852.

That front, familiar from a thousand flypasts, royal waves and fluttering flags hated by tabloid editors, was built as late as 1913 by Aston Webb. The Victoria Memorial in front of the palace, also designed by Webb, wasn't finished until 1924 in a last flourish of full-blown classicism – in this case Louis XVI French classicism.

From then on, after the First World War, the slow collapse of classicism was accompanied by the rise of modernism. You'll see the last vestiges of stripped-down classicism at the Cenotaph (1920). This memorial – its name comes from the Greek *kenos taphos*, meaning 'empty tomb' – was designed by Edwin Lutyens. Originally built in timber for a 1919 visit from American and French commanders, the Cenotaph was so popular that it was redone in stone. It didn't use any orders to support the coffin lying on top but its lines were subtly curved, based on the entasis of the Parthenon.

Although the Cenotaph's sides look straight and vertical, if you continued them upwards they would meet at a point a thousand feet up in the air. The horizontal lines curve around a point nine hundred feet below the ground.

The generation of architects after Lutyens's death was the first not to learn the classical orders rigorously; so, not surprisingly, these began to disappear from new British commissions. Only recently have they

The incredible shrinking building: Midland Bank (1929), King Street, Manchester, by Edwin Lutyens. Above the first floor, the walls narrow by one inch every 11 feet you go up.

Lutyens – The First and Last Architect

The words 'first' and 'last' can be used an awful lot of Sir Edwin Lutyens (1869–1944), Britain's last great classical architect. He built Britain's last castle, Castle Drogo in Devon, in the 1920s; it was also the first twentieth-century building acquired by the National Trust, in 1974.

Lutyens said of the orders, 'They have to be so well digested that there is nothing but essence left . . . the perfection of the order is far nearer nature than anything produced on impulse and accident-wise. Every line and curve the result of force against impulse through the centuries.'

You can see this stripped-down classicism in the Cenotaph and his government buildings in New Delhi, finished in 1929. Lutyens even invented his own Delhi order for the columns, incorporating little stone bells; when the bells started ringing, the story went, British rule in India would end. Eighteen years after the bells were sculpted, India celebrated its independence.

Lutyens showed how easily the classical era could mesh with the modern age. He was delighted to incorporate into his buildings the new steel frames: the first steel-framed building was built in London in 1906 (sadly not that useful as a dating tip because steel frames are hidden away from public sight).

In 1923 Lutyens built the Finsbury Circus façade of Britannic House, which, but for its steel frame, was still right in the mould of the classical tradition – a Baroque palazzo in the heart of the City of London.

Despite all these stellar – and relatively recent – triumphs, Lutyens never received much training, beyond a few years in his late twenties in an architect's office. Another 'last' then: Lutyens was one of the last architects not to be properly qualified as an architect by the new Registration Council, a system to which he thoroughly objected. And he wasn't the only one: the last significant church architect, Sir Ninian Comper, put 'architect, not registered' in his *Who's Who* entry.

begun to return. To see the full circle we have come, head on to Trafalgar Square and the 1991 extension to William Wilkins's National Gallery (1838) on the north side of the square.

This was the building whose original design by Ahrends, Burton and Koralek was condemned as a 'monstrous carbuncle on the face of a much loved and elegant friend' by Prince Charles in 1984 at the Royal Institute of British Architects Gold Medal award ceremony at Hampton Court.

Its 1991 replacement – Robert Venturi's part-classical, part-steel-and-glass extension – continues Wilkins's Corinthian order. The new Corinthian pilasters, though similar to the old ones, would not have gone down well with Inigo Jones or Andrea Palladio – they gather in a little cluster before breaking free in dribs and drabs, losing bits of their entablature along the way.

The extension reflects the halfway house of modern architecture – taking an uncertain step back from brutal modernism and dipping its toe gingerly in the old certainties.

29

Last Exit to Pont Abraham

The M4 Tour of British Buildings

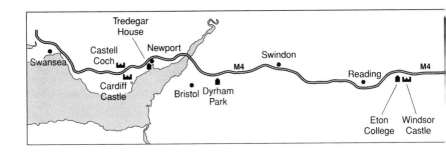

If well planned, a drive along the M4 can give you a quick guided tour to the architectural history of Britain. Not everyone uses the M4 and not everyone travels its full length from Exit 1 (Hammersmith) to Exit 49 (Pont Abraham service station). But all of our motorways – or any random two-hundred-mile stretch of road slicing through a country jam-packed with architectural gems – give you a flyover view of some of Britain's best buildings.

Most people travel along at least one motorway at least once a year. All it takes is a quick glance at the map before you get in the car. Look out for any little red cathedral, castle or country house signs within a fingernail's distance of the blue line of the motorway.

Even if you miss Much Garboldisham Castle – just there, on a line with your wing mirror – because you're too busy trying to eject your Edith Piaf CD, the exercise isn't wasted. There's something rather moving about drawing your finger along the blue motorway line and seeing what splendours you've been missing all these years.

Our drive along the M4, heading west from London, takes you chronologically through British architectural history from eleventh-century Norman, through fifteenth-century Gothic, seventeenth-century classical and on to nineteenth-century Gothic Revival.

The magical history tour begins with the biggest castle in the world. Three miles after Junction 5, look to your left and there you'll see it – the low-slung, fairytale skyline of Windsor Castle, particularly stirring at midday, when the sun is behind it. Or when the castle's on fire: the

M4 was a terrific viewpoint when the flames took hold at 11 a.m. on

20 November 1992 in the north-east wing – on the left of the castle as you look at it.

Even from two and a half miles away – as you are in your car – the full width of the castle is clearly, and breathtakingly, bigger than any other private house on earth. The full site covers thirteen acres. Stay in the slow lane at this point – then there are no cars between you and the castle.

Good of William the Conqueror to choose the castle site on a little cliff over a valley, so we can get a proper look at the silhouette. Good of him, too, to build up the motte – or mound – for us to see even more of the round keep he built on top of it.

From the motorway you can't see the three separate baileys, or wards, built by William. But even at seventy miles an hour, or more – naughty! – you can make out the changes that architect Sir Jeffry Wyatville made to the Norman castle for Queen Victoria.

The battle of beauty over defence in castle building had been won long before – castles were no longer needed for military reasons. So Sir Jeffry could go for the full Disneyland medievalisation. And he could sod the expense – the work for George IV, lasting from 1820 to 1830, cost £1 million.

Once Wyatville built up the castle walls and towers with his mock machicolations – which you can see cresting the horizon – the twelfth-century Round Tower, the castle's heart, suddenly looked a little fat dwarf by comparison with the rest of it. So he threw another thirty-three feet of stone on top of Henry II's tower base, in a collar shape that you can make out from the road. Bugger historical accuracy, thought Sir Jeffry – it's got to look right. So, although much of the silhouette you're looking at is actually nineteenth century, it's a pretty good nineteenth-century ideal vision of a Norman and early Gothic castle.

Once you've taken in Windsor, keep on looking out of the window – steady at the wheel – and, a few seconds later, just before Junction 6 (Slough and Eton), eyes left.

The motorway, usefully elevated at this point, gives a fine view of Eton College Chapel, built by Henry VI and place of worship for, *inter alios*, Prince William, George Orwell and David Cameron. Even from this distance you can make out the tall, prickly, slim profile of one of the best Perpendicular buildings in Britain. Completed in 1475, the chapel is similar in outline to its close contemporaries – its near neighbour, St George's, Windsor, the chapel of King's College, Cambridge and the Henry VII Chapel at Westminster Abbey.

There are lots of late Perpendicular details – buttresses, turrets, the battlemented parapet and crocketed pinnacles. You might even get a glimpse of the big Perpendicular east window with its strong mullions thrusting from bottom to top.

What you won't see, however slowly you're going, is the fan-vault ceiling – typical Tudor-looking work but actually inserted in 1958 to cover up a dreary 1699 roof.

Keep on going for an hour until you reach Junction 18 and Dyrham Park. You can't actually see Dyrham from the motorway because it's buried in its own little rounded dell. But no other National Trust house is quite so close to a motorway exit, and quite so easy to get to from that exit.

Head south towards Bath at Junction 18 and within a minute you'll see the sign, right, to Dyrham. Follow it, park your car and walk along the long drive that swishes from side to side along the humped chute of the valley.

And there, closing off the western view down to the Bristol Channel, is Dyrham, built in 1704, when Britain was perfecting its own unique form of classicism.

Throughout the house you can feel the free Baroque spirit that was pulsing round the country at the turn of the eighteenth century – driven by Sir Christopher Wren, Sir John Vanbrugh and Nicholas Hawksmoor.

Dyrham Park was where Anthony Hopkins and Emma Thompson filmed *Remains of the Day* (1993); the house stood in for Darlington

Just off the M4 – Emma Thompson's and Anthony Hopkins's last view of Dyrham Park, Gloucestershire (1704).

Hall, the home of Lord Darlington (played by James Fox), a fictional pre-war Hitler appeaser. It had several architects – one, Samuel Hauduroy, a Huguenot artist, built that French-looking garden front. The other, William Talman, did the front you see as you sweep towards the entrance.

There are Dutch tiles in the dairy and, in the stables, flourishes borrowed from Borromini, the Italian king of the Baroque, and his small masterpiece, San Carlo alle Quattro Fontane, Rome.

That church to the right of the house, St Peter, is a good link back to Eton. The porch with its quatrefoiled parapet, those straight-headed windows in the south aisle, the three-stage tower – all Perpendicular.

Back on to the A46, direction Cirencester. Then a minute later, left – or west – on the M4. Keep going for another half an hour or so – eyes peeled for Junction 28. Don't take the exit but, seconds after, look left as the motorway gently lifts a bit.

313

There, at the end of an oak-lined avenue carved in two by the motorway, is the best seventeenth-century house in Wales – Tredegar. Owned by Newport County Borough Council, Tredegar is on the edge of Newport, engulfed by housing estates and offices.

Because there's a close-up view of the house from the motorway, there's a pretty marvellous view of the motorway from the house. The road over which the M4 was laid was the main route to South Wales from England before Tredegar was built in 1688. Its owner, William Morgan, wanted to show his house off to passers-by, even if he didn't envisage you, me and 100,000 cars a day zipping past his bedroom window at eighty miles an hour. It's a mullioned and transomed bedroom window, by the way. The Morgans never fell for the sash-window fad that took off just as Tredegar went up.

It's not certain who built Tredegar, though the smart money is on the Hurlbutt brothers, Roger and William. They're not particularly well known, though they did build the grand houses of Maiden Bradley, Wiltshire, and Ragley Hall, Worcestershire. Whoever built it was awfully adept at handling the classical language of architecture. Just as at Dyrham Park, the architect has played around with that language confidently, avoiding any slavish copies of the Renaissance.

Even from the motorway you can make out the bold, creamy Bath stone enrichments against the pale-red brick of the house. The Corinthian columns around the doorcase are twisted and alluringly wrapped up in bay leaves. The rich pediment above the doorway, thick with animal and plant, is reflected in smaller pediments above each window.

It's now only another four exits until we reach the last stop on the magical history tour, Castell Coch. Seconds after Junction 32, look right and there, up on the hillside, is a Tinkerbell fantasy of a damsels-in-distress castle.

Fantasy is exactly what it is – an 1870 castle built by an intensely romantic Gothic Revivalist, William Burges (1827–81), for the Marquess of Bute, then the richest man in the world. His flourishing iron and coal docks – the biggest on earth in the late nineteenth century – gave Cardiff the nickname 'the Chicago of Wales'.

A short detour from the motorway, on the other side of Junction 32, takes you to Burges's other great commission for the Marquess, Cardiff Castle, a French medieval confection of plain walls, crested by machicolated towers capped with slim spires.

Just like Windsor, Castell Coch – Red Castle – was a Norman castle built on an artificial motte or mound. Unlike at Windsor, not much of the original Norman or later medieval stonework survived by the time Burges turned up. So he had even more room than Sir Jeffry Wyatville to indulge the full extent of his Gothic dreams. He borrowed from Swiss and French châteaux, as well as English castles, to produce a bewitching cocktail of arrow slits, candle-snuffer towers, merlons, corbels and oriels.

The interior is one of the great high Victorian Gothic set pieces. Its walls are rich in stencilled patterns and lurid heraldic colours, with glimmering stars and birds fluttering about all over the place. The towers are criss-crossed with rib vaults and lancets; the ceilings sprinkled with carved flowers and animals. Sleeping Beauty puts in an appearance at one point. The Victorian desire for the Middle Ages was never so strong.

30

Princess Diana's Walking Guide to Classicism

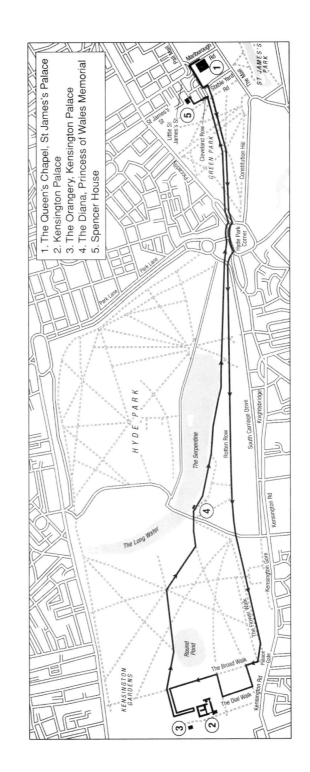

1. The Queen's Chapel, St James's Palace
2. Kensington Palace
3. The Orangery, Kensington Palace
4. The Diana, Princess of Wales Memorial
5. Spencer House

On the night of 5 September 1997, the body of Diana, Princess of Wales, lay in the Queen's Chapel, a handsome classical building opposite St James's Chapel. The coffin was presided over by the Reverend William Booth, the Queen's Chaplain, and Paul Burrell, her butler-cum-rock. Burrell had apparently placed in her hands some rosary beads, a present from Mother Teresa, who died in the same week as the princess. For her final outfit, Princess Diana had plumped for a black, long-sleeved Catherine Walker dress that she'd bought only a few weeks before.

It is appropriate that her penultimate resting place was classical – as indeed was her ultimate one, a wooden Roman Doric temple taken from the grounds of Admiralty House, London, which now stands next to the island at Althorp House, Northamptonshire, where she's buried.

The princess lived in a series of the greatest classical buildings in the country. Together they're a useful guide to the development of classicism from the early seventeenth to the early twentieth century.

Architecturally speaking, Princess Diana lived her life in reverse. Follow her life from death backwards, and you follow the life of classical architecture forwards. She spent her last night in London in one of Britain's earliest classical buildings. She was born and brought up in one of its latest ones, Althorp House, a Palladian house remodelled by Henry Holland in 1791.

The Queen's Chapel, where her body spent that last night in London, was the first classical church in the country, built by one of its greatest architects, Inigo Jones. He built the chapel in 1625 in an Italianate style appropriate to Charles I's Catholic Queen, Henrietta Maria. Their wedding was the first time a Protestant prince had married a Catholic princess, and the Pope had to give special permission for the union.

The only other classical building in London at the time was Jones's Banqueting House of three years earlier. But at least that was a secular building. For half a millennium, Gothic had been the accepted Christian style for churches. What a shocking sight the chapel must have been.

Stroll through Hyde Park and you come to the place where Princess Diana spent her last years – Kensington Palace. Largely rebuilt sixty-five years after the Queen's Chapel, Kensington Palace showed what a massive effect Jones had on those that followed him. By 1689 – when William of Orange headed for Kensington, fleeing the river dampness of Whitehall Palace that was so bad for his asthma – a new Anglo-Dutch classicism had developed.

At Kensington, Christopher Wren wrapped a country house of 1605 in an Anglo-Dutch classical skin – reflecting King William's Dutch origins. On the palace's south side you'll see a flat brick front with restrained pilasters – just like seventeenth-century Dutch buildings.

The palace was a bit of a jumble, despite the correct rules of its classical surface. This was partly because it was built round an old irregular house; partly because the palace had long been shared, as it still is, by an odd gang of grand residents with idiosyncratic architectural requirements. Edward VII called it 'the aunt heap' because it housed so many superannuated members of the royal family.

Move north up the east side of the palace, and you'll see how classical architecture developed over the next thirty years. Bang in the middle of that east side is a Venetian window from William Benson's 1726 rebuilding. The Palladians had arrived! That Venetian window is a dead giveaway to Palladian work.

As you continue walking north, Princess Diana's old private quarters are annoyingly out of sight to your left. Most tantalising of all is her private courtyard, hidden by those high walls, made out of slim, uneven, handmade seventeenth- and eighteenth-century bricks.

Inside the palace you'll see a mixture of seventeenth- and eighteenth-century state rooms, as well as a bare flat – number 1a – once lived in by Princess Margaret and Lord Snowdon.

This is where Snowdon installed an early minimalist room – a pared-down, ultra-sixties photographic studio – in among the rich Anglo-Dutch classical and Palladian state rooms. The studio has long since been removed, as were all Princess Margaret's fixtures and fittings when she died in 2002. All that's left to show Snowdon was there is a little square hole in one wall, through which he used to poke his projector on film evenings in the palace's mini-cinema. 'The place is absolutely filthy,' he said of his old flat on a return visit in 2007, 'It is disgusting. It is the first time I have been back for a very long time and I was shocked.'

Leave the palace, head north and you'll walk past a little side door in the wall. This is where Princess Diana sneaked into Kensington Gardens, sunglasses perched on forehead, Head tennis racket in hand.

Keep walking north and you'll see a rare chunk of early-eighteenth-century Baroque, the Orangery of Kensington Palace, built for Queen Anne in 1704. The architects of the Orangery were two of the greatest names in English Baroque – Sir John Vanbrugh and Nicholas Hawksmoor.

You can have lunch here – slow service, OK food, terrific baroque movement of planes and colours around the building, inside and out. While you sip your coffee, compare that movement of the brickwork – backwards and forwards, up and down – with the flat sides of Kensington Palace, and you get a feel for the agility of the Baroque; not as athletic as Italian or German Baroque, perhaps, but lively enough.

Next cross Hyde Park and Green Park, passing the Diana, Princess of Wales Memorial Fountain (2004), made of 545 leaking chunks of Cornish granite. Now aim for the Spencers' old London base, Spencer House, still owned by Lord Spencer but let on a long lease to Lord Rothschild. Built in 1754 by John Vardy and decorated in 1759 by James 'Athenian' Stuart, the house showed how far Palladianism had come since that Venetian window at Kensington Palace.

Here is an utterly symmetrical façade, with a vermiculated basement, rusticated ground floor, thoroughly Italian *piano nobile* and a
dominating central pediment. Where Palladian features were slapped
here and there on Kensington Palace's flat façade, the front of Spencer
House was one even, organically planned whole.

Inside, you begin to see the outline of the movement that followed
Palladianism – neo-classicism. As the nickname 'Athenian' implies,
Stuart was obsessed with the ancient world. He copied the frieze in
the hall from the Temple on the Ilissus in Athens; the Painted Room
he borrowed from Rome and Herculaneum. Compared to earlier, richer
Palladian work, the detail here is sparer – a glimpse of what was to come
in the later eighteenth century.

31

Railway to Heaven

The View from the Buffet Car on the Edinburgh Train

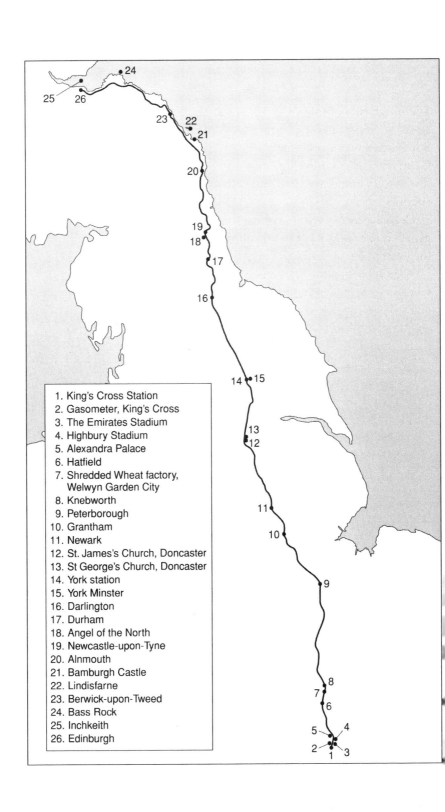

1. King's Cross Station
2. Gasometer, King's Cross
3. The Emirates Stadium
4. Highbury Stadium
5. Alexandra Palace
6. Hatfield
7. Shredded Wheat factory, Welwyn Garden City
8. Knebworth
9. Peterborough
10. Grantham
11. Newark
12. St. James's Church, Doncaster
13. St George's Church, Doncaster
14. York station
15. York Minster
16. Darlington
17. Durham
18. Angel of the North
19. Newcastle-upon-Tyne
20. Alnmouth
21. Bamburgh Castle
22. Lindisfarne
23. Berwick-upon-Tweed
24. Bass Rock
25. Inchkeith
26. Edinburgh

The rough rule of thumb so far has been: the later a big, grouped set of buildings are, the further they are from the centre of town. So, medieval houses, pubs and ancient church in the middle, Georgian terraces nestling close by, Victorian developments a bit further out, and Edwardian and between-the-war buildings in the suburbs.

Of course there were always lots of demolitions and rebuildings but, generally speaking, it got harder to do any large-scale new projects in the heart of our increasingly congested cities.

With one exception – the railways. Their wealth, power and usefulness meant that, through the second half of the nineteenth century, railway lines stretched right into the centre of most British cities, ending in a colossus of a station with a ringside view of the ancient parts of town.

While cars have been progressively fended off from cathedral closes by ring roads, pedestrianised areas and exorbitant parking fees, trains, for all their faults, still take you practically into the nave, right through the great west door.

The real highlights of this journey on the National Express line from London King's Cross to Edinburgh are the cathedrals: you get golden views of Peterborough, York Minster, Newcastle and, most spectacularly, Durham. And you also see some terrific church spires, from Grantham to Darlington.

Alongside the splendours there are the more day-to-day pleasures of staring into people's gardens, down deserted streets, into light industrial estates. (On the West Coast line near Preston, there's a splendid view of a gable with the advert – 'Uncle Joe Santos's Mint Balls Set You All Aglow' – in huge letters.)

On a train journey through Lincolnshire that began in Hull, Philip Larkin concentrated on all the weddings taking place on a Saturday afternoon, but he also took in the look of everyday Britain. The result was 'The Whitsun Weddings' (1958):

We ran
Behind the backs of houses, crossed a street
Of blinding windscreens, smelt the fish-dock; thence
The river's level drifting breadth began . . .
Wide farms went by, short-shadowed cattle, and
Canals with floatings of industrial froth;
A hothouse flashed uniquely . . .
An Odeon went past, a cooling tower,
And someone running up to bowl.

Try to get a seat in a nest of four on the right-hand side of the train as you head north – better sea views, more space on the table for your road atlas. Keep the atlas in front of you all the time and it's surprisingly easy to get your bearings, using roads alongside the track, other railway lines branching off to the side, place names on the edge of towns and, best of all, rivers and the sea.

My timings are based on the fast trains but beware: Passenger Announcement – times are approximate and subject to disruption.

All change at King's Cross

The line you're taking today, the old Great Northern Railway, was built between 1846 and 1850 by Sir William Cubitt (1785–1861), younger brother of Thomas Cubitt, the developer who built much of Bloomsbury, Belgravia, Clapham and Pimlico.

They were quite a family of builders. Their younger brother, Lewis Cubitt (1799–1883), built our starting point – King's Cross Station – in 1852.

At King's Cross the two wrought-iron-and-glass, round-arched roofs are supported by elegant arcades built of yellow, London stock brick. Cubitt also built the Italianate clock tower at the front of the station and the Great Northern Hotel (1854) next door – Italianate,

The other end of your gas pipe – Single Gasholder No. 8 (1880) next to its old dismembered companions, King's Cross, London.

too, with a fetching curved front, built to follow the bend of Pancras Road.

Just as you pull out of the station, on the left is Single Gasholder No. 8, built in 1880 – the last of a series of gasometers built by the Imperial Gas Light and Coke Company. These dignified skeletons, with three tiers of cast-iron classical capitals, once formed the biggest collection of gasometers in Britain. Decommissioned in the 1980s, they now lie dismembered in neat piles of columns in the shadow of the one survivor. The plan is to reassemble them as part of the new Regent Quarter in King's Cross.

Five minutes later, to the right, is the wavy steel-and-glass Emirates Stadium (2006), home to Arsenal Football Club, built for £430 million – the second-biggest stadium in the Premier League after Old Trafford.

Within seconds you'll see, also on the right, Highbury Stadium, Arsenal's old Art Deco home (see page 283), now clothed in a scaffolding cage while it is converted into flats. You get a good view of Claude Waterlow Ferrier's West Stand (1932).

327

A few minutes later, the distinct outline of Alexandra Palace looms on a hill to your left. Home to the first BBC Television broadcasts in 1936, Ally Pally has twice been ravaged by fire – in 1873, sixteen days after it opened, and again in 1980. The revamped building is a mixture of modern steel, glass and the original Italianate structure – itself built of materials salvaged from the South Kensington Exhibition building of 1862.

Around fifteen minutes later, to the right as you pass through Hatfield Station, you can glimpse the roof of Hatfield House, but only in winter when the trees thin out. The Jacobean prodigy house was built by Robert Cecil, the first Earl of Salisbury, in 1607–12. Arranged on the classic Elizabethan E-plan, it is still lived in by Cecil's descendant, the Marquess of Salisbury.

Moments after, as you pass through Welwyn Garden City, look to the right. Close to the line is an Art Deco industrialist classic – the flat-roofed, concrete, tubular Shredded Wheat factory, built in 1925 by Louis de Soissons, one of the architects behind the garden city.

Soon afterwards, just before Stevenage, on the right, Knebworth House pokes its head above the trees – a romanticised Victorian version of Tudor Gothic twirls and whirls. The 1820 rebuilding of a 1500 courtyard house also has later work by the first Lord Lytton – the novelist Edward Bulwer-Lytton (1803–73).

About half an hour outside London, just after Stevenage, brick gives way to stone.

Welcome to limestone country. We are now on that thick belt of stone which runs from the north-east of England down to the south-west. Look out for creamy yellow and light brown stone, particularly on tall, slim church spires.

Just before Peterborough Station, there's a view to the right of a big lump of cream-white and buff Barnack limestone, quarried a few miles north-west, near Stamford. This is twelfth-century Peterborough Cathedral, with its early thirteenth-century nave roof – the biggest in

Europe. That crossing tower was built in around 1325 – replacing the original Norman tower – but it retains a Norman-looking stumpiness. Catherine of Aragon was buried here.

At Peterborough Station, on the right, the Great Northern Hotel (1852) is a good example of a Victorian building that reflects the Italian palazzo roots of the classic British terraced house.

Grantham, Margaret Thatcher's home town, has a pair of fine churches. Just before the station, on the right, with four plain pinnacles, is St John the Evangelist (1841), a Victorian copy of an Early English church, as you'll see from those simple windows.

Just after the station, again on the right, is one of the most admired steeples in Britain, the 282-foot spire of St Wulfram's, a classic piece of early-fourteenth-century, Decorated work.

Since Margaret Thatcher's father, Alfred Roberts, was a Methodist, the family didn't worship in either of these churches. Instead they went to Finkin Street church (1840), a classic piece of semi-circular non-conformist church design – with polished mahogany pews ranged in front of a high pulpit, where Alfred Roberts often preached from. Margaret and her sister Muriel sat in the family pew in the fourth row from the front.

Leaving Grantham, more limestone spires dot the low-lying hills of the Vale of Belvoir – dream hunting country, by the way; so look out for immaculately maintained hedges, catnip to the rider.

Just past Grantham, beneath the horizon, eyes peeled for the Bellmount Tower – a folly on the Belton Estate (see page 125), built in 1757 by Samuel Smith. It's not really a tower, more a high arch with a Venetian window.

On the left, in Newark, just before the station, there's the soaring 237-foot-high spire of St Mary Magdalen, one of the best parish churches in Britain. It's a mixture of Early English, thirteenth-century work and fourteenth-century Decorated – look out for ogee tracery in the windows and much-crocketed gables.

Moments before you pull into Doncaster Station, on your right is the Victorian church of St James's (1858), built by the shareholders of the Great Northern Railway.

The architect was the most prolific church builder of the age, Sir George Gilbert Scott (see page 235). But he had to deal with much interference from Lord Grimthorpe, chairman of the Great Northern. Scott called him 'my friend and at the same time my tormentor'.

Those windows with lots of circles are imitation Geometrical work – that is, just on the cusp of Early English and Decorated, between 1250 and 1310; what Lord Grimthorpe called 'the exact climax of the Gothic styles'.

As you leave Doncaster Station, to your right, beyond Tesco, is the uplifting, bristling outline of St George (1858), also by Scott, but this time in the Perpendicular style of the medieval church that stood here before.

Next stop, York Station (1877), built by William Peachey of yellow Scarborough brick. Its marvellous 800-foot-long train shed, supported by pretty, slim Corinthian columns, runs along a stately, shallow curve.

Passengers on the three o'clock train to Edinburgh, transfixed by Darlington Station's half-fluted columns.

As you pull out of York, look to your right for the bunched trio of the towers of York Minster. The windows are twirly-whirly at the top with mullions soaring right to the top. So? Perpendicular. And, yes, the crossing tower and the west towers were built from 1407 to 1472, right in the middle of the Perpendicular period, although the earliest parts of the church above ground are early thirteenth century.

Soon after you leave York, off to the right, on the horizon, for quite some time you'll see the dark purple profile of the North York Moors, their humped back bristling with sitka spruce.

Darlington Station (1842) has good classical, red brickwork on its outside walls. Its iron and glass roof is carried over several bays by metal Corinthian columns – intriguingly fluted only halfway up their shafts.

As you approach Durham, to your right is one of the finest views in Europe. The marvellous thing is quite how high the railway line is here, on a level with Durham Cathedral and the monastery. The cathedral dominates the city, perched on its rock above the River Wear. Roger Whittaker (1936–) got the name of the river wrong in *The Leavin'* (*Durham Town*) (1969):

> When I was a boy, I spent my time,
> Sitting on the banks of the River Tyne.
> Watching all those ships going down the line, they were
>   leaving,
> Leaving, leaving, leaving, leaving me.
> Now I've got to leave old Durham town.

To the right are the twin towers of the cathedral's west entrance – a mixture of Norman and Early English work, with all those little rounded and barely pointed arches and windows. Slap in the middle of the towers, though, you'll see an enormous twirly-whirly seven-light window, a huge Decorated thing inserted into the Norman masonry by Prior Fossor in the middle of the fourteenth century.

331

Beyond the entrance towers is the 218-foot crossing tower – Norman below, fifteenth-century Perpendicular above (look for the ogees).

By the way, we have now moved out of the limestone belt. Durham Cathedral is built of local sandstone, most of it a dull buff colour.

Down to the left, by the Wear, is Durham Castle, built by William the Conqueror in 1072 on his return from Scotland. Lots of Norman work survives, encrusted with later Gothic additions.

A few minutes after Durham, off in the distance to your right, stands yellow and black Lumley Castle, with its symmetrical four towers and flag fluttering on the nearest tower. Built in the late fourteenth century, it was altered by Sir John Vanbrugh in the 1720s. Among other things, he inserted one of his favourite devices – a corridor – and installed sash windows throughout.

Just before Newcastle, up on the hill to your right, you get a momentary glimpse of *The Angel of the North* (1998) by Antony Gormley, built in Hartlepool of steel set into concrete foundations. Its 178-foot wingspan is wider than the Statue of Liberty is tall.

At Newcastle, just before the station, look right for one of the most thrilling sets of bridges on earth.

You are yourself travelling over Robert Stephenson's 1849 High Level Bridge, with the road deck slung below you by wrought-iron hangers.

There are ten bridges over the Tyne at Newcastle, but look out for these three to your right:

1. Down low, the Tyne Swing Road Bridge (1876) by W.G. Armstrong and Co.

2. Further away from you, the New Tyne Road Bridge (1928), designed by Mott, Hay and Anderson, with its two-hinged steel arch – a copy of Sydney Harbour Bridge, built by the same contractors at the same time.

3. And then, even further away, the hooped curve of the Gateshead Millennium Bridge (2001), built for pedestrians and bicycles. It flips

through forty degrees to let ships through, giving it the nickname 'the Blinking Eye Bridge'.

There's also a fine view on the skyline of the hulking steel-and-concrete outline of St James's Park, Newcastle United's stadium, and the third biggest in the Premier League. The 64.5-metre, steel-truss cantilever roof (1998) over the Jackie Milburn complex is the biggest cantilever in Europe.

Two churches jump out at you, too. Nearer to your right is the classical spire of All Saints, Pilgrim Street (1796), by David Stephenson. Look out for pairs of Tuscan columns on the lower stages of the spire, and single ones just below the obelisk.

Closer to the river are the arcing bows of the spire of St Nicholas's Cathedral, with its 193½-feet-high, fifteenth-century tower. Look closely at the top and you'll see four flying buttresses holding a pinnacled, battlemented square lantern, itself supporting four mini-buttresses with a crocketed octagonal spire.

Newcastle's first historian, William Grey, said of the spire, in his *Chorographia* (1649), that it 'lifteth up a head of majesty high above the rest, as a cypresse tree above the low shrubs'.

Straight ahead of you, soaring above the north bank of the Tyne, is the pencil-thin spire of Pugin's Catholic cathedral of St Mary's (1844), built in his favourite Decorated style.

The city's classical Central Station (1850) was built by John Dobson (1787–1865); again, like York, on a pleasing curve. Its train shed is an 800-foot-long marvel, covering three acres.

To your left, as you leave the station, there's a good, quick glimpse straight up Grey Street, much of it built by Dobson in the late 1830s. The handsome street bends gently as it rises, and is much enriched with Corinthian columns and pilasters.

Then, seconds later, to your right, is the Sage Gateshead theatre – aka the Slug – built by Foster and Partners in 2004 of curved glass and stainless steel.

A quarter of an hour after Newcastle, low to your right, the pastel-painted town of Alnmouth is wrapped in a fold of the coast. The spire of St John the Baptist – in simple Early English style – pokes above the terraces, failing to puncture the skyline. After Alnmouth Station, to your left, the ducal seat of fourteenth-century Alnwick Castle is just out of sight.

About ten minutes later, the mid-twelfth century Bamburgh Castle is to your right on its deserted shore opposite the Farne islands. The dozen or so round and square-headed towers make for a hulking great bar-chart outline against the North Sea.

Moments later, just before Berwick-upon-Tweed, Holy Island is off to your right – a small gathering of buildings rises just above the water; then, a little to the right of them, a jagged castle rises higher over the horizon.

The clutch of buildings consists of the thirteenth-century parish church, monastic quarters and the ruined Norman Priory Church of Lindisfarne (around 1100) – with round arches and fat pillars in blushing red sandstone, quarried at nearby Cheswick. The North Sea winds and saltwater have chiselled into the stone, giving it a ver-miculated effect.

Lindisfarne Castle was built in 1550 and adapted by Sir Edwin Lutyens in 1902 for Edward Hudson, the owner of *Country Life.*

In Berwick-upon-Tweed – on your right, just before you come into the station, just after the lighthouse – you cross the Tweed on Robert Stephenson's Royal Border Bridge of 1850. Look to your right, first at the not so handsome 1928 concrete bridge, then at the delightful old sandstone bridge (1626) beyond.

There are glimpses from the bridge, too, of the Elizabethan ramparts and medieval walls of the most vulnerable town in Britain – captured or sacked fourteen times in the three centuries leading up to 1482, when it became part of England for good.

A minute or so outside Berwick-upon-Tweed, welcome to Scotland! Look to the right at the cliffs here, and you'll see the local pink-red sandstone. A good rule of thumb about sandstone cliffs is that they move up and down, forwards and backwards, as sandstone is that much more prone to erosion than limestone. Harder and more durable, limestone cliffs are flat-topped things with more regular faces, and it's easier to walk along the top of them.

Up here on the north-east coast of East Lothian, near Dunbar, you get deep Dunbar Red Sandstone – the colour of rare roast beef.

Soon after Dunbar, off on the horizon, you'll glimpse Bass Rock, its soaring profile formed by a bulging plug of volcanic rock, now streaked with the guano of a million gannets.

To your right, looking across to Kirkcaldy, there's a lovely long view of the Firth of Forth, and, off on the horizon, the lighthouse island of Inchkeith.

As you come into Edinburgh look out for Arthur's Seat, a once-active volcano in this city of hard sandstone. Edinburgh Castle, with its much-battered melange of work from the Normans to the present day, stands on another old volcano, high above you.

You get a better view of the castle once you get out at our final destination, Waverley Station – named after *Waverley* (1814), Sir Walter Scott's novel about a young dreamer and English soldier, Edward Waverley, who was sent to Scotland in 1745, the year of the Jacobite Rebellion.

Waverley, built on the site of an earlier station in stages through the 1870s to the 1890s, is an unusually unsatisfactory railway station in such an uplifting city. One of the reasons is that the station is buried below Princes Street.

To get a good bite at the treasures of Edinburgh, you must climb up the stairs and out into the Athens of the North. There's also quite a lot of Rome there, a chunk of Gothic – original and revival – and a huge amount of window sills; quite enough to feed your lust for years to come.

Conclusion

Let the Scales Fall from Our Eyes

At the 2007 Festival del Mondo Antico in Rimini, I was struck by an Italian don from Bologna University reading Virgil aloud. With his thin white blouson, white pipe-cleaner trousers, candy-striped shirt, open to the navel, revealing a wiry chest tanned the colour of brown furniture by the Adriatic sun, he wasn't like your normal British academic.

He didn't read Virgil like one, either. *'Arma virumque cano . . .'* came out less like a retired optician from Malvern trying to buy stamps in Rome, and more like romantic, rat-a-tat Italian spoken by a Naples street urchin chatting up Sophia Loren.

Just as the professor from Bologna treated Latin like an everyday language, the Italians in Rimini were heroically indifferent to their ancient architecture. Twice a day, commuters into Rimini literally crossed the Rubicon – the river a few miles north of the city that Caesar crossed to fight Pompey in 49 BC. These commuters used the main bridge into town – a bridge dating from Caesar's time – as the principal thoroughfare during rush hour. Juggernauts and twelve-year-olds on tinny motorinos thundered across the bridge, coating the marble inscription to Caesar in a thin layer of soot.

Because they've got so much of this old stuff around, the Italians and the Greeks can be cavalier about it. For a long time the locals living near the ancient amphitheatre at Delphi, home to the most hallowed oracle of classical times, referred to it as 'the quarry'. Italians in particular really prefer new things – shiny suits, shiny cars, shiny motorinos, in fact – to old ones.

Well, the British aren't like that when it comes to antique buildings. Because we've got so few of them, we circle them with a fence and a Keep Off sign.

But, as soon as we get a strong suit in another set of buildings, we quickly become as indifferent as the Italians.

During a recent church tour in South Wales, I read this passage in a guide book called *Saints and Stones – Haven Ways and By-Ways in Pembrokeshire* (2006): 'On leaving the church, in the direction of Skomer, take a walk to Martin's Haven, and see a Celtic cross situated in the Deer Park wall just below the toilets.' Only in Britain do we direct people to ancient Celtic crosses by way of the nearest public convenience.

Even when we're not using lavatories to navigate our way to the nearest ancient building, we take our treasures for granted. We'll travel through the baking heat of a Tuscan summer to track down a Romanesque church with one spectacular thing in it – a Piero della Francesca fresco cycle, perhaps. But from year to year we ignore the equally spectacular Romanesque church in our next-door village. OK, it might not have a Piero della Francesca fresco cycle in it. But the chances are that it will be vastly richer than most Italian churches in its sculpture, inscriptions and architectural variety.

The same goes for our country houses, cathedrals, town halls, castles, palaces and terraced houses – the greatest collection of buildings in the world.

It isn't surprising that the country that has stayed richer longer than any other in history has a greater variety of architecture than anywhere else. But we refuse to acknowledge it.

Of course, there are places that reached more sophisticated heights of architectural achievement than Britain ever did – Italy during the Renaissance for one. We must be careful before we call Weymouth Bay 'the Naples of Dorset'. How often do Italians call Naples 'the Weymouth of Campania'?

Still, those Continental flourishes, however great, were often local and short-lived. Try to name a great Italian nineteenth-century architect. And then think of Pugin, Scott, Smirke, Barlow, Soane . . .

How little we take in the great beauties around us. Martin Amis said he only realised halfway through university how ravishing Oxford was, when he started looking properly at the place; and, in particular, started looking up. He was right. Take a look at anybody milling round a National Trust country house. The chances are they'll be looking at you, their feet, their children, their guidebook, or the bit of floor they're about to step on; and not at the Gainsborough over the fireplace, let alone the Adam cornice running round the edge of the ceiling.

Most of us spend our time looking into the middle distance at head height. Not only does that mean we waste a lot of hours looking at the back of other people's heads. It also means we devote our days to looking at the dreary necessities of everyday life – street furniture, cars, shop window displays.

And we're often looking at the dullest bits of buildings – their block-like bases, needed to support the rest of their frames. But look up and you remove the ephemeral dross. You see the lighter, more decorative parts. Spires, crockets and weather vanes aren't really necessary to a building but they are often crucial to their look, designed as they are purely for beauty.

Part of the reason we don't look up is that we don't know what to look for or what to appreciate. We take in the function of buildings, but not much else. So, when we give directions, we've noticed enough to say, 'Left at the church, right at the town hall.' How much richer our lives would be if, as we passed the church or town hall, we took in its details, too. That Venetian window to the left of the town hall's Doric porch. Or the Decorated window in the church's chancel, thick with ballflowers, and shaded by that much-crocketed pinnacle.

Now you know these words and their meanings, don't you delight in how bewitching they sound? Mullions, entasis, reticulated tracery and all that – your journeys throughout Britain, however pedestrian their aim, will be lifted everywhere by the knowledge of what lies behind these lovely words.

Look, and keep looking, and you will find extraordinary buildings, and extraordinary features on ordinary buildings, in every corner of Britain.

Glossary

I'm not going to include the obvious here, like basements and attics, naves or altars; nor obscure things like bucraniums (or bucrania) – the plaster ox skulls that decorate classical friezes. Instead, here's a list of the most important, lesser-known features to be found on our buildings, great and small. Italics within a definition indicate a related entry.

Aisle – a passage that runs parallel with the nave on either side of a church.

Ambulatory – a walkway behind the altar in larger churches and cathedrals.

Antae – simple *pilasters* at the front of a portico, usually at either end. When done like this, the thing to say is, they've been applied *'in antis'*.

Anthemion – a flower ornament on classical buildings, often honeysuckle.

Apron – a raised panel below a window, often in the same-coloured brick as the window surround. The apron keys the window into the façade.

Apse – a semicircular or polygonal space, usually added at the altar end of the church.

Arcade – a series of arches. If there's a wall right behind the arches, it's a blind arcade.

Architrave – the grand word for a lintel; the bottom, plainest part of the *entablature*.

Arrow slit – an opening only several inches wide on the outside of a castle but a foot wide on the inside, so that the archer can lean right into the wall cavity and get a proper look at his target.

When the crossbow appeared, the arrow slit grew a horizontal crossing line, often flaring out into circles at the ends to give more wriggle room for aiming and firing.

With the popularity of gunpowder, from 1660 onwards, the arrow slit was adapted into a gun loop with a big hole at the bottom.

Ashlar – expensive stonework with neat, square edges and flattened, even faces, found on grand churches and country houses.

Ballflower – a popular Decorated touch: little stone balls, each wrapped in a three-petalled flower.

Baluster – a single, usually small, pillar; gathered together, balusters form a balustrade.

Barbican – a double tower over a gate or bridge, protecting a city or castle.

Bargeboard – long board, popular on Tudor buildings, fixed under the eaves to protect the protruding rafters.

Baroque – a tricky word that covers a multitude of whirls and twirls. Strictly, it means a style that began in Rome in 1600, fitfully imitated in Britain from 1680 to 1720. Used more loosely to mean ornate and a little over the top.

Bartizan – think *Scots Baronial* tower: the little round, and sometimes square, turrets that jump out of the corners of McTavish Castle. There's a bartizan on the cover of this book – on the ornate house in the terrace, it's the little, rounded tower closest to you with a pair of crossed *arrow slits*.

Bay – each vertical stretch of a building, usually the width of a window, arch or pair of columns.

Belfry – the chamber in a church tower where bells swing and bats roost.

Boss – round or polygonal knot of wood or stone, seen where ribs gather together in a vault. Way up above you on cathedral ceilings, so bring binoculars.

Box pew – a pew heightened at front and sides to produce a box effect. It grew out of the parclose, the screen around chantries, side chapels in churches set up by families to commemorate distinguished relations.

Buttress – vertical stretch of stone used to hold up a wall. If the buttress is set in an arch between the wall and the ground, it's a flying buttress.

Byzantine – period of the Roman Empire from AD 330 to 1453; notable for clustered domes, tall, square, multi-coloured brick campaniles, and baldacchinos, or canopies, over the altars.

There was a brief neo-Byzantine period in Britain in the late nineteenth century, in the wake of the Gothic Revival. Notable buildings include Westminster Cathedral (begun 1895, still unfinished) and St Barnabas, Jericho, Oxford (1869), built by Arthur Blomfield.

St Barnabas was the model for St Silas in Thomas Hardy's *Jude the Obscure* (1895). During his earlier career as an architect, Hardy worked

The sun dies away,
His rays lying static at quarter to six
On polychromatical lacing of bricks.
Good Lord, as the angelus floats down the road
Byzantine St Barnabas, be Thine Abode.
Where once the fritillaries hung in the grass
A baldachin pillar is guarding the Mass.
                    John Betjeman, 'St Barnabas, Oxford', 1945

for the church's designer, Arthur Blomfield. In *Jude the Obscure*, he wrote of St Silas, 'High overhead above the chancel steps, Jude could discern a huge, solidly constructed cross. It seemed to be suspended in the air by invisible wires; it was set with large jewels which faintly glimmered in some weak ray caught from outside.'

Campanile – a bell-tower; thus campanologist, a keen bell-ringer.

Capital – the top section of a column (from the Latin *caput*, 'head').

Chamfer – the diagonal edge produced, usually on door frames, by cutting a corner at a forty-five-degree angle.

Chancel – the area towards the end of the church, usually the east end, in front of the altar.

Choir – in bigger churches and cathedrals, the area just before the chancel, where services are sung by the choir.

Clerestory – the highest level of the church or cathedral nave walls, with a series of windows.

Coade Stone – an artificial, hard-wearing stone manufactured by Eleanor Coade and her company from 1769 to 1840.

Colonnade – a series of columns in a line.

Composite – the only *order* invented by the Romans, in AD 82, this combines *Ionic* and *Corinthian*, so you get the twirly-whirly *volutes* and a sprouting mass of acanthus leaves.

Console – a curved, ornate bracket.

Coping – stones or bricks used to finish the top of a wall; thus coping stones.

Corbel – a little stone or brick that juts out from a wall to support a projecting tower, arch or chimney stack.

Corinthian – the last *order* to be invented by the Greeks, in about 400 BC. Thick with acanthus foliage and small *volutes*.

Cornice – the top section of the *entablature*. Also survives on its own, familiar from just about every sitting room in Britain – the decorative band which smoothes the transition from the top of the wall to the ceiling.

Course – a line of bricks or stones. A wall is made up of courses laid on top of one another.

Cove – a concave moulding, usually running along the top of a wall, where it meets the ceiling.

Crenel – a square gap in the stone on top of a parapet, through which you shoot burning arrows at seething hordes below. Thus 'crenellation' and 'crenellated tower'. When you've fired your arrow, take cover behind a *merlon*.

Crocket – leafy little hooks bristling in clusters around Gothic pinnacles, around the tops of tombs and so on. Look at a Gothic church against the setting sun, and you'll see the alluring jagged edge produced by heavy crocketing.

Crowsteps – imagine a crow climbing steps on either side of a gable.

Crypt – the basement of a church, from the Greek *kruptos*, 'hidden'. Because basements were dug out before the rest of the church was built, the crypt is the oldest part of the building. It might well have much more ancient vaulting and piers than the church above.

Cupola – the pretty little dome, often pierced with small windows, set on top of a bigger dome or turret.

Curtain wall – a wall connecting a castle's towers.

Cyclopean masonry – imagine the Cyclops, the clumsy, ham-fisted, one-eyed giant who kidnapped Odysseus in the *Odyssey*, building a wall, and this is the clumsy, ham-fisted result: big, irregular stones moulded together into a smoothly jointed wall. Perhaps Odysseus was responsible for the smooth joints.

Dado – the lower part of the wall in a formal classical room, railed off from the top part by the dado rail. The dado rail protected walls from scuff marks made by chairs drawn up to the edge of the room. Dado rails were often replaced by a picture rail just below the cornice in the Regency period, when chairs were left permanently in the middle of the room.

Decorated – also called Middle Pointed, and, as that name suggests, the middle period of Gothic architecture from 1290 to 1340. Look out for *ogees*, encrustations of *ballflowers* and tremendously twirly-whirly *tracery*.

Dentil – think dentist, think teeth, think Terry-Thomas. The little square blocks found in *cornices*, separated by symmetrical gaps – tooth, gap, tooth, gap. Rather like mini-*merlons*.

Diocletian window – a semicircular window divided into three. Also known as a thermal window because they were used in the *thermae*, or baths, of Diocletian in Rome (AD 306). The Palladians loved them.

Doric – the earliest of the *orders*, devised in the seventh century BC and used on the Parthenon in Athens. Just a simple plain ring for a *capital* on top of a fluted, often baseless column.

Dormer window – a little window that pokes out of a roof to light an attic.

Drum – the drum-shaped stage beneath a dome.

Early English – the first period of English Gothic architecture, 1190–1250. For the first time, windows and arches became pointed.

Eaves – the edge of a roof where it extends beyond the wall.

Egg and dart – the most recognisable decoration – egg, arrow-shaped dart, egg, arrow-shaped dart – that you see on a classical *entablature*.

Elevation – the face of a building.

Elizabethan – the period from Elizabeth I's accession, in 1558, until her death in 1603.

Entablature – the gubbins supported by a wall or *capital*. Divided into three sections: *architrave*, *frieze* and *cornice*.

Fluting – the vertical grooves of a column.

Four-centred arch – a giveaway to Perpendicular style. To build one of these low, flat arches, you had to draw curves around four different centres.

Frieze – the middle bit of the classical *entablature* between the *architrave* and the *cornice*. Usually decorated as a continuous strip or divided in *Doric* friezes into separate frames – metopes – by three fingers of stone called triglyphs. These are thought to reflect the old beam ends lying across the roof of the legendary primitive wooden hut – the supposed root of classical architecture.

Gable – at its most simple, the triangle shape made by your roof on the side of your house. Flemish or Dutch Gables have curving slopes on either side topped by a small pediment. The Jacobeans went nuts for gables on the *front* of their houses.

Gargoyle – before drainpipes came spouts, pouring water away from the roof. Gargoyles, which hid the spouts, were popular from the Normans onwards.

A devil with wings, fangs and claws was often used, notably at Lichfield Cathedral, Staffordshire. Versions of the devil include 'mouth-pullers', inspired by Satan, who was often shown sticking his tongue out at victims. The Green Man, a pagan symbol of fertility surrounded by leaves, was a popular subject.

Gable end, Conway Street, Belfast.

Gargoyles continued into the modern age – often modelled on cathedral employees. But their original role of hiding water spouts is long gone. Drainpipes took off from the thirteenth century onwards. In 1241 Henry III commanded the Keeper of Works at the Tower of London 'to cause all the leaden gutters of the great tower through which rainwater should fall to be carried down to the ground'.

By Tudor times, rainwater heads – open boxes to contain great quantities of water during deluges – were common, often marked with the coat of arms of the owner and a date. Be careful – the date is often the date of renovation, not of the original house.

Still, spouts flourished. In *Anecdotes of the Manners and Customs of London in the Eighteenth Century* (1808), J.P. Malcolm complained of the difficulty of walking through London in the early 1700s with 'a thousand spouts pouring cascades at [one's] luckless head'.

In 1724 the London Building Act ordered that every house had to have gutters and drainpipes. It wasn't until 1891 that, under London   347 regulations, waste pipes had to be on the outside of the house. In both cases, the rest of Britain soon followed.

Gazebo – a summer house raised to a prominent position (from the dog Latin for 'I will gaze').

Geometrical – the period of Gothic tracery on the cusp of *Early English* and *Decorated*, 1250–1310. Distinguished by lots of circles.

Giant order – a *pilaster* or column that rises through two or more floors. Michelangelo was keen on them.

Golden ratio – a ratio of around 1.618, regarded as having magically harmonious qualities when applied to the dimensions of buildings. Take one long line, *a*, and one short line, *b*. If *a* is around 1.618 times as long as *b*, then *b* will be to *a* as *a* is to *a* plus *b*. The Swiss architect Le Corbusier (1887–1965) was particularly keen on the golden ratio.

Hood mould – a thin protective band above a window or arch to throw off the rain.

Impost – a little flat shelf in a wall from which an arch springs.

Inglenook – a cave-like recess around a fire, wide enough to accommodate several stout yeomen.

Ionic – the *order* invented by the Greeks in the sixth century BC. The most feminine of the orders, it's slender with *volutes* reminiscent of a girl's curls.

Jacobean – the period from James I's accession in 1603 until his death in 1625 (from *Jacobus*, the Latin for James).

Jamb – the vertical side of a window (from the French *jambe*, 'leg').

Jetty – the bit of a pre-Great Fire of London building that juts out over the first storey.

Keystone – the heavy wedge-shaped stone at the top of an arch.

Lady chapel – during the late Middle Ages, before the Reformation, there was great devotion to the Virgin Mary – the lady in question. If the church itself was not dedicated to her, then the addition of a lady chapel was almost as good for the soul.

Lady chapels were built later than the bulk of the church, and often tacked on at the east end behind the main altar. This broke the chronological line of most cathedrals and big churches, which were built from the east – altar – end, in a westward direction. The façade of a church often ended up being built several centuries later than the altar end.

Once you'd got the altar up and running, you could then hold services, and it didn't matter too much if there were still workmen on tea breaks at the west entrance end. In Florence several great churches – including San Lorenzo, where Michelangelo sculpted his soft, fleshy marble nudes for the Medici tombs – have bare rubble façades, still yet to be decorated after half a millennium.

Light – the individual pieces of glass divided by *mullions* and *transoms* in a single window. Thus a two-light, three-light etc. window.

Lincrusta – a mixture of linseed oil and wood pulp, invented by Frederick Walton in 1877. Rich and garish, it was dyed and coloured to imitate metal and embossed leather. Popular on late-nineteenth-century pub ceilings and high-Victorian gentleman's clubs – the Garrick Club has plenty of it, below the dado rail.

Very OTT, it quickly went out of fashion. Lady Curzon said, on seeing the lincrusta interiors at the lodge belonging to the Viceroy of India in Simla in 1898, 'Oh, Lincrusta, you will turn us grey! It looks at you with pomegranate and pineapple eyes from every wall.'

Loggia – a gallery of columns or arches.

Machicolation – literally 'mashing device'; a projecting booth with holes in the floor to allow boiling oil/rancid cows to be dropped on the seething hordes below.

Merlon – a square chunk of stone on each side of a *crenel*.

Mezzanine – the low-ceilinged extra half-floor squeezed between two high-ceilinged main floors.

Misericord – monks in choir stalls often had to stand for hours on end. Thus the misericord, a crafty mini-seat built on the underside of the hinged choir stall. When the misericord was flipped up, the monk could sit while standing – thus the literal meaning of misericord, 'compassion'. Often carved into fantastic animals and grotesque caricatures.

Motte and bailey – the earliest and most basic Norman castle, consisting of a mound of earth – the motte – with a wooden tower on top of it. Around all this was a bailey – an enclosure surrounded by a palisade, a ditch and in some cases a bank.

349

In *Sir Gawain and the Green Knight,* when Sir Gawain sets off to fight the knight, he looked for him in a moated castle with a double ditch – a 'depe double dich' – and a drawbridge.

> De walle wod in de water wonderly depe,
> Ande eft a huge heit haled upon lofte.
> [The wall was wonderfully deep in the water,
> And it rose to a great big height above him.]

Mottes were later adapted to become stone castles or left to ruin. You can still spot the ruined ones – domed mounds surrounded with the vestiges of a ditch.

Mullion – the vertical strut of a window.

Newel – the thick, strong post of a staircase, on a corner, at its end or breaking up a series of thin banisters.

Oculus – a circular window.

Oeil de boeuf or *bullseye* – an oval window, with its long axis set to the horizontal.

Ogee – a trademark feature of the *Decorated* style, first seen in 1291 on the Eleanor Crosses erected along Queen Eleanor's funeral route from Lincoln to Westminster Abbey. A single ogee is a concave, then convex, line. An ogee arch joins two of these together.

Order – one of five architectural orders: *Tuscan, Doric, Ionic, Corinthian, Composite.*

Pebble-dash – small stones dashed at wet render to give an external wall a rough, varied look; also called roughcast.

Pediment – a big triangle, usually at the top of a classical building and supported by pillars. A crucial spot for figurative sculpture is inside the pediment or on its ends and apex.

Pendentive – the great Byzantine discovery: a concave triangular section. Four of these placed at the corners of a rectangular space allowed a dome to be built on top – a sleight of hand that the Romans never pulled off. Squinches performed the same role.

Perpendicular – the last stage of English Gothic architecture, 1340–1530; distinguished by tall, broad windows with straight-sided panels, and also notable for fan *vaults.*

Piano nobile – 'the grand floor' or first floor, where the best rooms with the highest ceilings and the tallest windows were.

Pier – a simple brick or stone pillar, often supporting an arch.

Pilaster – a flattened column with a flattened *capital*.

Pointing – the mortar between bricks and stones. Snail pointing is the distinct, raised, flat sort, imitating the course of a particularly single-minded snail. Flush and recessed pointing are self-explanatory. Tuck pointing used dark mortar that matched the brick; then a slim bead of white lime putty was laid on top to imitate fine-jointed brickwork.

Portcullis – an iron or wood grille mounted in vertical grooves, lifted and dropped by chains or ropes. There were often two at a castle's main entrance. By closing the inner and outer portcullis, you could trap the seething hordes and pour oil/burning arrows on their heads.

Portico – a porch, consisting of a series of columns usually topped with a *pediment*. Depending on the number of columns, it is tetrastyle (four columns), hexastyle (six columns) etc.

Putlog hole or *puthole* – a square hole, still visible in castle and cathedral walls, where beams were lodged to support early scaffolding.

Quoins – the distinctive long-short-long-short pattern of smartly finished, or 'dressed', stones on the corners of a building.

Rafter – a beam leading down from the top of a roof to the eaves, in parallel with others.

Regency – the period 1790–1830, even though George IV was only Prince Regent from 1811 to 1820.

Rendering – various coverings of outside walls, from stucco to the unfairly non-U world of pebble-dash and stone cladding.

Reredos or *retable* – an elaborately painted and carved screen behind and above the altar; much abused during the Reformation.

Rococo – think twirly-whirly, think wedding-cake decoration, curves, garlands and ribbons. Think 1720 to 1760. Think a lighter, frothier sort of Baroque. Think . . . not very much of it in Britain.

John Betjeman said that political history accounts for our failure to embrace Rococo. Because of the Civil War and gradual reform of Parliament, the aristocracy took a greater interest in politics here than on the Continent. There, blue bloods devoted their energy to full-blown Baroque and Rococo – which reached its rich, creamy, sugary, wedding-cake heights in Catholic Bavaria. As Betjeman put it, 'France was to pay for her Rococo: so were Italy, Germany, Austria, Spain and the rest of Europe. The educated [in Britain] ruled, but could not tyrannise.'

Romanesque – another word for Norman architecture: round-headed arches and round, fat columns. Popularised by William the Conqueror but outdated in the late twelfth century by *Early English* Gothic architecture and the pointed arch.

Rustication – the criss-cross pattern, sometimes with a rough surface, on the ground floor or basement of classical buildings, borrowed by terraced houses. When simplified down to horizontal grooves, it's called banded rustication.

Sacristy – the room in a church or cathedral where sacred vessels are kept.

Sanctuary – the raised, tiled area around the altar, often fenced off with altar rails. You're not really supposed to walk on this bit, but, if there's a knockout *reredos* to see, ruthless antiquarians will break rules.

Scots Baronial – you'll know this when you see it – the sort of pile Braveheart drags his mace home to after a hard day painting his face blue and picking off Sassenachs. Actually, Scots Baronial was a lot later than William Wallace (1272–1305). Its seminal decade was 1560–70, although it grew out of the peel towers familiar to Braveheart – simple three-storey towers, built from the thirteenth to the sixteenth century, with parapets carried on *corbels*, sprouting into *bartizans* at each corner.

From these towers the Scots Baronial house expanded, influenced by the chateaux of the Loire – plenty of French masons worked in Scotland. The towers were often in pairs connected by a central rectangular block – with towers at opposite corners, they ended up with a sort of Z-plan.

Other features Scots Baronial delighted in were little circular stair turrets that furled out of the house above the first floor. Throw in crow-stepped gables, candle-snuffer towers, round and square towers, and *dormer* windows jutting through the roof, and you end up with a deliciously jumpy roofline above a plain, solid castle below.

Screens passage – the gap between the medieval hall and the kitchens, fenced off by a screen. You enter Oxford or Cambridge dining halls by the screens passage.

Soffit – the underside of an arch.

Spandrel – the corner bits that fill the space between a rectangular hood and the arch it protects.

Squinch – an arch or series of receding arches inserted into the corners of a square tower to support a dome above.

Squint – a small hole, usually in the *chancel* wall, allowing a view of the altar from an otherwise obscured part of the church. Generous patrons built leper's squints for those unavoidably segregated from the rest of the congregation.

Stairs – made up of risers – the vertical face – and treaders, the things you tread on.

> **DATING TIP**
>
> The staircase's vertical struts, or *balusters*, were often vase-shaped from the late seventeenth century, with a swollen lower half. In the early seventeenth century the shape was the other way round: the top half bulged.

String course – a flat horizontal band on a wall, often marking where the plinth of a *pilaster* would have been.

Tracery – the window shapes caused by intertwining masonry ribs in a window.

Transept – if you imagine the typical church as a crucifix, the shorter bits on the right and left are the transepts.

Transom – the horizontal bars in a window.

Triforium – in grand cathedrals with three storeys along the nave, the middle storey is the triforium.

Tudor – the period that began with Henry VII's victory at the Battle of Bosworth in 1485, and, for architectural buffs, ended with the accession of Queen Elizabeth I in 1558, even though she was a Tudor, too.

Tuscan – the simplest of the *orders*, invented by Italian architectural theorists in the sixteenth century. Resembles a *Doric* column plus a base but minus fluting.

Tympanum – the large, semicircular stone above a doorway.

Vault – an arched roof of stone, brick or concrete, sometimes echoed internally in wood or plaster. The main types are:

353

Barrel vault: the earliest sort of vault, used by the Normans; as plain as plain can be, really no more than continuous semicircular arches.

Fan vault: expensive, as Wordsworth spotted. While other vaults support heavy ceilings, fan vaults add to the weight.

Groin vault: imagine one barrel vault crossing another and, at the intersection, you ended up with a groin vault – the result was four concave triangles of masonry meeting in the middle.

Rib vault: these ropes of masonry criss-crossing the vault were decorative as well as structural. They let the eye continue the line of stone up from the shafts supporting the vault, without disappearing into thin air.

Like pointed arches and flying *buttresses*, rib vaults supported a lot of weight. And, like them, they were a classic sign of early Gothic architecture. Durham Cathedral – essentially Norman, begun in 1093 – had rib vaults in 1104, earlier than anywhere else in the Western world.

There were many members of the rib family: transverse ribs, wall ribs, diagonal ribs, ridge ribs, tiercerons and lierne ribs. Here it's enough to know the basic rib vaults: four ribs – quadripartite rib vaults; six ribs – sexpartite rib vaults etc.

Church walls were thickest where they supported the greatest weight of the roof – that is, where the ribs on the vaults led the pressure of the roof down on to the walls. It's at these pressure points that you'll find piers on the inside and flying buttresses on the outside.

Stellar vault: a star-shaped vault.

Venetian window – invented by Donato Bramante (1444–1514) in Italy in the late fifteenth century and first used in Britain in 1630, at Wilton House, Wiltshire. Two flat-headed windows flank a taller, round-headed window. The Palladians loved them.

Vermiculation – little marks like worm tracks, sometimes found in stone or plaster panels formed by *rustication*.

Vestry – the room in a church where the vestments are kept. Often the door to the vestry is open and you can take a peek at the choristers' gowns hanging from their pegs, alongside the vicar's vestments. There you'll find things for making the tea, a little mirror for pre-sermon grooming and nostalgic group photos of the choir's trip to Jumièges in 1952.

Volute – twirly-whirly scrolls used on the capitals of columns, particularly *Ionic* ones.

Voussoir – a wedge-shaped stone used in groups on either side of a *keystone* to form an arch.

Weepers – the tragic little figures, often of dead or mourning children and wives or husbands, at the foot of medieval tombs. Also called mourners.

Windows – for our purposes, enough to know:

Bay window: a window that juts out from the face of a building. If it's rounded, it's a *bow window*, a curving window popular in the late eighteenth century. The bow window was an adaptation of the Elizabethan oriel window – rectangular or half-octagonal bay windows, dating from the fifteenth century, jutting out at first floor level or above. The bay window allowed views on three sides and so got more sun.

If a bay window has a straight front and sides at an angle, it's described as canted. The ordinary terraced houses shown on the front cover of this book have canted windows on their ground floors.

Bow windows on the first Barratt Home, Darras Hall, Newcastle, built for £2600 by the company's founder, Sir Lawrence Barratt, for his family in 1953.

Canted windows at Fawlty Towers – actually Wooburn Grange Country Club, Bourne End, Buckinghamshire, an Edwardian building, later Basil's Nightclub, before it burnt down in 1991. (BBC)

Rose window: a big round window, with *tracery* radiating from the middle, often at the west end of a cathedral.

Window tax – bear in mind that windows were often intentionally blind for aesthetic reasons – or because there was a solid mass of stone behind them – and not because of the tax inspector. Still, some people did block up their windows during the window tax years. The tax was

356

One of 'Pitt's Pictures' in Robert Adam's Charlotte Square (1791), Edinburgh. The middle window on the first floor has been painted black with fake white sashes on top to avoid window tax. The tax was introduced in Scotland by William Pitt the Younger in the 1780s.

introduced in 1696, with two rates: a flat rate of two shillings per house and a variable tax for any windows above ten windows. It continued in various forms until 1851, when it was replaced by House Duty.

Now turn back to page 11 and have another go at dating those Manchester buildings and putting them in the right order. The answers are on the next page.

The Manchester buildings were built in this order, with date of completion in brackets:

1. (B) Manchester Cathedral (late fifteenth century) – note the strong vertical axis of the Perpendicular tracery.
2. (D) Wellington Inn (1552) – note the gables, the black beams and the white wattle and daub.
3. (E) St Ann, St Ann's Square (1712) – note the pediment and the fluted Corinthian columns.
4. (A) Albert Memorial (1862) and Town Hall (1868) – both Gothic Revival, Manchester's Albert Memorial was built a decade before London's.
5. (F) John Rylands Library (1899) – Decorated Gothic Revival. Note the rib vaults.
6. (C) Central Library (1934) – Corinthian portico below and Tuscan order above reverse the hierarchy of the orders. Cenotaph and obelisks in front.

Acknowledgements

With thanks and love to my parents, Ferdy and Julia Mount, and my brother and sister, William and Mary Mount.

Deepest thanks to Richard Beswick, Iain Hunt, Bobby Nayyar, Susan de Soissons, Rowan Cope, Rachael Ludbrook, Linda Silverman, George Walkley and all at Little, Brown.

To Peter Straus of Rogers, Coleridge and White.

To Mungo McCosh for his fine cover picture, and Virginia Powell and Fred Phipps for letting me use their terrific terraced house pictures.

To Christopher Howse and Jeremy Musson who read the manuscript and made lots of life-saving changes.

To the late and much missed Dr Angus Macintyre.

To Nick Garland, who gave me his lovely Auberon Waugh picture and allowed me to reproduce it.

To Tony Ring, President of the International Wodehouse Association.

To Tristram Powell for advice on Osbert Lancaster. To Willa Beckett for her Holland Park insights.

To those who fed and watered me and had me to stay: Bella

Bathurst, Lindy Dufferin, Francie Mount, Christina Noble and Molly Watson.

To Sean Rafferty for his advice on Belfast buildings.

To Sarah Sands and Stuart Reid of *Reader's Digest*, John Goodall of *Country Life*, Sally Chatterton, Penny Cranford, Sam Leith, Charles Moore, Richard Preston, Simon Scott Plummer and Dr Damian Thompson of the *Daily Telegraph*, Michael Prodger of the *Sunday Telegraph*, Tobyn Andreae, Paul Dacre, Jim Gillespie, Leaf Kalfayan and Tom Utley of the *Daily Mail*.

Any mistakes are my own.

Venn Cottages, St Twynnells, Pembrokeshire
July 2008

We are grateful for permission to reproduce extracts from the following: 'The Stately Homes of England', by Noel Coward, courtesy of Methuen Drama, an imprint of A&C Black Publishers; 'Church Going' by Philip Larkin from *The Less Deceived*, courtesy The Marvell Press, England and Australia; from *Jeeves and the Impending Doom* / *Indian Summer of an Uncle* / *Company for Henry* / *Summer Moonshine* / *The Mating Season* / *Leave it to Psmith* / *Ring for Jeeves* / *Carry on, Jeeves*, all by P.G. Wodehouse, published by Hutchinson, reprinted courtesy of The Random House Group Ltd; from 'Churchyards' / 'A Few Late Chrysanthemums' / 'Summoned by Bells' / 'The Church's Restoration' / 'St Saviour's, Aberdeen Park, Highbury' / 'St Barnabas', all by John Betjeman, courtesy of John Murray, an imprint of the Orion Publishing Group; from *The Whitsun Weddings* by Philip Larkin, courtesy of Faber and Faber Ltd.

Index

365